NONE OF US IS FREE UNTIL ALL OF US ARE FREE

 NONE OF US IS FREE
UNTIL ALL OF US ARE FREE

NEW PERSPECTIVES ON GLOBAL SOLIDARITY

William Minter
In collaboration
with **Imani Countess**

Foreword by
Graça Machel

541 West Ingham Avenue, Suite B
Trenton, NJ 08638

Copyright © 2025, William Minter, ed. All rights reserved.

Book and cover design: Gail Oring, GO! Creative, LLC

Cataloging-in-Publication Data may be obtained from the Library of Congress

ISBNs: 9781569028711 (HB)
       9781569028728 (PB)

About reading this book
Almost all of the content in this book was born digital. The digital PDF version contains links not available in the printed version. To obtain a copy of the PDF for their use only, purchasers of the book should send an email including proof of purchase to wminter+allofusarefree@gmail.com.

About the title
The expression "None of Us Is Free Until All of Us Are Free" is attributed, with slight variations in wording, to many sources. These include Emma Lazarus, Fannie Lou Hamer, Maya Angelou, and singers Ray Charles, Eric Clapton, and Solomon Burke.

About the cover
The cover features persons whose voices on global solidarity appear in this book.
From left to right: First row: Rosebell Kagumire, Kumi Naidoo, Winona LaDuke, Adom Getachew
Second row: Angela Davis, Graça Machel, Greta Thunberg, Binyavanga Wainaina
Third row: Mia Mottley, Tokata Iron Eyes, Vanessa Nakate, Varshini Prakash

AFRICAFOCUS BOOKS AND AFRICA WORLD PRESS

AfricaFocus Books is a new imprint under the auspices of Africa World Press.

Africa World Press provides technical and business management. Kassahun Checole of Africa World Press and William (Bill) Minter of AfricaFocus Books have joint responsibility for editorial decisions.

After an initial period of up to 18 months for sales to libraries and other buyers to recuperate costs, the copyright license will transfer to Creative Commons License CC BY-NC 4.0 requiring attribution and non-profit use only.

None of Us Is Free Until All of Us Are Free is the first book to be published by AfricaFocus Books.

Praise for
NONE OF US IS FREE UNTIL ALL OF US ARE FREE:
NEW PERSPECTIVES ON GLOBAL SOLIDARITY

"The chapters in this collection provide a rich resource for those engaged in the hard work of creating and sustaining solidarity networks of activists, organizations, and institutions. ... The voices you will find in these pages well illustrate these connections across borders that teach and inspire us all."

— Graça Machel, first Minister of Education of Mozambique,
First Lady of Mozambique (1975–1986) and of South Africa (1998–1999),
and author of *The Impact of War on Children*.

"This powerful collection of essays and documents on Africa highlights the rich history and vital importance of transnational solidarity. The message and lessons could not be more timely. And who better to curate this collection of voices than Bill Minter—anti-colonialist, anti-racist, and long-distance runner in the global fight for freedom. Let this book inspire you to speak out and organize."

— Barbara Ransby, historian, activist
John D. MacArthur Chair and Professor at the University of Illinois at Chicago,
and author of *Making All Black Lives Matter*.

"Global solidarity, like local solidarity, requires stepping outside the boundaries of conventional wisdom fostered by the US media and government. These authors invite us to take grassroots democracy seriously, from encampments on university campuses in the USA to uprisings (intifada) against oppressive regimes in Palestine and around the world. Our collective liberation demands nothing less."

— Tiffany Willoughby-Herard, political theorist, poet,
Associate Professor of Global and International Studies at the University of California, Irvine,
and author of *Waste of a White Skin*.

"Building on what Graça Machel's description of the global anti-apartheid movement as 'the most successful transnational movement for justice that the world has ever seen,' this inspiring book offers us a guidebook on how to be global citizens. Minter and Countess supplement their own analysis with visionaries—from Angela Davis to Winona LaDuke—to expand our imaginations and offer the dynamic movements for racial, economic, gender, and climate justice of today a dazzling array of entry ramps into effective action for global justice."

— John Cavanagh, former Director of the Institute for Policy Studies and co-author
(with Robin Broad) of *The Water Defenders:
How Ordinary People Saved a Country from Corporate Greed*.

https://youtu.be/QGWG199bx88

https://youtu.be/GlSAY8GOkVo

TABLE OF CONTENTS

Acknowledgments iii

Foreword v

Introduction vii

PART ONE: Beyond Eurocentrism and U.S. Exceptionalism 1

    Chapter One: Starting Points for a Paradigm Shift
    from Foreign Policy to Global Policy 3

    Chapter Two: Green New Deal Can and Must be Global 11

    Chapter Three: National and Global Inequalities are Intertwined 17

    Chapter Four: Overhauling U.S. Foreign Policy 23

    Chapter Five: Making Rights Universal:
    The Contested Cases of Health and Workers' Rights 27

    Chapter Six: Racial Pandemic and Viral Pandemic:
    USA Is An Epicenter, But Both Pandemics Are Global: 33

    Chapter Seven: Divest From Violent Policing and Endless Wars:
    Invest Instead in a New Social Contract, Part One 35

    Chapter Eight: Divest From Violent Policing and Endless Wars:
    Invest Instead in a New Social Contract, Part Two 41

    Chapter Nine: Overhauling U.S. Foreign Policy 49

    Chapter Ten: Building Back a Better Africa Policy Should Not Mean
    Going Back to Old Ways 53

    Chapter Eleven: Africa/Global:
    "Daughter of Africa" Steps Up to Lead on Global Crises 57

PART TWO: From Global Apartheid to Global Solidarity 59

    Chapter Twelve: Confronting Global Apartheid Demands
    Global Solidarity 61

    Chapter Thirteen: Steve Biko Memorial Lecture 65

    Chapter Fourteen: Varshini Prakash on Redefining What's Possible 69

    Chapter Fifteen: From Disinvestment to Reinvestment 73

    Chapter Sixteen: African Young Women Resisting Beyond Borders 77

    Chapter Seventeen: African Feminist Charter 81

    Chapter Eighteen: Lessons Learned In Transnational Solidarity:
    Towards A Partnership of Equals 87

    Chapter Nineteen: African Trade Unions and Africa's Future 93

Chapter Twenty: Lawyers Crossing Borders 97

Chapter Twenty One: A Fuller Freedom:
The Lost Promise Of Pan-Africanism 101

Chapter Twenty Two: From Standing Rock To Line 3:
Indigenous Action to Save The Planet 105

Chapter Twenty Three: The Red Deal:
Moving Beyond the Green New Deal 111

Chapter Twenty Four: Pan-Africanist, Christian, and Queer 117

Chapter Twenty Five: We Must Free Our Imaginations 123

Chapter Twenty Six: Kumi Naidoo and Winona Laduke (Part 1) 127

Chapter Twenty Seven: Kumi Naidoo and Winona Laduke (Part 2) 133

Chapter Twenty Eight: Learning Lessons on Global Solidarity 139

Index 145

ACKNOWLEDGMENTS

Our thanks go first and foremost to the writers and activists whose voices are included in the chapters that follow. We encourage readers to look them up and learn more about their lifetimes of commitment to social justice. We are especially grateful to those who contributed original essays or interviews to the US-Africa Bridge Building Project: Donna Katzin, Rosebell Kagumire, Sahra Ryklief, Meredith Terretta, and Bishop Joseph W. Tolton.

We also thank Kassahun Checole at Africa World Press for making possible the publication of this book, and for his many decades as publisher of hundreds of books focused on Africa and the African Diaspora; and graphic designer Gail Oring, of GO! Creative, LLC, for her brilliant work in making this book a visual pleasure to read.

And finally, as editors, we are also grateful to those who fostered our values and provided opportunities for us to learn. Each of us owes enormous debts to family, friends, teachers, colleagues, and comrades, both those who are no longer with us and those still active in today's movements for social justice. Without them, we would never have had the experiences and contacts motivating us to compile this book.

Bill (William) Minter
Among those no longer alive, I am particularly thankful to:
- My parents David and Sue Minter, my aunt and uncle Elizabeth and John Minter, and my father-in-law Jim Sunshine;
- My teachers Paul Williams, Mrs. Celaya, Jacob Ajayi, Bernard Silberman, Paul Lehman, John Bennett, Ann Seidman, Joseph Miller, and Joseph Elder;
- My mentors on Africa and the world, including Paul Verghese, Margaret Flory, and Immanuel Wallerstein;
- My mentors in SNCC and FRELIMO, including Charles Sherrod, Eduardo Mondlane, Samora Machel, and Valeriano Ferrão;
- My friends and comrades Jennifer Davis and David Landes.

Among the living, to name only a few:
- My sisters Susan and Diane, my children Sam and Cynthia, and my ex-wife Ruth Brandon;
- My longtime friends and comrades Prexy Nesbitt, Elizabeth (Betsy) Schmidt, and Gail Hovey;
- My co-author and co-editor Imani Countess;
- My wife Cathy Sunshine, for companionship and insights over almost 40 years.

Imani Countess
Among those no longer alive, I am particularly thankful to:
- Professor Marie Perinbaum, who introduced me to Africa's rich and complex history and to the beauty and diversity of her peoples, cultures, and traditions;
- Jean Sindab, Jennifer Drayton, Damu Smith, Josephine Butler, Jack O'Dell, Jennifer Davis, and Keith Jennings, international solidarity activists on whose shoulders we continue to stand;
- William (Bill), Lucy, whose humor, humility, strategic thinking and commitment to human rights made him a hero of the labor and civil rights movements;
- Myesha Jenkins, feminist poet, anti-apartheid activist, always authentic and true.

Among the living:
- Scores of anti-apartheid, human rights, and economic justice activists and organizations, including the women and men of the Southern Africa Support Project, importantly Adwoa Dunn Mouton, Sylvia and Sandra Hill, and Joseph Jordan;
- Anti-racist, economic justice, and peace and solidarity activists, including Linda Burnham, Gerald Lenoir, Naima Natalie Bayton, Clarence Lusane, Peter Gribben, Loretta Hobbs, and James Early, to name only a few;
- The peoples of Southern Africa, who in their ongoing struggles for self-determination and human and economic rights continue to inspire;
- Friend and ally Prexy Nesbitt, who with great generosity and humor has always encouraged multiple generations to be the best that they could be.
- Individuals and institutions whose support was foundational to my ability to contribute to this book:
- The Open Society Foundations Fellowship Team: Alethia Jones, Stephen Hubbell, Milap Patel, Zachary Seltzer, Brian Bahe, and Mario Delgado and the 2019 – 2022 Economic Inequality Fellows cohort.
- The Building Bridges to End Illicit Financial Flows Advisory Group: William (Bill) Fletcher, Jr., William (Bill) Minter, Anyango Reggy, and Anita Plummer, along with the project's research assistants Nora Doyle, Seamus Love, and Kadidiatou Diallo.
- The US-Africa Bridge Building Project's first fiscal sponsor, the Fund for Constitutional Government, including former director Conrad Martin and current director Ian Gary.
- The US-Africa Bridge Building Project's research director, Bill Minter, for transforming the Transnational Solidarity Playbook from a vague idea to a well-conceived, comprehensive, and timely roadmap in part 2 of this book. And to Mary Semela for always being there.
- GO! Creative's Gail Oring and Holly Syrakos, who for decades have captured the essence and spirit of written words and enhanced them with beautiful designs.

Finally, I am extremely grateful to my siblings Gregory, Lisa, Kathy, and Jemal Countess and to my mother Colleen Countess. My children, Tendai and Tapiwa Chinhakwe, you keep me grounded, and to Albert Chinhakwe, no longer present but always with me – tozoonana.

FOREWORD

NONE OF US IS FREE UNTIL ALL OF US ARE FREE:
NEW PERSPECTIVES ON GLOBAL SOLIDARITY

Let me be frank. These are hard times. I am a Southern African. Our countries today are not the countries we fought to create a generation ago. Those of us who have been engaged all our lives in struggles for justice are too often reminded of truth by tragedy. In 2015, Mozambican Emmanuel Sithole was killed in a xenophobic attack in South Africa. At his memorial service, I had to speak. "Today," I said, "I want to make it clear and loud. I am a South African. I am a Mozambican, Zambian, Zimbabwean, Malawian. I'm Swazi, Sotho, Tswana." That day, I had to make it clear that the urgent problems faced in Southern Africa today could only be solved if we embraced a lived solidarity that transcended narrow nationalisms.

I first learned this solidarity with Frelimo in Mozambique as we fought to end Portuguese colonialism. With the support of allies from around the world, we gained our independence in 1975. I became the first Minister of Education. Education, especially for girls and women, has been my mission ever since. Education not just in knowledge and skills but in values. For us in Frelimo, one of our fundamental values was solidarity. After receiving it in our independence struggle, we offered it to freedom fighters from South Africa, Zimbabwe, Namibia and East Timor, sometimes at great cost to our own people.

Samora Machel, president of Mozambique and my husband, from 1975 until his death in 1986, said it this way:

> *"International solidarity is not an act of charity; it is an act of unity between allies who fight on different terrains for the same goals. The most important of these goals is to help the development of humanity to the highest possible level."*

Solidarity is an enduring foundation and goal, as the writers of this important collection make evident. Today we speak of Global Solidarity. It is required because what we face is Global Apartheid. As a Southern African, I experienced firsthand how South Africa's system of racial, economic, and social tyranny called apartheid, oppressed the entire region and cost the lives of millions of people, most of whom remain unknown. Yet, even during the wars to end colonialism and white minority rule, we understood that what we were experiencing was a microcosm of the whole world.

The history of European conquest and domination, the system of Western imperialism and global capitalism, ensured that wealth and power around the globe were structured to privilege one race over others and Europe and North America over all the rest. With the formal end of minority rule and colonialism, these structural inequalities did not end. They simply adapted to the new environment.

Saying this, I do not mean to take anything away from the great achievements of the late 20th century in defeating these centuries-old systems of oppression. On the contrary, the international anti-apartheid movement was the largest and most successful transnational movement for justice that the world has ever seen. Veterans of that movement who, in their courageous perseverance, along with generations of young people they have educated, are the voices you will find in this collection.

Here are stalwarts of international activism like Angela Davis and Kumi Naidoo. Here are young people, well known and not, Greta Thunberg and Tokata Iron Eyes. They focus on but are not limited to campaigns in Africa and between Africa and the rest of the world.

As I reflect on the triumphs we've experienced and the tragedies we've witnessed, I think of my friend Prexy Nesbitt. Our relationship captures in microcosm the kinds of personal and institutional connections that have sustained solidarity movements these many decades. Prexy is an American civil rights activist who came to Tanzania in solidarity with Frelimo in 1968. We began working together closely in the 1980s when he arranged for my travels to the U.S. to set up the Mozambique Support Movement.

A decade later, Prexy launched his program called Making the Road. He brought American young people to Southern Africa to meet their counterparts. It was my pleasure to welcome these groups to South Africa and to Mozambique, as I have met them in both countries. I tell them what a joy it is to see young people who are not convinced by the standard headlines in the U.S. about Africa: African hunger, African wars, African refugees. These are not who we are. These are the challenges we face. Challenges like those that Prexy and I have worked on together and separately now for more than four decades. We don't always know what we accomplish. But some of the Americans who came on Prexy's 2012 tour went home and later became organizers for Black Lives Matter. The torch is passed.

Prexy is the one who approached me about *None of Us is Free Until All of Us are Free: New Perspectives on Global Solidarity*. I commend to you the chapters in this collection. They comprise essays co-authored by William Minter and Imani Countess that appeared in a series in 2020 in AfricaFocus Bulletin, which Bill edits. They also include a series of web posts commissioned in 2021 and 2022 by the US-Africa Bridge Building Project, founded and directed by Imani. Taken together, they provide a rich resource for those engaged in the hard work of creating and sustaining solidarity networks of activists, organizations, and institutions.

Speaking at a rally against poverty in 2005, Nelson Mandela, president of South Africa, and my husband from 1998 until his death in 2013, spoke about a vision that is shared by the writers of this collection.

> *"As long as poverty, injustice and gross inequality persist in our world, none of us can truly rest. . . Overcoming poverty is not a gesture of charity. It is an act of justice. It is the protection of a fundamental human right, the right to dignity and a decent life. While poverty persists, there is no true freedom."*

These are hard times. The freedom struggles we fought and won did not create the just societies we sought. Still, our commitment to that just future, forged in struggle, is sustained by the solidarity we experience from friends and strangers around the world who keep the faith. The voices you will find in these pages well illustrate these connections across borders that teach and inspire us all.

Graça Machel

INTRODUCTION

GLOBAL CRISES CALL OUT FOR GLOBAL SOLIDARITY
WE CAN AND MUST WORK TOGETHER TO RESPOND

In the 21st century the scope of crises is global, encompassing the entire human race as well as other living beings and the earth itself. Climate disasters and pandemic threats mount. Violence escalates within households, on the streets, and on battlefields within and across national borders. Some are now calling this conjunction of crises a "polycrisis." Whatever the words used, the scale is unprecedented.

And each crisis intensifies existing human inequalities. These include the classic trinity of class, race, and gender; geographical divisions within and between nations; and countless other intersecting ladders of privilege, power, and abuse. For over five centuries, these have been embedded in an international system of global apartheid, reflecting the history of European conquest and domination.

Global Apartheid

The term "apartheid" comes from South Africa, notorious in the 20th century as the last stronghold of white minority rule. Political apartheid in South Africa ended in 1994 with free elections open to South Africans of all races. But South Africa and the world are still embedded in a global system in which wealth and power are still structured by race and place, both within and between nations. Moreover, exploitative relationships among human beings are paired with an extractivist approach to other living beings and the earth itself.

Apartheid is often understood as a simple dichotomy of white and Black. But even in the classic apartheid era in South Africa itself it was a complex ladder of privilege and mobilization of labor. English-speaking whites were at the top, followed by Afrikaans-speaking whites, then "honorary whites" such as Chinese, so-called "Coloureds," Indians and other South Asians, Blacks having residence rights in urban areas, Black migrant workers from the rural Bantustans, and "foreign natives" from neighboring countries such as Mozambique.

In Mozambique, as Samora Machel observed in a speech in Beira a few days before independence, there were "first-class whites" (born in Portugal), whites born in Mozambique, Asians, people of mixed race, "assimilated" Africans, and Africans regarded as "indigenous."

Similarly, global divisions can be seen as between "the West" and the rest of the world. "The West," in turn, can be conceived primarily as the Anglo-American world celebrated by Cecil Rhodes and Rudyard Kipling. Or it can be extended to the North Atlantic world, formalized in the North Atlantic Treaty Organization in 1949. The threat, it was clearly understood by the founders, included not only the Soviet Union, but also leftist forces in Western Europe and in Europe's colonial possessions.

Global apartheid, however, is not a dichotomy, but a complex set of ladders of inequality. These hierarchies cross national boundaries and change over time. But in the late 20th and early 21st centuries at least, the USA and the African continent epitomized the poles of inequality.

The USA and Africa

The United States of America became a global power after World War II. Its citizens trace their ancestral roots to all continents. But the self-description as "a nation of immigrants," featured by John F. Kennedy in his book with that title, masks a far more complex history.

Historian and activist Roxanne Dunbar-Ortiz put it clearly in her recent book *Not "A Nation of Immigrants."* Instead of being a land of opportunity for all, the USA was built on violent settler conquest of Native American peoples, slave labor of captives brought from Africa, and expansionist wars against territory controlled by other European powers. Subsequent 'immigrants' after 1776 were assimilated in different ways into a nation already defined by white supremacy.

Internal racial hierarchies within the USA paralleled the global hierarchies as successive European powers fought for preeminence. By the time of the 'scramble for Africa' at the end of the 19th century, the USA was already prominent enough to participate in the Conference of Berlin with 15 European powers, which laid out ground rules for completing the conquest of the African continent.

Under European colonial control of Africa until the 1960s, US and European political and intellectual elites, particularly in Britain but also on the European continent, shared common assumptions about white supremacy. They often drew from each other's thinking about how to manage subordinate peoples of African and other non-European origins. And as colonial and white minority rule held out for 30 more years in Southern Africa, both Republican and Democratic administrations were reluctant to break ties with the white regimes.

Despite all the achievement of formal political rights, the legacy of colonialism is still decisive in shaping internal inequalities in African countries and subordination to economic and political power structures in the Global North. Race remains one of the fundamental axes of inequality, both within and between independent countries.

Finding Distractions

Within such complex structures, privilege is relative. Almost everyone can find someone with greater privilege to envy or someone to look down on. Likewise, blame for one's own misfortunes can be aimed in many directions. Well-known examples include the long history of anti-Semitism in Europe and Korean merchants in Black urban areas in Los Angeles in 1992.

Within Africa, whether in the period of the slave trade or under colonial rule, conflict between ethnic groups could be fueled by explicit divide and rule strategies. But it also was built into economic and political structures of inequality allocating privilege and opportunity differentially. As better-educated groups took the lead in anti-colonial struggles, colonial authorities often found allies based in regions having less access to Western education.

In the USA today, there are two major alternative visions that serve as distractions from confronting the fundamental causes of national and global crises.

One is the Make America Great Again (MAGA) vision that finds threats to an imagined white Christian nation in both national elites and internal minorities. While Trump now personifies this vision, there are a host of others ready to tap these sentiments and a significant proportion of the population ready to listen. While clearly a minority, polls show this to be close to 40%. Opposition hovers at about 54%.

The other vision that is even more powerful is what might be called the Bipartisan War Party (BWP), bolstered both by the economic interests of the Military Industrial Complex (MIC) and the foreign policy establishment in the White House, Congress, and the media.

The influence of these militarist forces is visible in the extent to which the war in Ukraine has dominated U.S. foreign policy since the beginning of 2022. While media attention and public support for the war waned in 2023 and 2024, it has served as a distraction from other crises around the world and a prelude to the parallel bipartisan effort to promote a new Cold War with China.

Unity Without Uniformity

Outside Zambia, the contribution of President Kenneth Kaunda to Southern African liberation struggles is only rarely acknowledged, in comparison to the towering figures of Nelson Mandela of South Africa or Samora Machel of Mozambique. I never met him personally and have only been in Zambia for one brief visit in 1967.

But in reflecting on today's need for the kind of global solidarity that was a decisive factor in the defeat of white minority rule in Southern Africa, my thoughts turned to Kaunda's signature song Tiyende Pamodzi. I first learned the song from the version sung by the Mozambique Liberation Front (FRELIMO) in the war of independence from Portuguese colonialism. The refrain "tiyende pamodzi ndim'tima umo," which means "let us go together with one heart."

This became a theme song for national unity in Zambia as well as for unity against the white minority regimes in Southern Africa. Its success in Zambia is reflected in a profusion of covers of the song that one can find on Youtube.

Building unity, as President Kaunda demonstrated in Zambia, does not come from attempting to impose uniformity. It comes from joining with one heart to build a wider community and achieve common goals.

That was a challenging task for African nations built within borders shaped by outside powers. And it was even more difficult for bringing together the forces it took to overcome the last bastions of white minority rule in Southern Africa.

This Book

This book contains two series of posts.

The first series, published in 2020 in AfricaFocus Bulletin, focused on the major obstacles posed to global solidarity by the United States in particular. All were authored by William Minter and Imani Countess.

The second series, including both essays and other background documents, was published by the US-Africa Bridge Building Project between April 2021 and May 2022. It provided a range of diverse voices highlighting the potential for action to build social solidarity. Imani Countess directed the project and collaborated in the selection of authors and crafting of the essays. William Minter served as the editor of the series and Zeb Larson assisted with the editing of several of the essays.

The chapters in this book are the original text of the posts, as published. Although some details may now be dated, the fundamental realities presented then continue to be applicable today.

> Building unity...does not come from attempting to impose uniformity. It comes from joining with one heart to build a wider community and achieve common goals.

* William Minter is the editor of AfricaFocus Bulletin. Imani Countess is an Open Society Fellow focusing on economic inequality. This essay is the first in a multipart series beginning in January 2020. Thanks to Catherine Sunshine for editing some of the essays in this series.

PART ONE
BEYOND EUROCENTRISM AND U.S. EXCEPTIONALISM

CHAPTER ONE

STARTING POINTS FOR A **PARADIGM SHIFT** FROM **FOREIGN POLICY** TO **GLOBAL POLICY**

Since his election, Trump's erratic policies have aligned the United States with right-wing authoritarians across the globe, fed global currents of xenophobia and racism, and dismayed traditional allies. In 2019, nevertheless, foreign policy was a low priority in the 2020 presidential campaign. In January 2020, the administration's killing of Iranian leader Qassem Soleimani evoked widespread opposition amid fears of a wider war in the Middle East. Even so, evidence of new thinking on the U.S. role in the world, beyond opposition to Trump, remained sparse. Former Vice President Joe Biden called for a return to American leadership as it existed in an era "before Trump," and harked back to the "liberal" U.S.-led global order after World War II, which centered the alliance of Western democracies in the North Atlantic and the Cold War against the Soviet Union. But even Bernie Sanders and Elizabeth Warren only took tentative steps towards laying out an alternative foreign policy vision.[1]

Yet rising attention to the climate crisis, immigration, and economic inequality, while not categorized under "foreign policy," hints at a broader scope more attuned to a global vision. History, too, offers other options. Instead of only the North Atlantic, one can highlight the worldwide anti-fascist coalition in World War

The North Atlantic Treaty Organization was created in 1949 by the United States, Canada, and 7 Western European nations to provide collective security against the Soviet Union. Additional members brought the membership up to 27 by 2017. Credit: history.com.

II, the United Nations, international declarations on human rights, and the history of anti-colonial and anti-racist struggles around the world. In the era of African and Asian freedom struggles, Black American activists, but also many others, made connections between civil rights movements at home and their counterparts on other continents. This reached a height during the international anti-apartheid movement in particular. Activists today are beginning to make similar connections through their engagement in common struggles.

In exploring the options for new perspectives on national issues, activists and many other Americans are increasingly turning to a more critical examination of our history. Understanding the persistent legacy of slavery and colonial conquest is central to thinking about how to address contemporary domestic issues, including but not limited to racial justice issues.[2] A similar expansion of our time horizon, looking at how the past influences the present, is necessary for examining the causes of and solutions for today's global issues. This extends to the climate crisis, which is the result of more than two centuries of fossil-fuel-powered industrialization. It also applies to migration and economic inequality, which have been shaped by more than five centuries of conquest and colonialism by Europe and European settlers on other continents.

The two driving forces that shape U.S. foreign policy, eurocentrism and U.S. exceptionalism, are deeply rooted in U.S. history. The country began as a white settler state whose identity was formed by conquest of a continent and whose economy was built on slavery and appropriated land. Elite assumptions about a unique American destiny of unrivaled global leadership were solidified with the post—World War II global order. In recent years, many have criticized the current conventional wisdom, particularly its bias toward militarism, and offered new options for foreign policy.[3] But shifting the dominant framework is likely to require more than debate focused on foreign policy alone.

In 2020 and beyond, growing domestic social justice movements could provide a different starting point for shaping U.S. relations with the rest of the world. The global issues that are simultaneously domestic issues, we contend, must provide the overarching context for "foreign policy" toward specific regions and countries.

In conventional wisdom, foreign policy focuses on

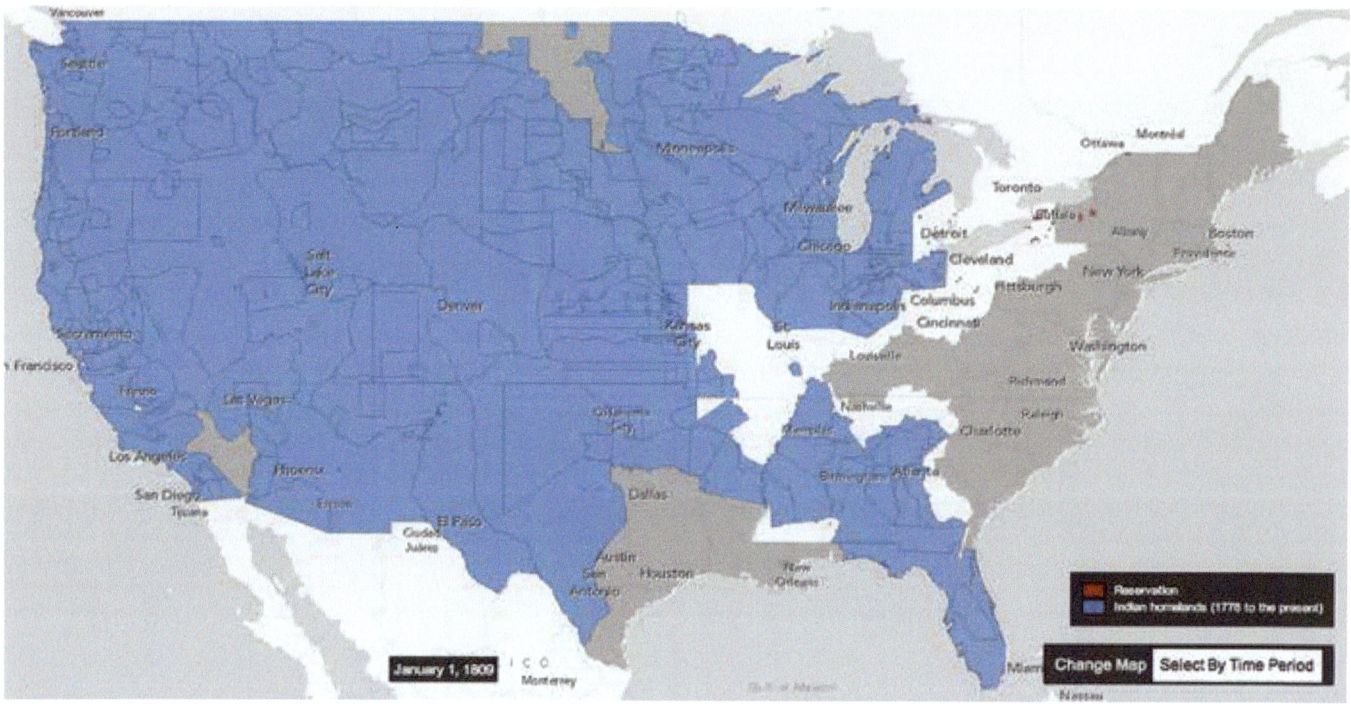

Interactive Time-Lapse Map Shows How the U.S. Took More Than 1.5 Billion Acres From Native Americans since 1776. Image shows map for 1809. For interactive map go to Slate.

geopolitics, economic competition, and military might, with a nod to diplomacy as well. All other issues, from climate change to human rights, migration, development, and economic inequality, are viewed as optional add-ons. A progressive alternative would give the highest long-term priority to these global issues, without ignoring the need to resolve immediate conflicts and manage state-to-state relationships with other countries. A "whole-of-government" approach, which has been most often applied to the national security sector, must put domestic and foreign policy within the same broader framework, one that prioritizes human security and human development at both national and global levels. Within such a perspective, foreign policy is not so much its own domain with separate rules, but rather a different arena in which the same issues must be addressed.

If one assumes a strict dichotomy of domestic policy versus foreign policy, it is natural that domestic policy will take priority in the eyes of most voters and politicians. Increasingly, however, almost all critical issues have domestic and international components and consequences that are closely intertwined. Climate change, to take just one example, is driven by emissions in the United States and multiple countries that rely on fossil fuels. It spawns lethal hurricanes in Texas and Florida and cyclones in Mozambique, wildfires in Australia and California. Nature does not respect national boundaries, and solutions must be implemented at all levels, from local to national and global. By taking our shared dilemmas into account, the United States can be better prepared to enter more productively into a truly reciprocal debate with other nations.

While the climate crisis is perhaps the clearest example, other issues are also closely linked across borders, blurring the distinction between domestic and foreign. Migration, a hot-button issue in many countries, has shared causes, including global inequality, wars and human rights abuses, and climate emergencies. The right-wing drive toward authoritarianism and unfettered corruption relies on divisive racial and ethnic appeals that have taken root in multiple countries. And secret financial flows across borders concentrate wealth in the hands of the super-rich, who use the proceeds to manipulate political systems in all parts of the world.

(L) Port Arthur, Texas underwater. Hurricane Harvey, 2017. Credit: SC National Guard / Flickr.
(R) Cyclone damage in Buzi, Mozambique. Cyclone Idai, 2019. Credit: Mozambique National Institute for Disaster Management.

What Do Democratic Candidates Say?

All of the leading 2020 Democratic presidential candidates understand that Trump's addictions to authoritarianism, racial and ethnic hatred, and the pursuit of wealth drive both his domestic and foreign policies. In this sense, the candidates do recognize the interconnections between domestic and global concerns. But a review of their foreign policy statements to date also shows significant differences in the ways they think about these issues.

Vice President Joe Biden, for example, calls for renewed American leadership and a return to pre-Trump normality, building on conventional foreign policy themes:

> "Today, Joe Biden laid out his foreign policy vision for America to restore dignified leadership at home and respected leadership on the world stage. Arguing that our policies at home and abroad are deeply connected, Joe Biden announced that, as president, he will advance the security, prosperity, and values of the United States by taking immediate steps to renew our own democracy and alliances, protect our economic future, and once more place America at the head of the table, leading the world to address the most urgent global challenges."[4]

He then lays out a long list of goals, but provides no vision of a common global effort in which the United States is a participant rather than a leader. There is neither a critique of past policies nor an analysis of how today's challenges differ from those of the past. In the summary on the Biden website, NATO is mentioned twice, and the United Nations or sustainable development not at all. Africa is cited only in the con-

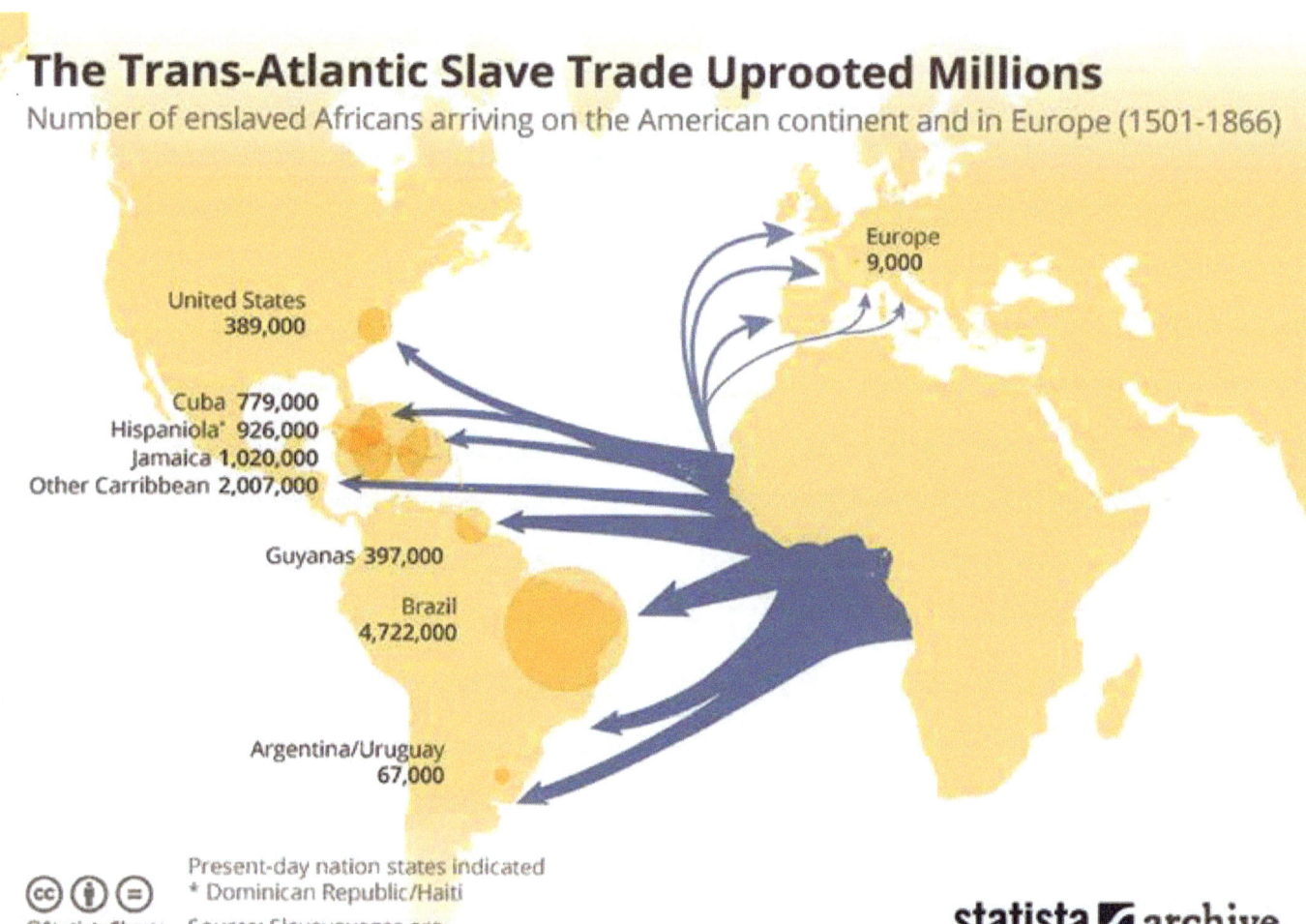

It is natural that domestic policy will take priority in the eyes of most voters and politicians. Increasingly, however, almost all critical issues have domestic and international components and consequences that are closely intertwined.

text of "integrating our friends in Latin America and Africa" into partnerships first defined by the North Atlantic partners.

Mayor Pete Buttigieg ambitiously titled his June 2019 foreign policy speech "America and the World in 2054: Reimagining National Security for a New Era." And the speech did include climate change and paragraphs on Latin America and Africa. Like Biden, Buttigieg called for American leadership based on American values. In addition, he advanced specific proposals on several topics. But there was no mention of the United Nations or of global action to address poverty and inequality, or of international collaboration other than rejoining the Paris climate accord.

As they do on domestic issues, both Senator Elizabeth Warren and Senator Bernie Sanders offer substantive new ideas on foreign policy, although their foreign policy visions are still incomplete. And the two candidates also contrast in similar ways on foreign as well as domestic policy. Sanders offers a more comprehensive and critical vision but lacks detail on alternatives. Warren has more detailed plans, but she has not yet addressed some of the critiques leveled by Sanders at conventional policy in the period since World War II.

Both Warren and Sanders share the critique of Trump's foreign policy advanced by other candidates. But they also give particular attention to the issues of economic inequality at a global level as well as domestically. While neither has advanced a systematic package of measures to address global inequality and sustainable development in order to narrow the wealth and income gaps between countries, Warren has incorporated key components of such a package into her plans under the rubric of economic patriotism.

The main pillar of that agenda is to protect and create American jobs. But in a supplementary plan for trade, Warren includes several provisions for using trade pacts to reinforce global standards, such as core labor rights and other internationally recognized human rights. She also proposes measures to address tax evasion and avoidance. In contrast to Biden's perspective, Warren's critique of previous U.S. foreign policy does not begin with Trump. In a speech at American University in November 2018, she described the postwar order as "not perfect." But, she added,

> "[B]eginning in the 1980s, Washington's focus shifted from policies that benefit everyone to policies that benefit a handful of elites, both here at home and around the world. Mistakes piled on mistakes. Reckless, endless wars in the Middle East. Trade deals rammed through with callous disregard for our working people. Extraordinary expansion of risk in the global financial system."

Warren went on, in this speech and in a contemporaneous article in Foreign Affairs, to lay out an agenda for "making globalization work" and "ending endless war." She also called for the United States to "work closely with allies to require transparency about the movement of assets across borders"—an issue that must be addressed to implement her well-publicized wealth tax of 2% on those with fortunes over $50 million. In December 2019, Warren launched her plan to address money laundering and related international corruption issues.

Sanders, for his part, stands out for his strong record on foreign policy since the 2016 election, including leadership in the fight to cut off U.S. support for the Saudi war in Yemen.[5] In September 2017 he spelled out his foreign policy vision in a speech at Westminster College in Fulton, Missouri, where Winston Churchill gave his famous "Iron Curtain" speech in 1946. Sanders linked domestic and global threats to democracy, warned about the limits and dangers of the use of military power, and highlighted key global issues, including climate change and economic inequality. And he stressed the importance of the United Nations, recalling Eleanor Roosevelt's reference to the organization as "our greatest hope for peace."

Among the candidates, Sanders has been alone in radically challenging American exceptionalism. In his 2017 speech, he hailed the reconstruction of Western Europe with the Marshall Plan and the fact that "there has not been a major European war since World War II." But he also recalled the history of "American intervention and the use of American military power … which has caused incalculable harm." He cited the Vietnam War along with U.S. interventions in Iran, Chile, and Iraq, and he castigated the counterproductive strategies of the global "war on terror." He concluded his speech with a call for "partnerships not just between governments but between peoples."

In the fall of 2018, Sanders further elaborated his vision in a speech in Washington and an article in The Guardian:

> *"On one hand, we see a growing worldwide movement toward authoritarianism, oligarchy, and kleptocracy. On the other side, we see a movement toward strengthening democracy, egalitarianism, and economic, social, racial, and environmental justice."*

The grand vision is inspiring. But Sanders is still silent on what forces might come together to form what he calls a "progressive international." As John Feffer points out in a commentary in Foreign Policy in Focus, "Sanders has a Eurocentric bias." Feffer notes that Sanders's speech in Fulton didn't mention Africa and hardly touched on Latin America or Asia. The principal partner in Sanders's progressive alliance is Yanis Varoufakis, the former Greek finance minister, who commented approvingly on Sanders's Guardian article and is engaged in building a progressive coalition in Europe.

Whether simply through the rejection of Trump or through the more developed insights offered by Warren and Sanders, all the Democratic candidates point in some way to the interconnection of domestic policy and foreign policy. Given the priorities of a presidential campaign, however, formulating and articulating a full, long-term vision is unlikely to be high on their agendas. Nor is it in any way a simple project to come up with a vision and a set of policies that are both persuasive and attentive to the complex and diverse realities of different policy arenas.

The Road Ahead

It's worth beginning to explore how a change in priorities on global issues might have implications for the conventional foreign policy framework based on geopolitics. This is relevant not only for the 2020 campaign, but for the development of social movements that can foster a richer conversation going beyond the conventional wisdom that currently prevails in political debate and among the foreign policy elite.

The following essays in this series focus first on the climate crisis and then on global economic inequalities, universal political and economic rights, migration, violence and security, and gender inequalities. A final sec-

> **The position of Africa in the global debate, diminished by bias and marginalization, closely parallels the treatment of African American experiences in U.S. policy more generally—another pivotal domestic-foreign link.**

tion considers how national history and national identity shape and define the United States' global role. We do not attempt the impossible task of providing a comprehensive analysis, but simply highlight some starting points for consideration within each issue cluster. Our approach does not center the big-power politics; instead we give more attention to the roles of multinational institutions, global civil society, and international social movements. We particularly highlight the centrality of the African continent to many of these debates. Not only is that our own background, but the position of Africa in the global debate, diminished by bias and marginalization, closely parallels the treatment of African American experiences in U.S. policy more generally—another pivotal domestic-foreign link.

In each case, we begin with recent shifts in the debate on national issues, shifts that have been fueled by progressive activist movements and have made their way into the Democratic primary debates. We lay out possible implications for foreign policy if similar changes were to be explored at the global level. And we contend that finding a new collaborative role for the United States on the world stage will require thinking that challenges conventional wisdom about our nation's history and national identity.

We begin, in the next essay in this series, with the climate crisis, where there has already been significant recognition of the intrinsic global connection.

Nelson Mandela, Deputy President of the African National Congress of South Africa, addresses the Special Committee Against Apartheid in the General Assembly Hall. 22/Jun/1990. *UN Photo/P Sudhakaran.*

We contend that finding a new collaborative role for the United States on the world stage will require thinking that challenges conventional wisdom about our nation's history and national identity.

NOTES

1. For summaries of candidates' positions on foreign policy, see articles in RollingStone and the Council on Foreign Relations. Summaries of election issues in The Guardian and Politico fail to mention foreign policy as an issue at all. Vox provides a regularly updated review of multiple issue areas, including foreign policy. This includes an article contrasting traditionalists Biden and Buttigieg with progressives Sanders and Warren. In December 2019, Indivisible released a scorecard that includes foreign policy and national security.
2. Two indispensable books for this historical examination are Roxanne Dunbar-Ortiz's An Indigenous History of the United States (2014) and Paul Ortiz's An African American and Latinx History of the United States (2018).
3. Our effort is not to substitute for these proposals but to complement them by highlighting social movements focused on national issues. One of the most comprehensive such frameworks is from Win without War. Phyllis Bennis of the Institute for Policy Studies covers a wide range of issues in an article in In These Times. Public Citizen concentrates on budget priorities with its People over Pentagon campaign. And the Quincy Institute provides a new forum for more restrained foreign policy views emphasizing statecraft and military restraint. The one recent essay we have found offering a similar approach to ours is a December 2019 article in the Guardian by David Adler and Ben Judah.
4. Quote is from the Biden website, accessed on August 4, 2019. The text is based on a speech given by Biden on July 11, 2019 at the City University of New York.
5. See the February 2019 essay in The Atlantic by Peter Beinart, "It's Foreign Policy that Distinguishes Bernie This Time."

CHAPTER TWO

GREEN NEW DEAL CAN AND MUST BE GLOBAL

January 27, 2020

July 2019 was the hottest month ever recorded worldwide, as a wide swath of the continental United States sweltered with heat indexes of over 100° F. This northern hemisphere summer also saw unprecedented heat waves in Europe and in the Arctic, from Alaska to Siberia. Greenland´s glaciers were melting at a unprecedented rate. Add in more frequent storms, flooding and wildfires, and the scale of the crisis is harder and harder to ignore, even in the United States, where climate denialism has been more prevalent than in any other major country.

In the 20th century, mainstream U.S. environmental organizations paid little attention to environmental racism, despite research and activist pressure highlighting the unequal impacts of environmental damage along racial and class lines. In the 21st century, and particularly since Hurricane Katrina submerged New Orleans in 2005, public awareness has grown substantially. Today's climate activists are homing in on climate justice issues, emphasizing how the climate emergency hits the most vulnerable populations with greatest force. Existing inequalities by race, class, and gender make recovery

Existing inequalities by race, class, and gender make recovery from disasters more difficult for minority communities, the poor, and women.

The Trump administration made its withdrawal from the global climate agreement official, but not before using its membership to block any meaningful progress at the 25th international climate summit in Madrid in December 2019. Nevertheless, the climate of opinion in the United States is shifting rapidly, spurred in part by the unprecedented wave of activism spearheaded by the youth-led Sunrise Movement. Public opinion polls show that a majority of registered US voters now favor the ambitious Green New Deal.

New social movements have expanded the horizon for debate on other issues in recent years: #OccupyWallStreet and the 2015 Sanders campaign on economic inequality, #BlackLivesMatter on racial inequality, #MedicareforAll on the right to health, and #MeToo on gender equality, to cite only a few. Yet the #GreenNewDeal and the climate crisis are the issue with the most easily understood links between "domestic" and "foreign" components.

from disasters more difficult for minority communities, the poor, and women. Women have fewer economic resources, face higher risks such as gender violence in disasters, and are left with greater responsibilities for care of children and the aged. And youth face a future with frighteningly greater climate risks.

Cyclone damage in Buzi, Mozambique. Cyclone Idai, 2019. Credit: Mozambique National Institute for Disaster Management.

All of these inequalities are accentuated at a global level, as illustrated by events in 2019.

Cyclone Idai struck Mozambique and neighboring countries in March 2019, leaving over 1,200 dead and some 2 million acres of crops destroyed by floods. Meanwhile, storms in the U.S. Midwest caused floods just as farmers were preparing to sow their fields. In each case the impact was devastating. Yet the toll was far greater in Mozambique, and the capacity to recover far less. Almost 150,000 people were displaced, and by the end of the year many were still in resettlement camps without permanent housing. In such contexts, in addition to the general misery, women and girls are particularly vulnerable to predators and opportunists.

The Rich Countries Must Step Up

The causal connection between climate change and extreme weather events is clear. The need for climate actions in both poor and rich countries is beyond dispute. These include mounting a sustainable response to crises, increasing resilience to the effects of climate change through adaptation, and rapidly accelerating action to cut greenhouse emissions from fossil fuels.

> The causal connection between climate change and extreme weather events is clear. The need for climate actions in both poor and rich countries is beyond dispute.

Whose responsibility should this be? At the 1992 Earth Summit in Rio de Janeiro, the first global climate agreement affirmed that much of the burden should be shouldered by the wealthy countries:

The Parties should protect the climate system for the benefit of present and future generations of humankind, on the basis of equity and in accordance with their common but differentiated responsibilities and respective capabilities. Accordingly, the developed country Parties should take the lead in combating climate change and the adverse effects thereof.

Greta Thunberg, 16, sits next to Tokata Iron Eyes, 16, during a panel at the Pine Ridge Reservation in South Dakota. Photo: Courtesy of Lakota People

The global climate agreement signed in Paris in December 2015 reconfirmed that, while all countries have obligations to act, rich countries have special responsibility for reducing greenhouse gas emissions and coping with the impact of worldwide climate disasters. Unfortunately, the agreement itself—which relies entirely on nonbinding voluntary pledges called Nationally Determined Contributions (NDCs)—does not include any provisions to ensure that rich countries meet this responsibility. According to analyses by civil society, rich country NDCs fall far short of what their "fair share" of global climate action should be.

Despite this, Donald Trump insisted that the Paris Agreement was "unfair" to the United States. Although the Trump administration has formally confirmed U.S. withdrawal from the agreement, to be fully effective in November 2020, all U.S. Democratic presidential candidates are opposed to U.S. withdrawal. But the next major opportunity to commit formally to stronger global action will be at COP26 in November 2020, before a newly elected U.S. president could take office.

In both its cumulative historical and current per capita emissions, the United States bears a major share of responsibility for the climate crisis. From the first use of in-

One of many #deCOALonize demonstrations in Kenya in recent years. "Coal ni sumu" means "Coal is poison." Credit: http://www.decoalonize.org/.

dustrial fossil fuels in 1750 through 2017, the United States contributed 399 billion tons of carbon dioxide—almost twice the 200 billion tons emitted by China. Germany, the United Kingdom, and India contributed 91 billion, 77 billion, and 49 billion tons, respectively, while the entire continent of Africa contributed only 43 billion tons (see the convenient summary charts from Our World in Data, a project of the Global Change Data Lab).

In carbon dioxide emitted per capita, with the exception of oil-rich Gulf states such as Saudi Arabia and Qatar, the United States also led the world in 2017, with 16.24 tons per person per year. Next in line were Japan with 9.45 tons, South Africa with 8.05 tons, and China with 6.98 tons. In contrast, most African countries, with the exception of major oil-producing countries, contributed less than half a ton per person per year.

Whether it falls under the label of Green New Deal or not, any major advance in the United States to curb use of fossil fuels and accelerate the transition to renewable energy will have significant impact worldwide. For U.S. climate activists, the highest imperative is making an impact on U.S. policy. Yet it is also essential from the start to put that campaign in global context and to acknowledge the initiatives being taken by activists around the world.

A solar-powered lamp allows this shopkeeper to stay open at night. Credit: Solarworks!

Grassroots Climate Actions

Most climate activists have come to understand, at least in principle, that it is the most vulnerable groups that suffer the greatest impact from the climate crisis, whether their disadvantages come from nationality, class, race, gender, or age. This disproportionate impact is reflected in the leadership and rank-and-file of climate activist movements around the world.

Women, particularly women of color and young women, are no longer only leaders behind the scenes, as they were in the civil rights movement and many other historical social moments. Instead they have become among the most prominent and visible spokespeople for climate change activism. African women activists have taken the lead in environmental struggles on the continent, such as the resistance to oil pollution in the Niger Delta and to the proposed coal plant in Lamu, Kenya.

The climate strike initiated by Swedish activist Greta Thunberg has gained supporters on every continent, including North America and Africa. While Thunberg has the most visible media presence, countless other activists, many of them indigenous, have been leading protests in various countries for years. Native American communities in the United States have been on the frontlines in seeking to block oil pipelines, linking these struggles to their own centuries-long commitment to protecting land and water. Teenage Lakota activist Tokata Iron Eyes spoke with Thunberg at the Pine Ridge Reservation in South Dakota in October 2019. "Indigenous people have been leading this fight for centuries," Iron Eyes told the audience.

Minimizing future climate damage depends on stopping the use of fossil fuels, most urgently coal. In China and the United States, as well as Western Europe, the decline of coal is well under way, a response to its inefficiency and the health damage from air pollution. But these major economies are also still financing and exporting coal technology. In June 2019, local activists in Kenya won a national court ruling that blocked a proposed Chinese- and American-backed coal plant in Lamu, on Kenya's coast. Significantly, this was the result of local activist initiatives in Lamu, bolstered by strong links with national and international climate activist groups.

Kenya is also one of the countries leading in innovative forms of renewable energy. Most popular is off-grid solar energy, which is now lighting homes for millions of rural consumers in Africa and South Asia who otherwise would have no access to electricity. Some 5 million households in Africa and South Asia have enough power to serve appliances as well as simple lighting. Growth is rapid, but the potential market of people lacking access to electricity worldwide is still over 800 million. International donors, including the US Agency for International Development (USAID), are supporting off-grid solar, although Obama's Power Africa Initiative primarily backed fossil fuel projects using natural gas.

There is great potential for further innovation in renewables. For example, cooking with solar electricity instead of wood or charcoal could help curb deforestation and prevent deaths caused by pollution from indoor cooking fires. To accelerate innovation, there is a need for collaborative transnational research that links technologically advanced countries with local researchers.

Implications for Multilateral and Bilateral Foreign Policy

If the United States were to give priority to the climate crisis, this would not only have implications for global climate policy; it would also affect our foreign policy more narrowly defined, reshaping bilateral relations with both large and small countries.

The effect of activist mobilization and lobbying is already apparent in the Democratic debate, with the campaign plans of both Bernie Sanders and Elizabeth Warren being particularly attentive to international obligations. When the Sunrise Movement decided this month to endorse Bernie Sanders, its statement also praised Elizabeth Warren, and its scorecard rated both candidates highly. Both candidates recognize that global commitments are essential to their visions of a Green New Deal. Sanders's plan envisages a $200 billion commitment to the UN's Green Climate Fund, while Warren's plan includes $100 billion for a Green Marshall Plan.

Climate activists realize, of course, that implementing such ambitious plans will require not only presidential action but also parallel legislation from Congress. They already have congressional allies, who have introduced legislation affirming a 10-year commitment to fund the Green Climate Fund at levels appropriate to the international need. But the fate of such legislation, and its funding at a level approaching either Sanders's or Warren's proposals, depends on changing the composition of Congress. That is why activists are campaigning not only for Democratic victories in the Senate and the House, but also in the primaries for candidates who are champions of action on climate.

In bilateral relations as well, taking climate into account would have consequences. For example, the effects of Trump's trade war have increased the costs of renewable energy goods dependent on U.S.-China trade. As rival global powers, the United States and China will inevitably have tensions in their relationship. But the potential for collaboration on renewable energy could be a strong countervailing force and a striking contrast to U.S.-Chinese collaboration on the climate-destroying Lamu coal plant. Corporations and scientists in different countries often collaborate even as they compete, and government policies can make working together either easier or harder. Among various factors that could put the brakes on a warming planet, few are as critical as a cooperative relationship between the U.S. and China, as noted by Wood Mackenzie Energy Transformation Outlook in August 2019.

Similarly, a comprehensive U.S. strategy aimed at curbing the use and production of fossil fuels in favor of renewable energy could lessen the intense geopolitical focus on Middle Eastern oil producers such as Saudi Arabia. This could potentially ease, though by no means solve, the complexities of that region. Unlike fossil fuels, whose distribution rewards some countries and penalizes others, renewable energy options such as solar and wind are more evenly distributed around the world. Moreover, when one country makes more use of sun and wind, it benefits the entire world as well. Mutually beneficial transfer of technology could take priority over competing for sales and access to fossil fuels.

> **A comprehensive U.S. strategy aimed at curbing the use and production of fossil fuels in favor of renewable energy could lessen the intense geopolitical focus on Middle Eastern oil producers such as Saudi Arabia.**

Admittedly, smart green growth, with its heavy reliance on information and communication technologies, also makes use of raw materials such as cobalt and rare minerals, the scarcity of which poses its own problems. But those problems can be addressed, for example, by research into alternate battery technologies, which is already motivated by the shortage of cobalt and by public protests against human rights abuses in cobalt mining.

Maximizing New Technologies Requires Political Choices

Carlota Perez, in her pathbreaking studies of the role of technology in history, argues that a technological revolution based on prioritizing knowledge rather than material goods has the potential to address not only the climate crisis but also global inequality. This will only happen, Perez stresses, if states take the initiative in planning to maximize benefits to the wider society, instead of only considering profits to private enterprises. Advocates of the Green New Deal in the United States stress that this change requires paying attention both to those affected by the transition and to those who are particularly disadvantaged because of deeply rooted structural inequalities. Similarly, according to Perez, smart green growth will be impossible without a radical shift on a global level to involve the majority of the world´s population as both consumers and producers. "The technologies capable of driving a sustainable global golden age are available," concludes Perez. "Unleashing them successfully requires an understanding of the historical moment and the willingness to make a clear socio-political choice."

First, though, we have to build broad political support for such a choice. This requires us to understand not only the competing technologies of the past and future, but also the structural inequalities, both national and global, that have been violently imposed throughout history and that still shape the present. In the past decade, the United States has seen significant social movements emerge to confront the domestic inequalities of race, class, and gender. But the United States and other privileged countries have hardly begun to confront the parallel global hierarchies built on centuries of conquest, slavery, colonialism, and patriarchy. Understanding and contesting global inequality must go hand in hand with developing technological solutions to the climate crisis.

There is great potential for further innovation in renewables. For example, cooking with solar electricity instead of wood or charcoal could help curb deforestation and prevent deaths caused by pollution from indoor cooking fires.

CHAPTER THREE

NATIONAL AND GLOBAL INEQUALITIES ARE **INTERTWINED**

February 24, 2020

The recession that began in 2008 brought new life to the public debate on class inequality in the United States. The #OccupyWallStreet demonstrations in 2011 may have left no institutional legacy, but they shined a spotlight on a yawning wealth gap and the role of the "one percent."[1] In 2020, these themes are being sounded in national media and even on the presidential debate stage.

At the same time, complacence about racial inequality is being challenged. Thanks to the activism of #BlackLivesMatter and other racial justice groups, there are perceptible shifts in public opinion, including among some whites and particularly among youth. The racial justice movement initially focused on police violence but rapidly extended its vision to fundamental issues of inequality and national identity. The impact on mainstream opinion was symbolized in 2019 by the 1619 Project, a New York Times Magazine feature reflecting on 400 years of the impact of slavery.

Gross economic inequality in the United States by class and race is not new, but it has increased rapidly in recent decades. Wealth inequality is far greater than income inequality, though both are on the rise. Economists Emmanuel Saez and Gabriel Zucman have compiled extensive data sets on wealth distribution since 1913. After wealth concentration peaked in 1929, the trend was toward greater equality until the late 1970s. Since then, though, inequality has increased steadily. Two factors among many are the declining strength of unions and tax policies that advantage the rich, enacted under both Republican and Democratic administrations.[2]

In 1979, in the United States, the top one-tenth of one % owned 7% of the wealth; this tripled to 22% by 2012. The share of wealth held by the bottom half of the population is almost net zero, as debts balance out assets. So the losses have hit the top 50% to 90% of families. The effects on minority populations have been particularly extreme.

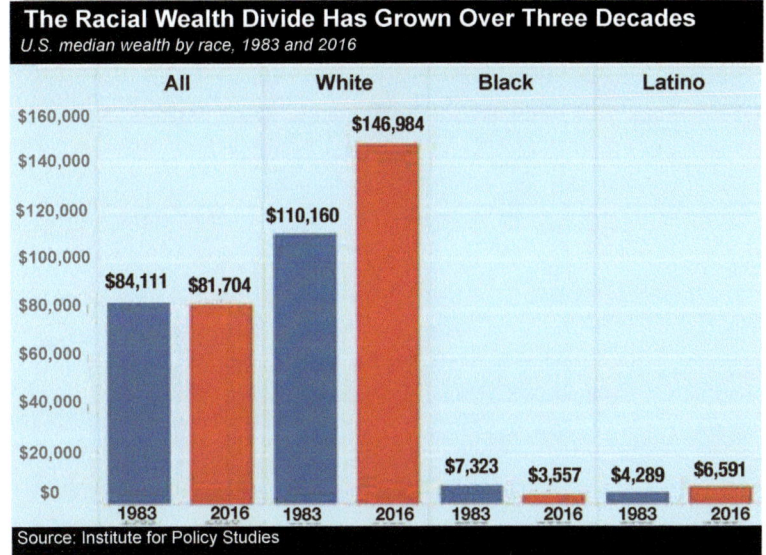

Public awareness of inequality, like awareness of climate change, was rising even before President Trump took office. But his administration's sharp turn toward denial and regression on both issues has spurred active opposition and cut into the complacency of conventional Democratic Party politics.

However, while most people understand the climate issue as global, the U.S. debate on national inequality between rich and poor households has not yet broadened into a conversation about global inequality between rich and poor countries. This theme remains muted at best, even among progressive activists.

What would it take to start such a conversation? An understanding of history, for starters:

- Slavery and its lasting impact, so well documented in this 400th year anniversary, was not just a U.S.

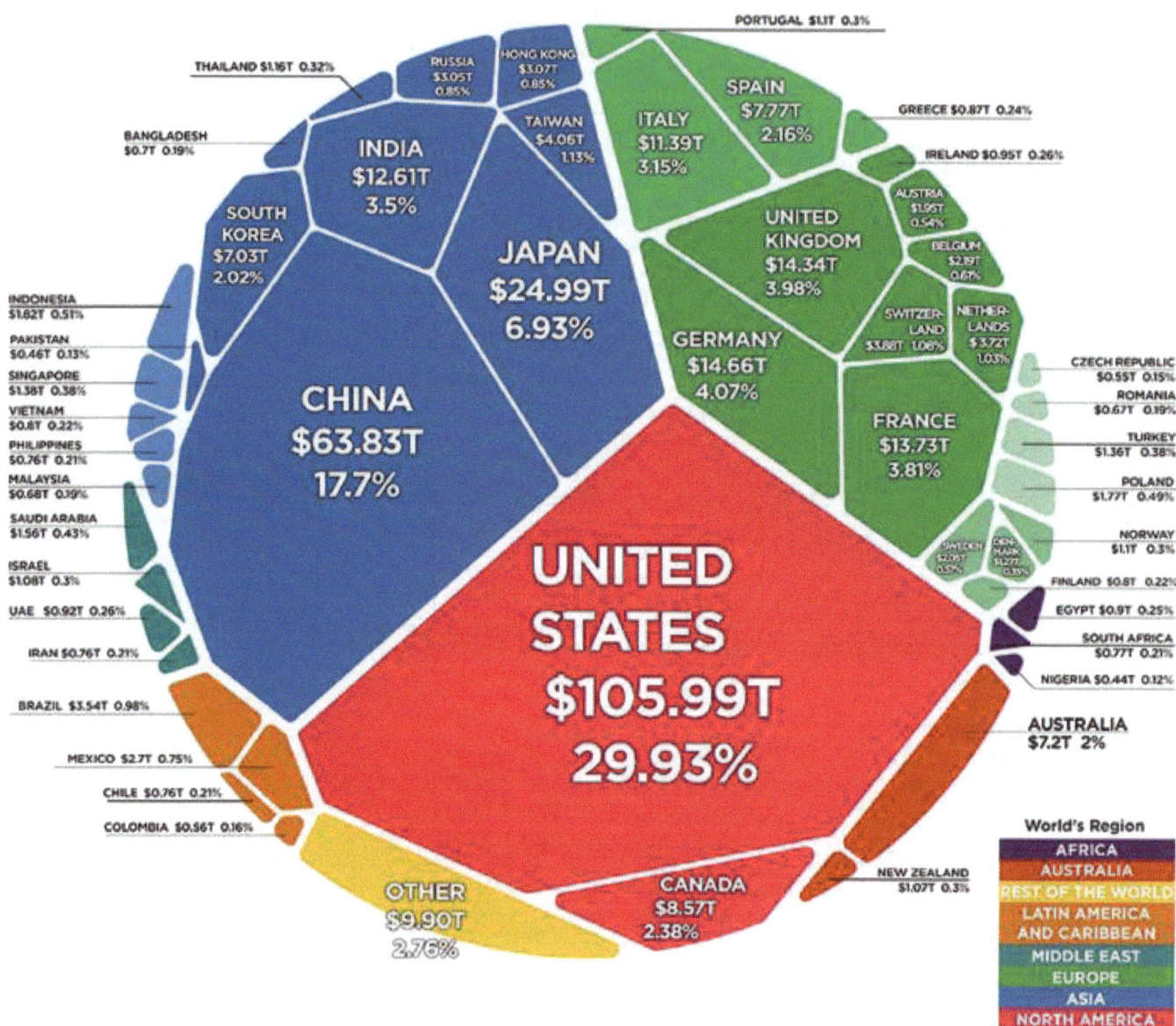

experience. It was shared by other countries in the Americas, based on a global capitalist system that included trade in slaves, sugar, and cotton. This trade was central to building the wealth of the United States and leading European countries.[3]

- The slave trade was followed in the late 19th century by European conquest of almost the entire African continent. Colonial economies were based on extraction of raw materials, shaping Africa's subordinate role in the world economy. Moreover, the post-colonial independent states still reflect, in large part, the authoritarian political legacy of the colonial state. African elites stash much of their wealth outside the continent.[4]

- After independence, African countries remained part of a global hierarchy dominated both politically and economically by the European and North American countries. While China has a seat on the United Nations Security Council and Japan is part of the Group of 7, these forums exclude Africa, Latin America, and the Middle East. These regions are also underrepresented in the powerful World Bank and International Monetary Fund.

- The U.S.-led "Western liberal world order" that followed World War II had two faces. On one hand, it was built on a foundation of white supremacy and market capitalism, while on the other hand, it enshrined values of anti-colonialism and universal human rights, reflected in the expanding United Nations system. In recent years a rising tide of ethnonationalism and right-wing authoritarianism is undermining this postwar liberal order, despite pro-democracy protests in every region of the world.

Global Inequality: Wealth Vs. Work

Beyond a grasp of history, U.S. activists need to understand how corruption, oligarchy, and inequality at the national level are tied to similar patterns around the world. Abundant evidence on rising global economic inequality is available from prominent academic sources.[5] Nongovernmental organizations focused on development, such as Oxfam and ActionAid, highlight not only global poverty but also the extremes of wealth and the rapidly widening the gap between the ultra-rich and everyone else. Tax justice organizations in Europe, North America, and Africa show how tax resources needed for public investment are hidden in tax havens around the world—not just in small countries such as Luxembourg and Bermuda, but also in major financial centers such as London and New York. The International Consortium of Investigative Journalists and related groups have done detailed reporting on secret transactions revealed in leaked documents such as the Panama Papers.

In January 2020, to coincide with the Davos World Economic Forum, Oxfam published its latest comparison. It observed that "In 2019, the world's billionaires, only 2,153 people, had more wealth than 4.6 billion people.... The richest 22 men in the world own more wealth than all the women in Africa." The previous year's Oxfam report noted that a wealth tax of 0.5% on the richest 1% of the world's population could "raise an estimated $418 billion a year—enough to educate every child not in school and provide healthcare that would prevent 3 million deaths."

Compared to income, the distribution of wealth by country and region is far more unequal. In 2019, the median wealth per adult in Canada and the United States amounted to $69,162, almost ten times the global median of $7,087, according to Credit Suisse. For the African continent, including North Africa, median wealth per adult was only $1,219. Thus the inequalities of history continue to affect the resources available to countries today.

Gender and Work

At every level of the global hierarchy, wealth inequalities intersect with inequalities based on race, ethnicity, and gender. Those who are rich can accumulate even more wealth over their lifetimes or over generations. Those who depend primarily on income earned from work struggle to stay afloat and are constantly vulnerable to losing their jobs.

According to Oxfam, "At the top of the global economy a small elite are unimaginably rich. Their wealth grows exponentially over time, with little effort, and regardless of whether they add value to society. Meanwhile, at the bottom of the economy, women and girls, especially women and girls living in poverty and from marginalized groups, are putting in 12.5 billion hours every day of care work for free, and countless more for poverty wages. Their work is essential to our communities. It underpins thriving families and a healthy and productive workforce."

> At every level of the global hierarchy, wealth inequalities intersect with inequalities based on race, ethnicity, and gender.

Oxfam calculates the monetary value of women's unpaid care work globally as at least $10.8 trillion annually—three times the size of the world's tech industry. Those laboring at low-paid jobs in health, education, and other essential sectors are also disproportionately women. Changing that reality requires public investment to provide public goods such as health, elder care, and child care, and ensuring that decent jobs with ade-

Credits: amandla.mobi and Labour Research Service.

quate pay are available to all. And checking the further growth of inequality, as technological change reshapes the global job market, requires government action to protect workers' rights and provide economic opportunities. It also requires adequately financed universal social protection systems to protect both those who work and those unable to work for reasons of age, disability, or other limitations.

Domestic workers in South Africa, as in most countries around the world, are underpaid and are often not protected by legislation covering the formal work sector. Unions have campaigned to expand such protections, with some success.

Technological innovation—automation, the internet, smartphones, and more—continues to accelerate. The impact on the workforce, in terms of who reaps the benefits and who is further disadvantaged, is highly unequal. The gig economy, subcontracting, and remote access to work over online platforms open up doors for some. Meanwhile, formal work protected by strong unions and government regulation is everywhere in decline. That is why those who study the "future of work" stress the urgency of collective action. The Global Commission on the Future of Work, for example, lays out ten principles that should be adopted, including a universal guarantee of basic workers' rights and social protection from birth to old age. Fulfilling these principles, however, requires both political will and financial resources.

Where's the Money?

Almost 10% of the world's wealth is held offshore, where it is shielded from the tax authorities of rich and poor countries alike. "Offshore," however, is not a physical location but rather a fiction of legal paperwork. Ultra-rich individuals, aided by bankers, lawyers, and other financial agents, hide their money in a web of shell companies, while multinational corporations mask profits through accounting sleight-of-hand. Countries desperately need revenue to support economic and social development, but the information necessary to locate and tax the money is rarely accessible. The facts of who actually owns the wealth and where it is earned remain hidden, becoming visible only when revealed in court or outed by whistleblowers or investigative journalists.

Credit: https://afrique.latribune.fr/

This is one of the key reasons why it is difficult for campaigns against global inequality to gain traction. Action must come from national governments, requiring political pressure focused on a single country. But the targets are elusive and their money easily takes flight across borders.

The latest and most sensational case is #Luanda-Leaks, from the International Consortium of Investigative Journalists (ICIJ) responsible for the #PanamaPapers and other previous exposés.

Africa's richest woman, Isabel dos Santos, daughter of the man who served as president of Angola for 38 years, used her family connections to siphon off wealth into a network of more than 400 companies in 41 countries. The story is told in detail on the ICIJ website and in other press reports. The ICIJ documents how this fortune was built with the collaboration of leading Western firms, who helped dos Santos move money, set up companies, and avoid taxes. They include two of the four major global accounting firms, PwC and KPMG, as well as the Boston Consulting Group, one of the three top global management consulting firms. Although dos Santos faces confiscation of some of her properties following the scandal, there is no sign that her global enablers will suffer any serious penalty.[6]

Recovering the Money for Public Goods

Governments in many countries are starved for resources to meet public needs, such as health, education, and other essential investments. But the need, and the hemorrhage of resources, is most blatant on the African continent. Estimates of illegal transactions in Africa show a loss of at least $50 billion to $80 billion in wealth every year, a figure that would be incalculably more if transfers made legal by loopholes and unfair treaties were included. Some flows are only seen as "legal" because the laws are written and interpreted by those who profit from the system. Nevertheless, even the outflow of clearly illegal funds is far greater than the estimated $40 billion a year that Africa receives in official development assistance.

Despite corruption at the top in many African countries, networks of civil society activists and honest public servants are organizing to expose and curb illicit financial flows—money that is illegally earned, transferred, or used. They are aware that the culprits are not only corrupt national leaders but a global system, requiring a global response. In 2015, a coalition of six Pan African activist networks launched #StoptheBleeding Africa in Nairobi to mobilize global support to end illicit financial flows.

African countries are taking action on their own to tighten controls on revenue losses. And dedicated civil servants in many African governments are coordinating these efforts through the African Union and the United Nations Economic Commission on Africa.[7] But their leverage is limited without support from the rich countries that shape global rules and host much of the stolen wealth. In the 1960s wave of African independence struggles, and again during the 1980s global anti-apartheid movement, African initiative spurred global solidarity, notably among African Americans as well as others in the United States. But illicit financial flows, despite their massive impact, lack the clear visibility of those earlier struggles.

Still, the issue is rising, both in the U.S. and globally, as demands for new public investments run up against the obstacle of where to find the money to pay for them. The logical answer, already surfacing prominently in the U.S. presidential campaign, is fairer taxation, targeting multinational corporations and the extremely rich.[8] This implies reversing the trend to minimize taxes on the rich which has accelerated since the 1980s. According to Emmanuel Saez and Gabriel Zucman, the average tax rate on income from capital dropped from a peak of 46% in the early 1950s to under 30% in 2018. Reformers are demanding a return to higher top rates for both individual and corporate taxes, as well as demanding new taxes, such as wealth taxes on the ultra-rich and the RobinHood tax on stock transactions.[9]

In addition to political will, two steps are essential to ensure that hidden wealth, estimated at anywhere from $9 trillion to over $21 trillion, is available for taxation. First, to ensure that multinational corporations don't conceal their profits by transferring them to low-tax or no-tax jurisdictions, there must be a legal requirement for public country-by-country reporting. This needs to include transparency on where money is earned, where workers are employed, details of taxes paid, and other key data, in public financial statements reported to the U.S. Securities and Exchange Commission.

Second, all corporations and other business entities must be required to make public reports on who really owns and controls them. The United States is one of the easiest places in the world to form anonymous shell companies. A requirement to report beneficial ownership would make it possible for tax authorities, lawmakers, and the public to "follow the money" and conduct informed debate about fair rates of taxation.

Steps toward these goals are gaining bipartisan support in the U.S. Congress, as well as among many investors and business leaders. According to an April 2019 report from the U.S.-based Financial Accountability and Corporate Transparency (FACT) Coalition, the trend is in the right direction. "The evidence suggests we are quickly reaching a turning point," said Christian Freymeyer, author of the report. "Investors see the value, policymakers see the benefits, and businesses see the inevitability of greater transparency. It's only a matter of time before tax transparency is accepted and expected of financial disclosure."

Freymeyer's analysis may err on the side of optimism, given the continued opposition from those with vested interests in tax avoidance. But the argument is gaining ground. Even limited actions will assist U.S. taxpayers and those in other countries seeking to tax resources extracted from their economies. Significant action will depend above all on the outcome of the 2020 elections. But it will also depend on continuing pressure from social movements, insisting that the U.S. government take responsibility for addressing inequalities not only in income and wealth but in access to fundamental human rights.

NOTES

1. See the website Inequality.org, especially the section on wealth inequality.
2. See the 2014 working paper by Saez and Zucman as well as their book The Triumph of Injustice: How the Rich Dodge Taxes and How to Make Them Pay. Saez and Zucman have advised 2020 presidential candidates Bernie Sanders and Elizabeth Warren on their proposed wealth tax plans.
3. See the special issue of AfricaFocus Bulletin, From Wakanda to Reparations. The New York Times 1619 Project included an essay by Matthew Desmond highlighting the fundamental role of slavery in the formation of American capitalism.
4. Recommended reading includes Walter Rodney's How Europe Underdeveloped Africa. On the continuing transfer of wealth out of Africa, see The Looting Machine, by Tom Burgis. A short essay by William Minter, Africa, Race, and World Order, is available on the AfricaFocus Bulletin website.
5. For a graphic overview, see Facts on Global Inequality on the Inequality.org website. For a summary based on data through 2005 from former World Bank economist Branko Milanovic, who pioneered the study of global income inequality, see the AfricaFocus page on national and global inequality. The issue has drawn enormous attention following the 2014 bestseller by Thomas Piketty, Capital in the Twenty-First Century. The latest data from Piketty and colleagues is available in the World Inequality Report, summarized by AfricaFocus in 2018.
6. See 3-minute vido Luanda Leaks Is a Global Story.
7. Initial findings were presented in the 2015 "Mbeki report." See also a 16-minute video presentation on the issue as well as ongoing coverage in AfricaFocus Bulletin.
8. This was spurred most dramatically by Warren's proposed 2% wealth tax. Sanders also offered a similar proposal. Other Democratic candidates, such as Biden and Bloomberg, also support more income taxes on the rich, although they stop short of advocating a wealth tax.
9. For an on-line tool to explore various plans as well as the current status quo, visit this site which accompanies the book by Saez and Zucman.

CHAPTER FOUR

OVERHAULING U.S. FOREIGN POLICY

Originally published in Organizing Upgrade
March 25, 2020

The COVID-19 pandemic is global, but national responses have spanned a wide spectrum. After initial denial, China mobilized massively and appears to be winning its battle against the virus. Several close neighbors of China—Hong Kong, Singapore, Taiwan, and South Korea—reacted quickly and decisively, taking advantage of systems set up to counter earlier epidemics.

But Italy and other European countries, as well as Iran, were slow to respond, and the United States is even more laggard, making these all countries vulnerable to exponential growth.

African countries, with the help of the World Health Organization, responded quickly, and the case count at this writing still mainly consists of imported cases from Europe. But the rapid growth that is almost inevitable in Africa could quickly overwhelm poorly resourced health systems. And social distancing is impossible for the majority of Africa´s population.

On March 23, South African President Cyril Ramaphosa announced a 21-day nationwide lockdown intended to curb the virus, with plans to mobilize national resources to protect South African formal and informal workers as well as businesses. His speech, available on YouTube and was detailed and determined. But implementation will be extraordinarily difficult.

Much of Latin America and South Asia is in a similar situation, along with many countries in other regions. And, as in the United States, investments in public health institutions have been eroded by austerity policies in countries around the world.

The Trigger, Not the Cause

At national and global levels, the pandemic has already led to drastic economic consequences, for the stock market and for the real economy. But the disease is the trigger rather than the only cause of these problems, notes Marxist economist Michael Roberts in an extended blog post. "That's because … now the profitability of capital is low and global profits are static at best, even before COVID-19 erupted. Global trade and investment have been falling, not rising."

Households and government institutions at all levels face challenges that are coming fast, and a fast learning curve is imperative if we are to survive. At an individual level, we are learning rapidly that social distancing, which is really physical distancing, is essential. Along with reaching out to our families and personal networks, we know we must mobilize support for essential health workers, grocery workers, and others

Policy debates show sharp contrasts between those who would use the crisis to blame others and accentuate inequalities and those who are questioning entrenched assumptions about the role of government in defending common interests.

who are required to work on the frontlines despite personal risks. One among many such creative efforts is a project in New York City that organizes unemployed gig drivers to deliver meals to vulnerable seniors.

At national level, the pandemic is revealing the failures of our institutions and testing their capacity to adapt. Policy debates show sharp contrasts between those who would use the crisis to blame others and accentuate inequalities and those who are questioning entrenched assumptions about the role of government in defending common interests.

Resistance to learning lessons is most firmly entrenched in the Trump administration and the Republican Party. But the pressure to bail out the rich and neglect the most vulnerable is widespread, despite calls for a different course, such as Senator Elizabeth Warren´s conditions for corporate bailouts, or this proposal to follow Denmark´s ambitious stimulus example.

At the global level, it is past time both for mutual learning and for solidarity. And on both counts, the United States is behind the curve.

Global Learning

Within specialized scientific communities, scientists from China, the United States, and other countries are in contact regularly to share research about the virus. "Preprint" articles appear daily on sites such as medRxiv. Although these articles have not been formally peer reviewed or published, they are an important means of airing new ideas and receiving scientific feedback. When one such article in early February sparked the viral spread of a conspiracy theory on Twitter, pushback was immediate, and the faulty article was withdrawn within days of its release.

At the policy level, however, ingrained institutional and cultural biases block rapid learning. This is particularly true in the United States, with its longstanding hubris and belief in U.S. exceptionalism.

Mainstream commentators, such as foreign policy veteran Dennis Ross, are already lamenting the U.S. failure to provide global leadership. But their emphasis is on how the United States is losing geopolitical ground to China rather than on the missed opportunity to learn from other countries´ experiences, including South Korea as well as China. Such learning is happening, but the pace is still limited by assumptions of U.S. exceptionalism and the lack of established bilateral channels at the level of governmental institutions.

There is also the need for more fundamental questioning of the models of industrial agriculture that analysts say have fueled the rise of zoonotic diseases, as natural habitats are invaded by human populations. According to a new report from the African Centre for Biodiversity:

> Like the climate crisis and economic inequality, the COVID-19 pandemic may not at first glance seem to be a "foreign policy" issue. But it powerfully points up the need to forge a global perspective—and global alliances—without delay.

"Most pandemics in fact, including HIV/AIDS, Ebola, West Nile, SARS, Lyme disease and hundreds more, have their roots in environmental change and ecosystem disturbances. These infectious zoonotic diseases originate from animals, wild and domesticated. These diseases are magnified through the erosion of ecosystem health, deforestation, biodiversity loss, ecosystem destruction and the removal of essential, natural, protective barriers."

https://youtu.be/Rd039yrRLuA

The point is also developed in a recent interview with Rob Wallace, author of Big Farms Make Big Flu.

Analyst Walden Bello argues that both Western and Chinese models of capitalism share this extractivist orientation.

Global Solidarity

With the United States struggling to confront the coronavirus at home, the country´s capacity to provide solidarity to other countries is very limited. Help will have to come from elsewhere when, as expected, the global pandemic and its economic impact land with full force on Africa and other vulnerable regions. If the United States wanted to help efficiently, it could immediately provide additional financial support to multilateral agencies such as the World Health Organization, UNICEF, as well as a UN special fund being launched.

The UN Secretary General on March 19 eloquently called for global solidarity:

"We are facing a global health crisis unlike any in the 75-year history of the United Nations—one that is spreading human suffering, infecting the global economy and upending people's lives. A global recession—perhaps of record dimensions—is a near certainty."

Saudi Arabia, the current chair of the G-20 group of major economic powers, has called a virtual summit for this week at the urging of India. Although the potential for agreement on common action is uncertain, it is very likely that China will play a major role, and that the United States will be irrelevant at best.

Already China is taking the lead, not only in dealing with the virus at home, but also in providing supplies and expertise to other countries. Initiatives are coming both from the Chinese government and from the Chinese private sector. Billionaire Jack Ma, for example, has provided 500,000 test kits and 1 million masks to the United States. He has also shipped 1.1 million testing kits and 6 million masks to Ethiopia to be distributed by Ethiopian Airlines around the African continent.

Cuba is not a member of the G-20, but it has continued its decades-long tradition of medical solidarity. When a British cruise ship in the Caribbean was denied entry by the United States and other countries, Cuba accepted the almost 1,000 passengers, including 50 with symptoms of coronavirus, and provided secure transport to meet chartered planes to fly them back to Britain. And last week, Cuba sent more than 50 doctors to northern Italy to join the battle there against coronavirus. A Facebook video of their arrival on March 22 gained almost 4 million viewers within 24 hours.

Like the climate crisis and economic inequality, the COVID-19 pandemic may not at first glance seem to be a "foreign policy" issue. But it powerfully points up the need to forge a global perspective—and global alliances—without delay. Progressives must lead the way, and the coronavirus is an immediate opportunity to change the way we think to always recognize domestic and global realities as intertwined. Both self-interest and moral values make this imperative.

Households and government institutions at all levels face challenges that are coming fast, and a fast learning curve is imperative if we are to survive.

CHAPTER FIVE

MAKING RIGHTS UNIVERSAL: THE CONTESTED CASES OF HEALTH AND WORKERS' RIGHTS

May 12, 2020

The global COVID-19 pandemic has made clear that the right to health is not just an aspirational value. Suddenly, it's a matter of desperate self-interest for everyone, except, perhaps, those insulated by enormous wealth. The same is true for the rights of workers in the United States and worldwide: their work and their consumer power are indispensable to a global economy facing recession. The current crisis thus presents an opportunity to expand the recognition and exercise of these pivotal rights, accelerating efforts that were already underway before the virus hit. But all too predictably, these efforts are running up against stubborn resistance from forces that benefit (or think they benefit) from the status quo.

In the 20th century, World Wars I and II spurred the formation of global organizations whose mandates included expanding "universal" social justice and human rights. Yet implementation lagged far behind formal commitments, and even those commitments limited both the rights that were included and the people to whom they were presumed to apply. Thus the International Labour Organization, founded in 1919, opened its constitution with the claim that "universal and lasting peace can be established only if it is based upon social justice." But the covenant of the League of Nations, founded the next year, failed to include the right of self-determination for all nations. Only two African countries, Liberia and Ethiopia, were members of the League. And campaigners for the rights of women, Blacks, and indigenous and colonial peoples found little sympathy among the architects of these new global organizations.

The interwar period saw the growth of right-wing authoritarian movements and states, and eventually the return to war. But at the same time, anti-colonial, civil rights, and labor movements around the world gained new momentum after World War I. Among the protagonists were war veterans of color who had been mobilized to fight overseas even though they lacked political rights at home. President Franklin Roosevelt also took steps toward expanding rights, although his New Deal was marred by the restriction of many of its programs to white men. An executive order in 1941 barred discrimination in the defense industry. And in his 1944 State of the Union message, President Roosevelt laid out a "second bill of rights" to apply to "all, regardless of station, race, or creed."

After World War II, the United Nations and the Universal Declaration of Human Rights embodied a similarly expansive view of human rights. But the commitment to these principles by member countries, including the United States, was hedged by many limitations.

A "Liberal International Order"

Fresh from the Allied victory over Nazism in World War II, the United States was a moving force in creation of the United Nations in 1945. The UN's initial membership of 51 nations included Ethiopia and Liberia in Africa, China, India, and the Philippines in Asia, and almost all the Latin American countries. Ironically, white-ruled South Africa was also a member, and its leader, Jan Smuts, played a prominent role as statesman, even though the state he led was based on white supremacy. Indeed, white supremacy at home and abroad continued to be the de facto norm for the United States and other Western powers.

The "liberal international order," according to Brookings Institution scholar Thomas Wright, is "generally defined as the alliances, institutions, and rules the United States created and upheld after World War II." Its pillars are the security order centered in NATO and the UN Security Council, and the economic order defined by the Bretton Woods institutions (the World Bank and International Monetary Fund). In all of these, the United States and its Western allies have played and still play dominant roles. Whether this order can be preserved or adapted, in the face of the Trumpian onslaught, is a point of current debate among the U.S. foreign policy establishment.[1]

Human rights is generally included as only a minor theme in establishment discussion of this postwar order. Nonetheless, international human rights law and associated United Nations institutions have outlined a global agenda encompassing social, cultural, and economic rights as well as civil and political rights. This agenda is buttressed by a host of international agreements on women's rights, workers' rights, and more.[2] It forms a framework for global consensus and an inspiration for civil society activists around the world. Yet in most aspects of this movement, the United States is at best a reluctant participant.

This was not always so. The negotiations toward the adoption of the Universal Declaration of Human Rights in 1948 were led by Eleanor Roosevelt. Much of the language echoed lofty ideals from the Atlantic Charter and the "Four Freedoms" speech of President Roosevelt, both in 1941, which had inspired people around the world during World War II.[3]

Subsequent decades featured more hypocrisy than dedication to human rights ideals, both globally and in the United States. At the same time, the rapidly expanding membership of the United Nations provided a sympathetic forum for advocacy of universal ideals. The U.S. civil rights struggle and global anti-colonial struggles both reinforced and paralleled each other in demanding that the freedoms fought for during World War II should apply to all human beings without exception.

Yet it took decades of struggle before the landmark expansion of political rights in the 1960s was achieved in the United States and Africa. White-minority resistance remained a powerful force, delaying the fall of white-minority regimes in Southern Africa to the last decade of the 20th century. In the United States, determined campaigns of voter suppression never stopped, despite the Voting Rights Act of 1965.

Subsequent decades saw the Republican Party's transformation into a white-minority bastion. The most extreme opponents of human rights for all, though they are a minority even among white Americans, now have a firm grip on political power in the Trump era.

A Spectrum of Rights Affirmed in Principle

The rights in the Universal Declaration were enumerated in 30 articles with a wide scope, including political, social, cultural, and economic rights. Although the generality of the language allows for diverse interpretations, subsequent international conventions have fleshed out the details of international human rights norms. Specialized international agencies offer guidance and coordination, although implementation is up to the signatory states.

The right to health, for example, is spelled out in many international agreements, including those mandating the responsibilities of the World Health Organization (WHO). The International Labour Organization (ILO), made up of representatives of governments, businesses, and trade unions, provides guidance on workers' rights, based on eight fundamental conventions and a host of other conventions and recommendations. The United States has only ratified two of the eight fundamental conventions and 12 of the other 182 conventions. Although ILO conventions are separate from the UN human rights framework, a 2016 UN Special Rapporteur's report spelled out how workers' rights are also inescapably human rights.

As documented by recent historians,[4] human rights activists as well as states have been selective in choosing which rights to prioritize and what standards to use to judge compliance by states. In part, this is normal human hypocrisy, visible in the foreign policies of all countries. It is far easier to stress the faults of others than to apply the same standards to oneself. During the Cold War, the United States and its allies emphasized the lack of political rights in the Soviet bloc, while the Soviet Union and its allies pointed to the United States' denial of civil rights to African Americans. For the U.S. government, tolerance of gross rights abuses in allied states of strategic importance has been standard practice since World War II.

What Kind of Rights?

Yet there are also substantive ideological disagreements in rankings of different human rights, by human rights activists as well as by governments, and these are apparent in the different levels of support for the international treaties that have been added to human rights law over time. A key distinction is between civil/political and economic rights. The United States is a party to the International Covenant on Civil and Political Rights of 1966, along with 172 other countries. However, it has signed but never ratified the International Covenant on Economic, Social and Cultural Rights, which has 170 countries as full parties to the treaty. It has also not ratified the majority of additional international human rights treaties adopted by the international community.

Thus, while according a modicum of formal recognition to civil and political rights, the United States has been an outlier in failing to support economic, social, and cultural rights, and specifically workers' rights, even in theory. In contrast to civil and political rights, where the main need is to protect against abuses by the state, the second set of rights requires proactive state responsibility for their fulfillment. Strikingly, the most prominent international human rights organizations, such as Amnesty International and Human Rights Watch, have also generally limited their portfolios to civil and political rights.

In recent decades, the principal challenge to a broad concept of human rights has come from the right, as a well-orchestrated intellectual and political campaign has elevated the rights of property ownership above all other rights.[5] Instead of expanding the U.S. debate on human rights to meet international standards, the trend has been to roll back the limited achievements of the 20th century that expanded, however tentatively, the state's responsibility to protect citizens' rights. This retrogressive campaign has reached new heights under Trump, and resistance has had limited success. Yet this may be changing, for structural and demographic reasons and, most recently, because of the COVID-19 pandemic.

New Focus on Health and Workers' Rights

The shifting landscape is most visible in revived demands for the right to health and for workers' rights. Both fall under the category of social and economic rights, and both offer the potential to link domestic struggles for human rights to a global agenda. The potential for shaping public opinion is well illustrated by the role of National Nurses United (NNU), one of the most politically engaged unions in the United States today.

With some 150,000 members, NNU represents only a small fraction of the 12.5 million workers in AFL-CIO—affiliated unions. But nurses consistently rank first among professionals in respect from the public. The NNU has strategically maximized its impact, not only by actively organizing in the workplace, but also by targeting key public policy issues. Working with the Bernie Sanders presidential campaign, it has spearheaded the campaign for Medicare for All. And it has successfully campaigned for state-level standards for safe staffing ratios of nurses to patients. The NNU has played a key role in changing the public debate on the right to health to make this a fundamental commitment for Democratic politicians.

Accepting health and workers' rights in principle, including the assumption that government action is necessary to implement these rights, is the foundation for applying these rights globally. Civil and political rights often receive attention in foreign policy because extreme cases of abuse are highly visible, particularly when spotlighted by media coverage and by local and international activists working in tandem to raise the issue.

April 20 - Nurses in South Korea, one of the countries with the most successful response to COVID-19, send a video message of solidarity to the National Nurses Union.

In some cases, workers laboring in the same industry on different continents have been able to build solidarity and confront multinational corporations. But the majority of workers worldwide are now service workers, many in the health and education sectors, or ´precarious workers´ in the informal sector. Government action, both national and international, is fundamental to any effective action to ensure their rights. Global union networks, such as Global Nurses United as well as Public Services International, which includes 700 trade unions representing 30 million workers in 154 countries, provide a framework for campaigning for the implementation of global standards. Such campaigns can stress the dual objective of serving public needs and ensuring the welfare of public service workers.

U.S. campaigns for implementation of human rights at home should begin to break from U.S. exceptionalism and draw inspiration from global standards developed through international collaboration. While implementation of rights always depends on mobilization to influence national governments, participation in the international dialogue provides access to new thinking about changes that are taking place at a global level. Thus, the recent Global Commission on the Future of Work lays out a "human-centred agenda for the future of work" to meet the challenges of globalization, automation, and rise of precarious labor. The goal of decent and sustainable work for all requires both public investment in people´s capabilities and changes in the institutions that manage work, in both rich and poor countries.

The first prerequisite for government action, in turn, is a strong union movement. And despite the low rate of unionization in the United States, compared to most other developed countries, there are some encouraging signs of revival. In 2019 a Gallup Poll showed the %age of Americans approving of unions rising to 64%, the highest rate in 50 years. Although union strength is still at a low ebb, new energy is visible in the autoworkers´ strike, campaigns such as the Fight for $15 minimum-wage campaign, and the wave of teacher strikes in both blue and red states. Within the Democratic Party, notably, political support for unions has been reviving, with increased attention from presidential candidates. And there is recognition that changing the legal framework to support workers´ rights is a high priority.

A key factor behind these changing attitudes is the demographic and occupational transformation of the working class. While the white male manufacturing worker remains the iconic image favored by pollsters and the media, it is nurses, teachers, and other service workers who are becoming the visible face of working-class activism. And that face is diverse. Some blue-collar occupations are now predominantly female,[6] and almost all include large numbers of people of color and immigrants. The three largest unions in the country are all composed of service workers, and the trend toward more service jobs is sure to continue. Moreover, to the extent that programs such as the Green New Deal and Medicare for All advance domestically, there will be a further boost in service jobs, including those in public service, from local governments to federal agencies.

This changing workforce can potentially provide a growing constituency for global perspectives. The trade union movement faces many internal issues, including with hierarchy, patriarchy, and racism. But progressive unions such as the NNU, the Chicago Teachers Union, and others, as well as parallel campaigns such as Fight for $15 and Jobs with Justice, are having a grassroots impact. Many of their leaders and members are also open to a transnational perspective, influenced by shared objectives with workers in other countries and by the increasing numbers of recent immigrants in their ranks.

What Difference Does a Pandemic Make?

Even as these changes reshape the U.S. workforce and labor movement, the COVID-19 pandemic has shined a harsh light on U.S. denial of the right to health and workers' rights—and the impacts of this denial on the whole society.

At this writing in May 2020, the need for massive government action to address the pandemic is widely recognized, except by those at the top levels of the Trump administration. The crisis has shocked many Americans into a new awareness of the inequalities of race, class, occupation, and place, factors that to a large extent determine who bears the greatest burden and greatest risk. Front-line medical workers and essential workers in meatpacking plants and in agriculture, for example, are disproportionately people of color, many of them from immigrant communities.

Around the world, many nations and multilateral institutions are mobilizing to respond to the virus. Promising experiences can be found in countries such as South Korea, New Zealand, and others, and in breakthroughs such as the rapid testing kits developed in Senegal. Africa overall, despite many vulnerabilities, has had excellent leadership from multilateral institutions such as WHO and Africa CDC, as well as from some governments such as South Africa and Senegal. African countries have so far managed to stay ahead of the virus curve, although the continent, like other developing regions, is hit hard by the economic impact of national shutdowns, as well as by fallout from the global recession.

Yet the Trump administration, instead of learning from other countries and advancing plans for controlling the virus and expanding stimulus and recovery measures, is ramping up denial. It is shifting responsibility to the states while denying them needed resources. It casts blame on China and on the World Health Organization, seizing the opportunity to further weaken global institutions. Fortunately, other nations are stepping up to support WHO, and the organization's COVID-19 Solidarity Response Fund has raised over $200 million from almost 300,000 donors.

While some U.S. states, particularly the early responders on the West Coast, may have flattened the curve, most have not. And by prematurely reopening their economies, some are courting renewed exponential growth of the virus, egged on by President Trump and by protesters mobilized by far-right networks. While no one can accurately project the future, most experts expect that the national toll of the pandemic will remain at the current level or even continue escalation into next year.

Democratic members of Congress can propose actions, such as additional stimulus bills to aid states and local governments and even more ambitious plans such as an essential workers' bill of rights. But further action also depends on concessions by the Republican-controlled Senate and the administration. And even implementation of measures passed is limited by incompetence and by ideology and built-in bias.

It is clear that neither confronting the virus nor absorbing the lessons it can teach can rely on the White House. Instead, leadership is falling to state, city, and local governments, along with an outpouring of mutual aid efforts. These responses, shaped by politics, are highly uneven, with Republican-controlled states less likely to take strong action. But as the virus spreads in red and rural states over the coming months, mounting deaths in these areas may eventually convince some skeptics that government has a role to play.

The toll of COVID-19 deaths is revealing in real

time the deadly effect of right-wing Republican policies. As the impact continues to mount in red states as well as blue, the impact will still be unequal by race and class. But whites who have supported the right-wing agenda will not be spared by the virus.

The contrast between governors and mayors who act to protect their population and those who do not will be inescapable. Despite efforts to divert the blame to foreigners and minorities, the virus will continue to expose the failures of the anti-government message and enhance the case for inclusive government responsibility.[7]

Changing minds to accept the right to health and workers' rights as fundamental principles, and even more changing government policies, still face enormous obstacles. But accepting these rights at home, in the context of a global pandemic, should be and hopefully can be, a first step toward accepting its application to the entire human community living on one planet.

Note: Links to books in this essay are to the new nonprofit http://bookshop.org, which provides support to local independent bookstores, as well as providing an affiliate option for others who want to promote books without reinforcing Amazon's monopoly power. Disclosure: AfricaFocus Bulletin is an affiliate of Bookshop.org and will earn a small commission if you click through and make a purchase.

NOTES

1. For example, see the article just cited by Thomas Wright, and a summary article by Graham Allison in *Foreign Affairs*, July/August 2018.
2. Data on the treaties included and their status by country are available at http://indicators.ohchr.org/.
3. The central role played by Eleanor Roosevelt is summarized in a recent article by the United Nations Foundation and vividly portrayed in a 2018 5-minute video by UN Web TV for the UN 70th anniversary, using archival footage as well as contemporary commentators.
4. For a clear account of an expansive human rights vision in the 1940s and one more focused on gross abuses in the Soviet Union and Latin America in the 1970s, see Mark Philip Bradley, *The World Reimagined: Americans and Human Rights in the 20th century* (excerpt here). Human rights scholar Samuel Moyn, in his recent book *Not Enough: Human Rights in An Unequal World*, writes less clearly than Bradley but presents a strong critique of the limits of actual human rights language in addressing global inequality.
5. See the detailed account by Nancy MacLean, Democracy in Chains: The Deep History of the Radical Right's Stealth Plan for America. MacLean recounts economist James Buchanan's opposition to school integration in 1950s Virginia, linked to wider rejection of the role of government to tax to benefit the majority. Buchanan's career as well as dissemination of this ideology was promoted for decades by the Koch brothers network of rich donors.
6. This is also true globally, as illustrated by statistics on gender breakdown for health workers and education workers.
7. See "The Race-Class Narrative and Eroding the Racist Right" by William Minter and Prexy Nesbitt, reviewing two new books relevant to the potential for change, Merge Left and Dying of Whiteness.

CHAPTER SIX

RACIAL PANDEMIC AND VIRAL PANDEMIC: USA IS AN EPICENTER, BUT BOTH PANDEMICS ARE GLOBAL

June 8, 2020

The twin pandemics of racism and coronavirus are colliding, in reality and in metaphor. Anti-racism scholar Ibram X. Kendi writes in the Atlantic of "the racial pandemic within the viral pandemic." And the meme of "America's two deadly viruses" has gone viral on Twitter. But while one is a literal (and new) virus and the other an endemic condition that has persisted over centuries, the scope of each spans the range from local communities to the entire planet.

The footprint of these intersecting pandemics differs by geography and by the distribution of vulnerability along many lines of inequality. Actions of resistance also vary from place to place and over time. But there are, nonetheless, common threads in the global response, eloquently summed up in an online monologue by Trevor Noah, the South African comedian who has become one of the most incisive media commentators on American society. His comments were entitled "George Floyd and the Dominos of Racial Injustice."

"You know what's really interesting about what's happening in America rights now is that a lot of people don't seem to realize how dominoes connect, how one piece knocks another piece that knocks another piece, and in the end creates a giant wave."

> Each story seems completely unrelated and yet at the same time I feel that everything that happens in the world connects to something else in some way, shape, or form.
>
> While everyone is facing the battle against coronavirus, Black people in America are still facing racism and coronavirus."

In June 2020, the United States is an epicenter of both pandemics. The outcomes here will have deep effects not only on this country but around the world.

Demonstrators in many countries are mobilizing in solidarity with the US-based Black Lives Matter movement. On June 2, 105 African writers expressed this global solidarity in an open letter:

"As African writers without borders who are connected beyond geography with those who live in the United States of America and other parts of the African diaspora, we state that we condemn the acts of violence on Black people in the United States of America."

The letter went on to cite the names of those killed most recently, such as George Floyd and Breonna Taylor, followed by a long list of others; it also acknowledged the many unnamed. The writers added:

"We note in dismay that what Malcolm X said in Ghana in 1964 that 'for the twenty million of us in America who are of African descent, it's not an American dream; it's an American nightmare' remains true for 37 million in 2020."

This global response is not only a matter of empathy, spurred by the explicit video of George Floyd's murder, which was viewed worldwide. It is also a recognition that anti-Black racism is global, not confined to any one country. This racism shows itself in the treatment of Africans and Afro-descendants in a wide range of countries, even those without large Black populations, such as China. It is reflected in the position of the African continent in the global hierarchy, and in the racial hierarchy within the global institutions that make up the postwar order.

Around the world, the impact of the coronavirus pandemic within each country intersects with that country's specific structural inequalities. In countries that are relatively homogeneous in racial terms, such as most African countries and many Asian countries, the most

Credit: "The George Floyd Murals of Minneapolis: A Demand for Justice, Hope and a Better Humanity" thirdeyemom, June 9, 2020

salient division may not be race. But in every country, sickness and death from the virus, as well as income losses and medical costs, have inflicted disproportionate suffering on the most vulnerable. Each society's response in turn reveals the weaknesses or strengths of its governmental institutions.

A few countries across the political spectrum have managed the viral threat with relative success: Taiwan, South Korea, Vietnam, New Zealand, Cuba, Norway, and Senegal, among others. Among those that have failed most spectacularly are the United States and Brazil, two countries with vast racial and other social inequalities linked to a history of conquest and slavery. In the United States, the Trump administration has refused to respond constructively to the pandemic even as it undermines global institutions, such as the World Health Organization, that are attempting to do so.

But all countries face or soon will face the cumulative impact of global recession as well as the continued threat of a virus that is not going away any time soon. Meanwhile, the clock is ticking for effective action to curb the coming apocalypse of climate change.

All of us—in local communities, popular organizations and movements, national governments, and multilateral institutions—must think deeply and imaginatively about the destructive institutions inherited from previous generations. Institutions at all levels must decide whether to fund state violence or public health and, more broadly, whether or not to curb private greed for public good. Corporations and governments must choose whether to destroy the planet with fossil fuels or speed a transition to renewable energy. Returning to the previous status quo is not an option. We can increase the damage by resisting structural change, or we can move decisively toward new inclusive and sustainable societies.

CHAPTER SEVEN

DIVEST FROM VIOLENT POLICING AND ENDLESS WARS: INVEST INSTEAD IN A NEW SOCIAL CONTRACT, PART ONE

August 24, 2020

The Black Lives Matter protests following the murder of George Floyd in May 2020 have been the largest wave of protests in American history, according to calculations by the New York Times. They have erupted across the country in red states and blue states, in big cities and suburbs and small towns. This uprising, sparked by racial disparity in police violence, is playing out against a national backdrop of striking racial inequality in COVID-19 illnesses and deaths. Multiple surveys have documented significant recent shifts in public opinion on race, including among many white Americans.¹

> The current wave of protests in the United States has received intense exposure in the global media. The whole world is watching, as it was during the massive protests of the Vietnam War years.

Going beyond a long history of failed reform efforts will be difficult. But the debate has been intensified and deepened with calls for action at local, state, and federal levels to defund the police and invest in positive rather than punitive programs to ensure public safety. The Justice in Policing Act, passed in June by the US House of Representatives, offers a limited set of reforms. The broader scope of activist demands is illustrated by the Breathe Act, proposed by the Movement for Black Lives, which calls for divesting federal resources from incarceration and policing and investing in new approaches to community safety.²

Such a comprehensive approach, with massive budget implications, is unlikely to win approval even from a majority of Democrats in Congress. But it sets a visionary benchmark for a direction that is increasingly accepted. This direction is reflected in incremental steps being taken in localities around the country, from major cities such as San Francisco to smaller communities such as St. Petersburg, Florida.

Protesters and even some establishment figures, their voices amplified by the mainstream media, warn that current efforts will again fall short unless the nation confronts its legacy of white supremacy, so deeply rooted in history. Symbolic measures are coming first. Confederate monuments and flags, at the forefront of the debate, represent the nation's original sin of slavery. But statues of Columbus have also been targeted for removal, reflecting the recognition that white supremacy is also based on the nation's other historical sin: conquest. Andrew Jackson, celebrated by President Trump, symbolizes these twin pillars of white supremacy; his statue was recently removed from the Mississippi city named for him.

The current wave of protests in the United States has received intense exposure in the global media. The whole world is watching, as it was during the massive protests of the Vietnam War years. The response abroad reflects the empathy and solidarity that many people feel with respect to Black struggles for justice in the United States. But there is also a recognition that anti-Black racism is global and not confined to any one

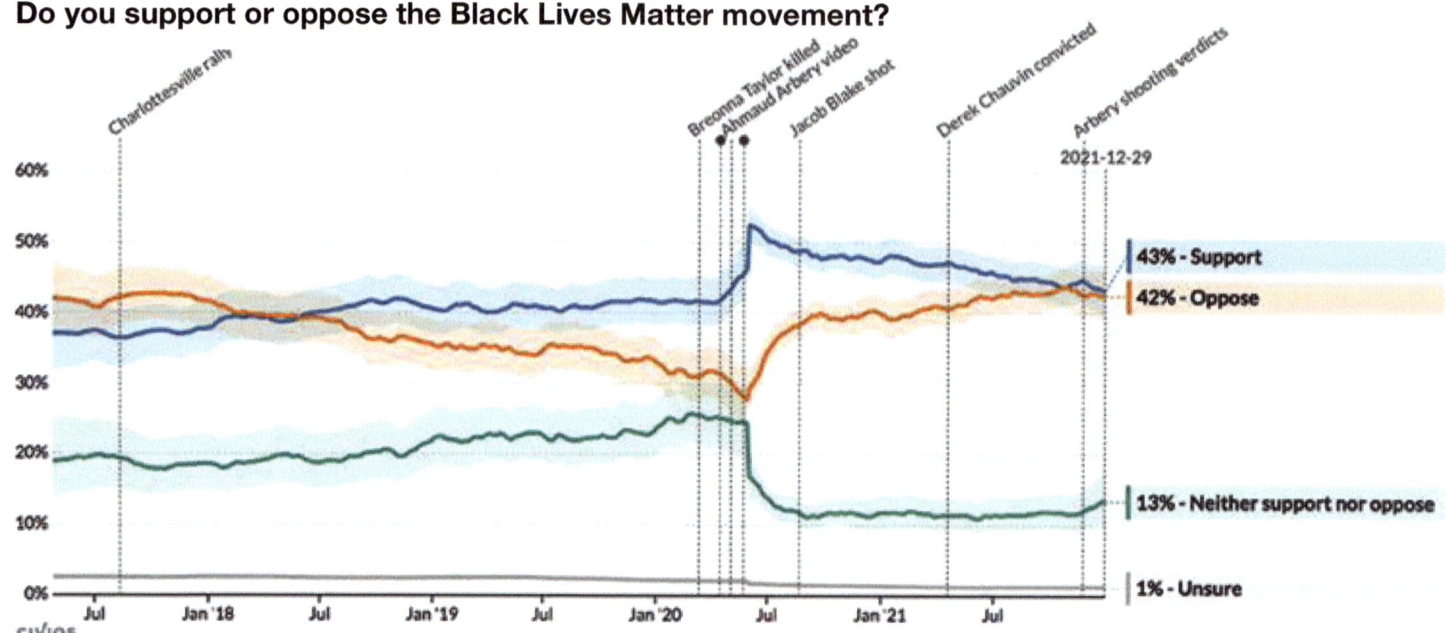

country. This racism shows itself in the treatment of Africans and Afro-descendants in a wide range of countries, even those without large Black populations, such as China. It is reflected in the position of the African continent in the global hierarchy, and in the racial hierarchy within global institutions.

Despite the heightened attention to police violence in recent years, reporting and statistics from around the world are patchy and inconsistent. Even global human rights organizations, such as Amnesty International, only feature systematic documentation for a few countries, despite the existence since 1979 of an internation-

Police killings amid pandemic shutdowns in Kenya and South Africa have raised the question of whether Black Lives Matter to African governments; so has the ongoing police violence against civilians in Nigeria.

Protesters outside the United States insist that the history and practices of their own countries must also be questioned. As Kenyan analyst Nanjala Nyabola wrote in Foreign Affairs, the police in Kenya and other African countries continue the colonial practice of institutionalized brutality. In Europe, where demonstrators have denounced police violence and racism, protesters toppled the statue of slave trader Edward Colston in Liverpool, England. Police killings amid pandemic shutdowns in Kenya and South Africa have raised the question of whether Black Lives Matter to African governments; so has the ongoing police violence against civilians in Nigeria.

al code of conduct for law enforcement officers. It is generally recognized that police violence is a common feature of authoritarian regimes and of countries engaged in civil wars. But the reality of police violence, disproportionately inflicted on the most vulnerable, is often hidden from public view in most if not all countries around the world.

Nevertheless, looking at the United States in comparative perspective, three points are clear. First, the country consistently ranks highest among developed countries in killings by police relative to population. Second, the pattern closely parallels that of other white settler societies and other countries that were part of

European colonial empires, most notably the extreme cases of South Africa and Brazil. And third, global police practices during the 20th and 21st centuries have been and are still deeply influenced by the U.S. example, both through official government links and through the U.S.-based International Association of Chiefs of Police.

In the following section, we review briefly the significant changes in the narratives about police violence and racism that have taken place in recent months. These changes are the result of scholarly critique and activist protests that have mounted steadily for more than a decade.

Changing the Narrative on Police Violence and Racism

In mid-August the Civiqs daily tracking poll showed that support of Black Lives Matter among registered voters overall was still at almost 50%, compared to 37% opposition. But among whites, levels of support first rose to exceed opposition 44% to 34% before dipping again to 40% support against 46% opposition. Among white Republicans in particular, opposition to

> In mid-August the Civiqs daily tracking poll showed that support of Black Lives Matter among registered voters overall was still at almost 50%, compared to 37% opposition. But among whites, levels of support first rose to exceed opposition 44% to 34% before dipping again to 40% support against 46% opposition.

In a second part of this essay, sent out separately, we first sketch some of the key stages in the evolution of white supremacy and state violence stemming from slavery, conquest of a continent, and overseas empire building. We then look at how the current framework for global military security, prominently including but not limited to the United States military, reflects a destructive logic similar to that of domestic policing

Black Lives Matter dipped to a low of 59% in late May, but rose again by mid-August to 78%.

Even if the November election sweeps new leadership into the White House and Congress, entrenched racism within the police and other institutions of power will pose a formidable obstacle to change. And even as protests continue, unexpected events and Republican messaging may fuel the backlash in favor of white rac-

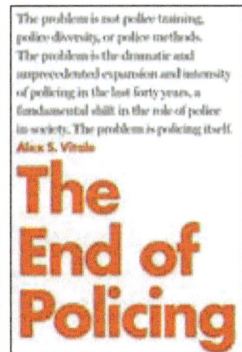

Chapter 7: Divest from Violent Policing and Endless Wars: Invest Instead in a New Social Contract, Part One

Credit: WDRB News

ism. The movement, it is clear, must have staying power if it is to accomplish its goals.

The foundation for such staying power consists has been built by than a decade of work by scholars and activists, and on the intersection of Black Lives Matter with a wide range of issues and organizations. It is not concentrated in only one organization but in mutually reinforcing local and national networks sustained and expanded by personal connections, by social media, and by common narratives.

Recent surveys of scholarship undergirding demands for radical change in policing cite dozens of authors.[3] One could fill a small library with widely praised books on police violence and racism published in recent years, beginning in 2010 with The New Jim Crow by Michelle Alexander and The Condemnation of Blackness by Khalil Gibran Muhammad, both recently republished. Other noted titles include White Rage (2016), by Carol Anderson; From #blacklivesmatter to Black Liberation (2016), by Keeanga-Yamahtta Taylor; and Making All Black Lives Matter (2018), by Barbara Ransby. In The End of Policing (2018), Alex Vitale provides a concise account of how the expansion of policing in recent decades has accentuated rather than ameliorated the fundamental problems.

In the early years of President Obama's first term, the most visible protests were from the right, with the rise of the Tea Party. This pattern reflected and intensified the long-standing white backlash against the civil rights advances of the mid-1960s. The murder of Trayvon Martin in 2012 and the acquittal of his murderer in 2013, however, sparked what came to be called #BlackLivesMatter. That movement grew rapidly after the police killing of Michael Brown in 2014. And it has continued to grow, forcing widespread media and public recognition of the reality of disproportionate and unjust police violence against Black men and women. Significantly, the movement, with Black women and LGBTQ people playing central roles, has also modeled an inclusive vision aimed at justice for all, across all the barriers of structural inequality in society.

Also essential to the impact and sustainability of the Black Lives Matter protests is the fact that the movement is rooted in long-standing local campaigns against police violence. To cite just one example, the police station at Homan Square in Chicago had been notorious since the 1960s for systematic brutality, including torture. The abuses were exposed publicly in 1983, and in 1993 the commander, Jon Burge, was fired. In 2014, following appeals from Chicago activists, the United

Nations issued a condemnation citing violation of international anti-torture statutes. And in 2015, sustained community campaigns led to a Chicago city council resolution approving a reparations package. In 2020, victims were still waiting for a promised memorial to be constructed.

It is local organizers in Chicago and in cities and towns around the country who have kept Black Lives Matter campaigns going, even during times when the national spotlight was focused elsewhere. At the national level, the Movement for Black Lives, a broad coalition of national organizations and local groups, issued in 2016 a platform of demands, including community control of law enforcement agencies and an end to the war on Black people. Many similar demands were echoed in the plans for criminal justice reform outlined by Democratic presidential candidates, particularly Bernie Sanders and Elizabeth Warren. Even more significantly, activists in other social movements—as well as majority of the Democratic Party—have increasingly been forced to recognize that fighting systemic racism must be part of their agenda as well.

The Sunrise Movement, focused on the climate crisis and the Green New Deal, has been composed mainly of young white people, along with some non-black people of color. But its activists have stated explicitly that climate justice implies a commitment to fight environmental racism. It is no accident that local hubs of the Sunrise Movement have been actively engaged in the latest round of Black Lives Matter protests.

The overt racism of the Trump administration has encouraged violent threats and actions by its white supremacist supporters. This in turn has spurred anti-Trump forces to recognize that combating racism is essential to the mobilization against him. The persistent organizing work of the Black Lives Matter network prepared the ground for the participation of many whites, especially youth and women, in anti-racist efforts. Organizational networks such as the Indivisible Movement were also ready to reinforce the message in the streets and in local political arenas.

As protests continue in communities around the country, such as those in Louisville, Kentucky, around the murder of Breonna Taylor, there are many remind-

Also essential to the impact and sustainability of the Black Lives Matter protests is the fact that the movement is rooted in long-standing local campaigns against police violence.

Thus when high school students led national protests for gun control after the killing of 17 people in 2018 in Parkland, Florida, young Black activists reached out to them about the killings in their own communities. Gun violence, the Black youth made clear, is not just a matter of school shootings, but of pervasive racism, a point that the white activists acknowledged. These protests marked a turning point in national opinion, and by the end of 2019, polls showed solid majorities for common-sense gun control measures such as universal background checks and a ban on assault weapons. Gun control activism also primed the young protesters for participation in a wider movement.

ers that opposition to reform remains strong. Indeed, the response to protests in Portland, Oregon, shows the ominous potential for federal intervention deliberately aimed at inciting further violence. The images of heavily armed local police and federal agents on the streets of Portland and other American cities have prompted much discussion of the militarization of law enforcement. Through an array of programs, the U.S. government funnels hundreds of millions of dollars in military surplus to local police departments each year.

The notion of policing as a war, in which more lethal force will lead to more security, is not a recent development, but is deeply rooted in U.S. history. The police and the military share the country's legacy of white supremacy and violence against racial others, which has also given rise to mob and individual violence by white civilians. Both domestic law enforcement and the conduct of foreign wars continue to reflect the history of conquest, slavery, and U.S. empire of earlier centuries.

For the second part of this essay, go to http://www.africafocus.org/docs20/viol2008-2.php

NOTES

1. See news reports in the Washington Post and New York Times, as well as more detailed poll results from Pew and Civiqs. The Civiqs results are updated daily.
2. Whether one uses the term "divesting," as in the Breathe Act proposal, or "defunding," as in the hashtag and street slogan #Defundthepolice, activists realize that this is a process that must take place step by step, as positive actions to protect communities gradually replace violent policing. The goal of full abolition of violent policing, almost all proponents agree, is a vision that will be difficult to achieve in practice even if the political will is there. In the title of this essay, we use the terms "divest" and "invest" together to emphasize that the two processes must be simultaneous.
3. See, for example, the recent series by Boston Review on policing. For books, see The Best Histories of U.S. Policing in New York magazine.

CHAPTER EIGHT

DIVEST FROM VIOLENT POLICING AND ENDLESS WARS: INVEST INSTEAD IN A NEW SOCIAL CONTRACT, PART TWO

August 24, 2020

Policing and Empire: A Deadly Feedback Loop

The interactions between policing, racism, and the U.S. military vary enormously across time and place. In some instances the relationship is positive. In particular, the two world wars of the 20th century led to advances in international human rights law, such as the Geneva Conventions and the global human rights system constructed after World War II. Both within the United States and around the world, veterans of color returned home to demand that they and their communities should enjoy the same rights that they had been fighting for. Their actions contributed decisively both to the U.S. civil rights movement and to anti-colonial movements around the world.

Nevertheless, violence against racial "others" has been pervasive, with the history of conquest and slavery feeding into contemporary policing and U.S. wars. This is amply confirmed by recent scholarship and commentaries on the history of U.S. policing, usefully summarized in a New Yorker article by Jill Lepore.

> The elephant in the room in these debates has long been what the armed militias of the Second Amendment were to be used for.

A few examples, ranging over the course of U.S. history up to the present, well illustrate the point.

Let us briefly consider the iconic Second Amendment, the violent displacement of Native Americans over centuries, the territorial expansion of U.S. empire in the late 19th century, and the growth of domestic policing and its international expansion in the 20th century.

The Second Amendment was adopted in 1791, after almost two centuries of colonial settlement in what was to become the United States. It reads in full: "a well regulated Militia, being necessary to the security of a free State, the right of the people to keep and bear Arms, shall not be infringed." As historian Roxanne Dunbar-Ortiz explains, this historical context is still relevant despite the passage of more than two centuries and the expansion of U.S. power across the continent and around the world:

"The elephant in the room in these debates has long been what the armed militias of the Second Amendment were to be used for. The kind of militias and gun rights of the Second Amendment had long existed in the colonies and were expected to continue fulfilling two primary roles in the United States: destroying Native communities in the armed march to possess the continent, and brutally subjugating the enslaved African population."[1]

The violent displacement of Native Americans within the territory that is now the United States began with Spanish settlers in Florida and New Mexico in the late 16th century, even before English settlers first arrived in Virginia in 1607. The violence continued with conquest of the East Coast and New Mexico in the 17th and 18th centuries. Then came the forced expulsion of

Native Americans from the South in the infamous Trail of Tears, under the Jackson administration in the 1830s, to make way for white settlers to occupy the land and grow cotton on plantations using slave labor.

The conquest of the American West, then home to many of the continent's indigenous peoples, followed in the second half of the 19th century. The assault on Native lands continued in the second half of the 20th century with displacement for construction of dams and, in recent years, pipelines—intrusions that are still being contested.[2]

From the Spanish-American War of 1898 onward, U.S. wars included not only the iconic World Wars I and II, but also the construction and defense of a formal and informal empire that spanned the globe.

August Vollmer is not a household name, but his career trajectory reflects the historical links between policing and the military. He served as the police chief of Berkeley, California, from 1909 to 1923. Vollmer was influential in shaping law enforcement around the country, becoming known as the father of modern American policing and a pioneer in the academic field of criminal justice. His drive to professionalize the police was built on his experience in counterinsurgency in the Philippines after the Spanish-American War.

Vollmer was not an exception. According to historian Stuart Shrader, writing in 2014 in the wake of the killing of Michael Brown in Ferguson, Missouri:

"A close look at the history of US policing reveals that the line between foreign and domestic has long been blurry. Shipping home tactics and technologies from overseas theaters of imperial engagement has been a typical mode of police reform in the United States. ... From the Philippines to Guatemala to Afghanistan, the history of US empire is the history of policing experts teaching indigenous cops how to patrol and investigate like Americans. ... But the flow is not one-way: these institutions also return home transformed."

This mutual influence has manifested itself in open wars in Southeast Asia in the 20th century and in Iraq and Afghanistan in the 21st century. But it has also spawned pervasive global structures to manage not only these wars, but also the war on drugs, the policing of immigration, and the post-9/11 war on terror.

A Global Military

The Breathe Act, proposed by the Movement for Black Lives, includes a demand to dramatically reduce the budget of the U.S. Department of Defense. This is echoed in more detailed proposals put forth by antiwar activists and defense analysts. The global reach of the Black Lives Matter movement implies that a similar reckoning must come for the global security system. Progressives must scrutinize, expose, and challenge the endless wars pursued by the United States military along with the parallel failures of global counterinsurgency and counterterrorism strategies.

> From the Spanish-American War of 1898 onward, U.S. wars included not only the iconic World Wars I and II, but also the construction and defense of a formal and informal empire that spanned the globe.

United States military spending far exceeds that of any other country, adding up to more than the total of the next nine countries. Despite rising criticism of wasted money and endless wars, however, in late July 2020 significant majorities, including Democrats as well as Republicans in Congress, defeated an amendment to cut 10% from the total Pentagon budget of $740.5 billion. The vote was 324 to 93 in the House of Representatives and 77 to 23 in the Senate.

In contrast to the Vietnam War era, there is currently no strong antiwar movement in the United States with links to progressive movements focused on domestic policy. The default assumption in public debate is that U.S. wars are waged in order to protect the security of the United States. And with no military draft to

   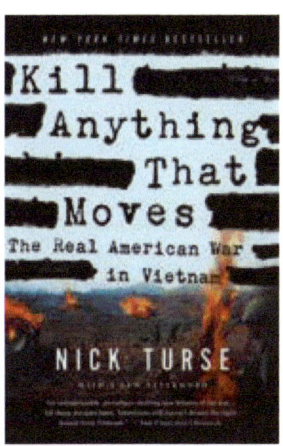

spread the pain widely throughout society—as during the Vietnam War—the loss of U.S. lives in wars abroad remains largely invisible to the media and the public. Nonetheless, there are abundant critiques, across a wide political spectrum, of the U.S. military posture, and a widely shared uneasiness about "endless wars."[4]

> Much more common, throughout the years of the Cold War as well as the post-9/11 era, is U.S. complicity with authoritarian regimes to wage aggression without the presence of large numbers of U.S. troops on the ground.

The toll of U.S. wars, of course, is by no means limited to the U.S. personnel who lose their lives. The wars involve a scale of violence against civilians that systematically violates international human rights law, primarily targeting those seen as racially "other." In the Indochina wars of the 1960s and 1970s, in covert interventions throughout the post-World War II period, and in the Middle East wars and the global war on terrorism of the years since 9/11, there has been little accountability to international standards.[5] Moreover, U.S. policy systematically rejects any international obligation to allow independent review of the U.S. military presence around the world.

Violent Repression But No Security

Impunity for abusive state violence and failure to provide security are more common around the world than respect for the rule of law. The United States is no exception. It is important to explore the unique U.S. history and legacy of white supremacy that underpins the resistance to change. But it is also important to recognize that the United States, however powerful, is far from alone in its failures. No nation can claim to have found the solutions or to be above the need for accountability.

Because of the global scope of its military force, the United States is indeed the largest force for state violence outside its own borders in the current era. But in many active conflicts this country is neither the exclusive nor even the primary factor driving these wars, which are also shaped by internal forces and by other outside actors. As Elizabeth Schmidt has extensively detailed in her two-volume study, the scope, nature, and impact of foreign intervention in Africa varies enormously across cases.[6] However iconic, U.S.-dominated interventions such as those in Afghanistan and Iraq are the exception rather than the rule worldwide.

Much more common, throughout the years of the Cold War as well as the post-9/11 era, is U.S. complicity with authoritarian regimes to wage aggression without the presence of large numbers of U.S. troops on the ground. U.S. involvement in such cases can unfold largely without attracting the attention of the U.S. media. The slaughter of as many as one million Indonesians in 1965—1966 has no resonance in U.S. public memory, unlike the Vietnam War. But U.S. officials both encouraged and collaborated with the slaughter of as many as half a million people, directed by the military forces that brought General Suharto to power and kept him in office for 31 years. "Jakarta" became a code word in Latin America for anti-communist mass killings, which the United States supported over decades.[7]

> Because of the global scope of its military force, the United States is indeed the largest force for state violence outside its own borders in the current era.

Whether the United States is actively involved or plays a secondary role to other actors, however, the post-9/11 counterterrorism and counterinsurgency wars tend to operate with the same logic. With a relatively low toll in American lives, they have little visibility to most of the U.S. public. But these forever wars have produced mounting costs in U.S. resources as well as violence and insecurity in the nations where the wars are staged. At best there have been occasional military victories and temporary restoration of a semblance of normality. More often, escalation has increased insecurity and civilian suffering, whether or not U.S. involvement is front and center.

In sub-Saharan Africa, the region with which the two of us are most familiar, that pattern is most visible in three long-running conflicts: the Nigerian army against Boko Haram in Nigeria, the African Union military mission in Somalia, and French and regional military forces fighting in Mali and other countries in the West African Sahel. In all these cases, unlike in the Middle East and Afghanistan, the United States has a minimal presence of combat troops on the ground. But U.S. involvement is significant nonetheless: the United States is training African military forces, flying armed as well as reconnaissance drones, and mounting occasional actions by special forces, most notably in Somalia. Neither the U.S. government nor the affected African governments are willing to prioritize diplomacy and development over military aid and arms sales.[8]

During the Cold War, extreme repression sometimes bought years or decades of stability for authoritarian governments at the expense of their citizens. In the period following the Cold War and particularly in the post-9/11 period, even nominal stability is elusive, as state violence often provokes increased insurgent violence and/or the growth of organized criminal violence, such as drug trafficking.

This then provides the incentive and the excuse for security forces to double down on violence. Despite revelations by investigative journalists, monitoring by human rights organizations, and calls for reform, the mission and the organizational culture of both the police and the military ensure that reform efforts are strong on rhetoric and weak on implementation.

Structural Obstacles Thwart Internal "Reforms"

To some extent, racism, violence, and impunity can be tempered by reforms within police and military institutions, such as policies to encourage diversity in the ranks and to prohibit or change certain practices. The U.S. military is subject to codes of conduct such as the Geneva Conventions, the United Nations Convention against Torture, and the U.S. Uniform Code of Military Justice. Some local jurisdictions have attempted to reform their policing through measures such as barring chokeholds, requiring use of body cameras, and establishing civilian review boards to investigate misconduct.

These reforms can have some limited effects, but they are by no means universally applied. There are significant differences among agencies, within both law enforcement and the military, with respect to the rule of

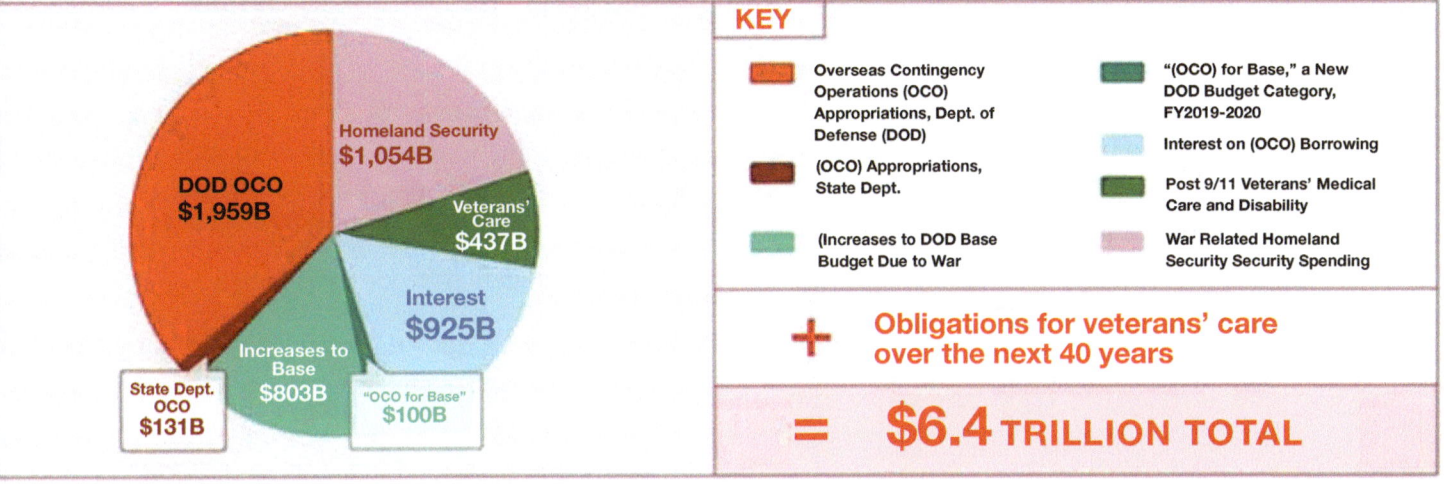

Estimate of U.S. War on Terror Spending, in $ Billions FY2001-FY2020

Credit: Costs of War Project

law. Many officers in the U.S. military hold strong personal commitments to professional codes of conduct; this is reflected in the rising tensions between some levels of the military and the lawless Trump administration.[9] Among federal and domestic law enforcement agencies, norms, policies, and practices are highly variable. In times of crises, these differences between agencies will continue to be central in the choices either to escalate violence or to deescalate violence while considering alternatives.

However, the organizational culture of security agencies is most often highly resistant to significant reforms or checks, and credible penalties for violations are rarely enforced. Moreover, the criteria for "success" in achieving their missions—numbers of enemy forces killed in war, arrests made in policing—are not measures of success in achieving actual security. Continued threats are turned into justification for increased budgets and for doubling down on failed strategies.

Without external accountability for violations of human rights and for ineffective policies, internal reforms can only have marginal impacts. And vested interests in violent organizational cultures, growing in proportion to exorbitant budgets, create strong incentives for politicians to avoid enforcing outside accountability.

Shifting Resources Through Divestment and Investment

The domestic debate on police violence has significant momentum, with continuing local protests and high national visibility. A central question is whether, how, and to what extent localities should divest from violent policing and reinvest some funds in alternative means to ensure community security.

With U.S. military engagement abroad largely invisible to the wider U.S. public, there is no parallel, high-profile debate on the role of the U.S. military in fomenting global violence, nor much public discussion of redirecting the Pentagon's budget or priorities. The U.S. military itself is unlikely to question the fundamental premises of its global engagement, which centers on the competition with major powers such as Russia and China. The traditional conception of security—as protection against violent threats from enemies—largely persists. And the vested interests and policy assumptions that protect funding for the military-industrial complex are even more strongly entrenched than those that defend local police budgets.

But there is also a strand of strategic thinking and internal criticism within the defense community that is open to considering other threats to security, most notably global disease pandemics and climate change. A notable example is the internal military investigations of the impact of climate change. In his new book All Hell Breaking Loose, Michael Klare analyzes internal Pentagon documents, finding evidence that "of all major institutions in U.S. society, none is taking climate change as seriously as the U.S. military."[10]

> No single conflict, in Africa or elsewhere, currently has the potential to shift thinking about fundamentals of the U.S. global military posture.

Military planners realize that they must prepare for complex clusters of climate disasters, such as the sequence of Hurricanes Harvey, Irma, and Maria in 2017. Such events have already stretched the military's capacity for humanitarian response and pose a growing threat to military bases, both within the United States and around the world. The military has focused its planning more on adaptation to climate change than on mitigation by reducing carbon emissions. But it has also taken steps to diminish its reliance on fossil fuels through proactive research and investment in renewable energy. And it is acutely aware of the likely increase in instability due to the effect of climate crises in areas already plagued by other causes of conflict.

These Pentagon reports and their implications have not been widely publicized, given the imperative not to openly contradict the climate-denying commander-in-chief. But under different national political leadership, some military voices could potentially be advocates for addressing the causes, rather than only the consequences, of rising conflicts. This would also require rethinking the mission of counterterrorism and counterinsurgency.

No single conflict, in Africa or elsewhere, currently has the potential to shift thinking about fundamentals of the U.S. global military posture. Even Saudi Arabia's war in Yemen, which earned bipartisan condemnation, is discussed only as an exceptional case. Nor is the movement to curb violence within the United States likely to fully extend its scope to the global arena. What can have significant effects, however, are the fiscal pressures from new initiatives on other issues, such as the Green New Deal and Medicare for All. And changes in the Pentagon's priorities may also come, in indirect ways, from its own research and planning to deal with the climate crisis, the threat of pandemics, and other humanitarian crises. Those factors, together with the emerging consensus against endless ground wars, have potential to eventually change the minds of Republican as well as Democratic voters.

The costs of the post-9/11 wars have been well documented by the Brown University Costs of War Project, with a budgetary cost of $6.4 trillion through fiscal year 2020. Peace activists and analysts have advanced credible alternatives to save on military spending.[11] Polls from foreign policy establishment organizations may highlight support for ongoing military alliances as essential to U.S. global engagement. But when other pollsters asked more detailed questions, 58 % of Republicans and 79 % of Democrats supported ending U.S. ground wars.

When asked to identify the top threats to our security, a plurality of voters (46 %), and 73 % of Democrats, said that the US primarily faces nonmilitary threats. In light of the COVID-19 pandemic, along with disastrous hurricanes, fires, and floods, public pressure for spending on such other threats is likely to grow. And critics will find many in the military who agree with them.

Trump has vowed to end wars, but this is a false promise, notes Peter Certo in Foreign Policy in Focus. Democratic candidates, for their part, have not yet taken full advantage of public disenchantment with shooting wars to advance a robust agenda of funding for alternative security initiatives.

A New Social Contract?

In the previous essays in this series, we argued that significant shifts in views on the home front open an opportunity for similar changes in policy paradigms at the global level. Such is the case for action on the climate crisis, gross economic inequality, and economic rights, such as the right to health and the right to a living wage. The major obstacle is political will rather than lack of compelling alternative visions, which are now highly visible in public debate. The same applies to state violence, although the potential for domestic change on this front is still much more visible than the alternatives to global U.S. military overreach.

The current convergence of global crises, none of which shows any signs of ending, threatens mass devastation on the scale of the Great Depression and World War II, in the United States and around the world. In rapid succession in 2020, the COVID-19 pandemic, its economic repercussions, and resistance to state violence have had unprecedented cumulative effects. While further turmoil is inevitable, this might also offer the opportunity for fundamental changes—if urgent demands for immediate action are grounded in an understanding of the deep roots of injustice and the global scope of the challenge.

One of the most striking signs of hope is the fact that progressive activists as well as many mainstream analysts are seeing the issues not as isolated and competitive but as linked and complementary. The Black Lives Matter movement has continuously stressed the intersectionality of identities and issues. More and more activists are following their lead, which implies focusing on providing mutual aid and solidarity across boundaries of all kinds, including national borders.

Policy changes to implement such a vision will not be easy. One measure of success, whether at the local, national, or global level, will be to what extent government budgets begin to shift from investing in state violence to social investment in fulfilling a new social contract.

> The current convergence of global crises, none of which shows any signs of ending, threatens mass devastation on the scale of the Great Depression and World War II, in the United States and around the world.

NOTES

1. The quote comes from page 203 in the conclusion to Dunbar-Ortiz's short book Loaded: A Disarming History of the Second Amendment, published in 2018. She addresses the same theme in a January 2018 article on settler colonialism and the Second Amendment.
2. For an indispensable overview, read Roxanne Dunbar-Ortiz, An Indigenous Peoples' History of the United States. For the conquest of the inland South and the expulsion of Native Americans to lands west of the Mississippi, see the recent detailed accounting in Unworthy Republic, by Claudio Saunt. In an eloquent account entitled Our History Is the Future, Nick Estes highlights how the displacement of the peoples of the Dakotas, as well as their resistance, continued in the 20th century and into the present.
3. Schrader is also the author of the 2019 book Badges Without Borders: How Global Counterinsurgency Transformed American Policing.
4. For a sampling of recent commentaries, see articles in the Boston Review, Foreign Policy in Focus, Just Security, and Common Dreams. A similar vision is available in the recent paper proposing a feminist foreign policy for the United States, paralleling similar proposals in other countries.
5. Particularly useful recent accounts include Nick Turse's Kill Anything that Moves: The Real American War in Vietnam and the edited volume by Mark Pavlick and Caroline Luft reminding us that the unrestrained violence of the U.S. wars extended beyond Vietnam to other countries in Southeast Asia. For post-9/11 counterterrorism interventions, Jeremy Scahill provides a wide-ranging account in Dirty Wars.
6. Schmidt's two volumes on foreign intervention in Africa cover the period after World War II up to the Cold War and the post-Cold-War period. The second is available for free download from the publisher.
7. See the new book by Vincent Bivens, The Jakarta Method.
8. See in particular the second volume by Elizabeth Schmidt, cited above. For more current material see the work of Nigerian journalist Obi Anyadike on Boko Haram and on the Sahel. On Somalia see the recent article by Paul Williams and the review by Alex de Waal of the book by Williams on AMISOM. For additional resources on conflicts in specific countries check the country pages of the International Crisis Group and African Arguments, and search the New Humanitarian news service. On U.S. involvement in particular, see the 2015 book by Nick Turse, Tomorrow's Battlefield: U.S. Proxy Wars and Secret Ops in Africa, as well as the many recent articles available through his website. For Turse's most recent investigative report, see the August 8, 2020 issue of The Continent.
9. It is significant that the federal forces deployed to Portland, Oregon, and other cities include agencies particularly notable for their lack of such professional codes. The US Border Patrol, for example, despite the fact that over half its agents are Latino, has a long history of racial profiling and violence, as detailed in the classic history Migra by Kelly Lytle Hernández. And the Federal Protective Service is primarily composed of private contractors who have no professional codes of conduct at all.
10. For a brief summary, see the September 2019 review and interview in Rolling Stone.
11. See, for example, the specific suggestions from defense analyst William Hartung, as well as the overview from the Friends Committee for National Legislation.

CHAPTER NINE

OVERHAULING U.S. FOREIGN POLICY

Originally published in Organizing Upgrade

September 22, 2020

The most consequential election year in most of our lifetimes has featured stark crises unspooling against a backdrop of vigorous activist mobilizations and simmering public outrage. While the first essential step for progressives is to prevent the re-election of President Trump, that will not be enough. We need fundamental change rather than a return to the status quo ante.

Climate change, public health, police violence, and the systemic racism manifest in all policy areas are on the November 3 ballot. On these issues and others there is already significant mobilization to hold an incoming Democratic administration accountable.

This will not be easy, especially when it comes to foreign policy. The Democratic Party platform says that "we cannot simply aspire to restore American leadership. We must reinvent it for a new era." But it fails to question the legitimacy of American preeminence and exceptionalism or, more broadly, the understanding of the world as an arena primarily for competition rather than collaboration.

Credit: The Star (Kenya), June 13, 2020.

Challenge Militarism

Despite rising criticism of wasted money and endless wars, in late July significant majorities in the U.S. Congress, including Democrats as well as Republicans, defeated an amendment to cut 10% from the $740.5 billion military budget. The vote was 324 to 93 in the House of Representatives and 77 to 23 in the Senate.

There are critiques across a wide political spectrum of the U.S. military posture, and widely shared uneasiness about endless wars. But there is still no strong antiwar movement with links to progressive movements focused on domestic policy. The default assumption in public debate is that U.S. wars were and still are aimed at protecting the security of the United States. Military spending to defend against "adversaries" takes priority over spending that would enable the U.S. to play its part in combating common global threats and investing in human security.

> We should reinforce the message from climate justice organizations, such as the Sunrise Movement and 350.org, that the Green New Deal must be global.

Foreign policy veterans of the Obama-Biden years vary significantly in their views. Some acknowledge that policy cannot just return to the status quo before Trump. Yet even those who are most critical of previous policy still speak of "rebuilding the city on a hill"—the United States as leader and shining example for the world. Few are willing to engage in fundamental questioning of Washington's global role.

Andrew Bacevich, a longtime critic of militarism, and others at the Quincy Institute for Responsible Statecraft are bringing options for anti-militarist positions into the establishment debate. But more substantive change is only likely to happen with greater pressure from progressive voices that are now largely outside the foreign policy establishment.

> Today, as our military engagements drag on with dwindling media attention, there are fewer dramatic headlines to propel global issues into mainstream media and political debate. This makes it difficult, though by no means impossible, to build wider consciousness of global issues.

To be effective, mobilization must be broad, extending beyond foreign policy-focused constituencies to engage large swathes of the U.S. public. This vast reach marked the movement against the Vietnam War and the solidarity movements with Southern Africa and Central America in the 1970s and 1980s. Those mobilizations, however, were largely driven by external events and nightly news coverage that made the U.S. role impossible to ignore.

Today, as our military engagements drag on with dwindling media attention, there are fewer dramatic headlines to propel global issues into mainstream media and political debate. This makes it difficult, though by no means impossible, to build wider consciousness of global issues.

Forge National-Global Connections

As progressives, we can educate ourselves now to advance a global perspective and help pave the way for lobbying campaigns by progressive organizations seeking to influence a new administration.

As a first step, activists and organizations working primarily on domestic issues and those working on global or foreign policy issues should build closer links of understanding between them, even as they recognize the need to work along parallel tracks. Examples include the recent article on the urgency of Internationalism on Organizing Upgrade, the wide range of organizations involved in the National Priorities Project, and the inclusion of action against militarism among the key demands of the Poor People's Campaign.

> As indicated by actions around the world in solidarity with #BlackLivesMatter, activists here need to recognizethat anti-Black racism is global and not confined to any one country.

We should focus on issues, not on personalities. Defeating Trump is a prerequisite for advancing a progressive agenda. But opportunities for influencing a future Biden administration will depend on the strength of movements that put forth compelling alternative visions on key issues.

We should reinforce the message from climate justice organizations, such as the Sunrise Movement and 350.org, that the Green New Deal must be global. Among the specific implications: multilateral and bilateral collaboration with China is imperative, while a strategic partnership with the oil-rich Gulf autocracies is obsolete.

The COVID-19 pandemic makes clear that action to protect the right to health must be global. Among the specific implications: the United States must not only support the World Health Organization, but must learn from countries as diverse as Cuba, Vietnam, New Zealand, and South Korea, to name only a few.

> Progressives should prioritize support for members of Congress willing to speak out against foreign policy taboos, such as those in "the squad," the Congressional Black Caucus, and the Congressional Progressive Caucus.

As indicated by actions around the world in solidarity with #BlackLivesMatter, activists here need to recognize that anti-Black racism is global and not confined to any one country. This racism shows itself in the treatment of Africans and Afro-descendants in a wide range of countries and is reflected in the position of the African continent in the global hierarchy.

Call Attention To Fundamental Parallels

Both domestic law enforcement and the conduct of foreign wars continue to reflect the history of conquest, slavery, and U.S. empire of earlier centuries. The continuing effects of the "original sin" of slavery are now widely recognized; the effects of our imperial past on indigenous populations and the world receive less attention. Both domestic and global inequalities of all kinds are rooted in the history of conquest and empire as well as of slavery.

Follow the money! In communities around the country, local authorities are being challenged to divest from over-policing and invest in community needs instead. The same scrutiny and demands should apply to the federal budget, redirecting resources away from the military and toward investment in global public goods that advance human security.

It is also essential to address tax injustice by applying higher rates to the ultra-rich and by pursuing the wealth hidden in offshore accounts by corporations and wealthy elites around the world. This loss of capital is particularly acute for African countries, where local elites are conniving with a global network of facilitators to loot the continent. Efforts to curb such looting, by locating and taxing hidden wealth, would free up funds to be invested in Africa's urgent needs. The Stop the Bleeding campaign of African civil society groups, coordinated by Tax Justice Network-Africa, is working toward this aim with support from the Global Alliance for Tax Justice.

Reject Foreign Policy Taboos

We should not shy away from confronting tough political issues with alternative frameworks. An area of particular concern, given current political biases among Democratic as well as Republican establishments, is support for justice in Palestine and Israel through global solidarity, including Palestinian, Jewish and other activists in the United States. We also need to mobilize resistance to the bipartisan trend toward a new Cold War with China, and support partnership for justice based on reliable information rather than arrogant unilateral intervention in crises such as those in Venezuela and Ecuador.

Progressives should prioritize support for members of Congress willing to speak out against foreign policy taboos, such as those in "the squad," the Congressional Black Caucus, and the Congressional Progressive Caucus.

Don't Be Afraid To Dream

To challenge a new Democratic administration and inspire progressive mobilization, we should advance not only practical policy goals but also new visions of mutual cooperation beyond those presently thinkable. One clear albeit difficult example is the case of Cuba, where U.S. policy has been paralyzed for decades by right-wing pressures.

> While the first essential step for progressives is to prevent the re-election of President Trump, that will not be enough. We need fundamental change rather than a return to the status quo ante.

A progressive agenda for U.S.-Cuban relations should begin with the reversal of new restrictive measures imposed by the Trump administration and progress toward full elimination of the trade embargo and travel restrictions that have defined U.S. policy for almost six decades.

A more ambitious goal would be to stress U.S. collaboration with Cuba in promoting global health, as happened in the case of Ebola in West Africa. The United States should be prepared to accept future Cuban offers of assistance with disaster relief and preparedness, an offer that the George W. Bush administration rejected in 2005 after Hurricane Katrina. Most visionary, but also beneficial to both countries, would be for the United States to ask Cuba for technical assistance in developing equitable public health policies in this country—and to pay generously for such assistance. That could promote mutual understanding as well as begin to pay for repairing the damage done over many decades of U.S. intervention in Cuba.

CHAPTER TEN

BUILDING BACK A BETTER AFRICA POLICY SHOULD NOT MEAN GOING BACK TO OLD WAYS

On security, economy, and heath: we need to think about new frameworks rather than retreating to policies of the past.

Originally published in Responsible Statecraft.

November 25, 2020

President Trump's overt contempt for Africans is encapsulated in his famously crass remark about African countries. But the principal damage to Africa has stemmed from his administration's broader policy choices, such as the disastrous rejection of the World Health Organization and the Paris climate accords; harsh curbs on legal immigration and asylum; and gutting of gender equality programs.

Most recently, Trump's remarks supporting Egypt in its dispute with Ethiopia over the construction of a dam on the Nile River have inflamed tensions in a volatile region. And now his administration's failure to call for de-escalation and dialogue in the conflict in Ethiopia's Tigray region is likely to have disastrous consequences in fueling expanded war.

Credit:

> The record of both Republican and Democratic administrations, over more than six decades, has been mixed, ranging from destructive interventions to neglect to—far less often—productive collaboration with Africans on common goals.

Nevertheless, the Biden administration should not merely go back to the pre-Trump status quo. As noted by John Campbell at the Council on Foreign Relations, the Trump administration has made fewer changes to Africa policy than expected. Campbell calls for a "reset." We argue that an even more fundamental questioning of U.S. Africa-related policy is needed.

The record of both Republican and Democratic administrations, over more than six decades, has been mixed, ranging from destructive interventions to neglect to—far less often—productive collaboration with Africans on common goals. If the Biden mantra of "Build Back Better" is to be applied to Africa, we need to think about new frameworks to guide policy rather than retreading the shibboleths of the past.

The new administration should abandon the temptation to offer lessons to Africa. Instead, the United States should strive to understand African realities and address problems in a spirit of collaboration and mutual learning. This requires rebuilding the capacity for diplomacy and also taking account of how other U.S. government agencies and institutions outside the foreign policy arena directly affect Africa's future.

The following guidelines are essential for not repeating the many mistakes of the past.

First, Do No Harm

Avoid counterproductive military engagements, a point made by earlier commentators in Responsible Statecraft. Whether in the Sahel, Nigeria, or Somalia, counterinsurgency efforts and government repression have fueled rather than quelled Islamic insurgencies. Analysts are virtually unanimous that foreign intervention to counter the growing insurgency in Mozambique's Cabo Delgado province would be a disaster.

There are no easy answers to such conflicts. But the U.S. priority must be to support multilateral initiatives in conflict resolution and peacekeeping, as well as humanitarian relief. Rather than assuming that Washington knows best, the incoming administration should heed advice from knowledgeable sources, such as the recent letter from over 80 African studies scholars responding to police brutality in Nigeria.

Do not subordinate Africa policy to a new cold war with China. For decades, U.S. Africa policy was harnessed to the Cold War with the Soviet Union. This led to disastrous interventions in the Congo and to the de facto alliance with apartheid South Africa. The competition with China in Africa is economic rather than military, but a blinkered vision ignoring Africa's own interests is self-defeating. It also misses the opportunities for cooperation as well as competition with China.

U.S. policymakers should recognize that, despite the wide disparities in size and power, African countries, like the United States, must find their way in a multipolar world. This requires managing opportunities for cooperation, as well as threats, from a wide range of external powers, and is incompatible with simplistic binary choices.

Do not impose the false gospels of austerity and privatization on African countries. In developed and developing countries alike, market fundamentalism—denying the essential role of government in promoting development—has failed to deliver. The International Monetary Fund and the World Bank have begun to admit this failure, but old guidelines are still applied to countries too weak to determine their own policies.

U.S. policymakers should instead learn from African thinkers such as Thandika Mkandawire and the economists at the Addis Ababa—based U.N. Economic Commission for Africa. They share the growing global consensus that state investment in public goods and strategic state leadership in development strategy are prerequisites for sustainable and equitable development. This thinking is reflected in a new co-authored book, "African Economic Development: Evidence, Theory, Policy."

Then, Think Globally and Work Collaboratively

The United States and African countries face many of the same global issues, and these must be addressed at multiple levels. Coordination is complex and always imperfect. But collaboration is essential, both with African countries and, to the extent possible, with multilateral agencies and other external actors.

The U.S. Contribution Can Be Significant in Three Areas:

Global health: Despite lack of resources, African countries have done better than the United States and many European countries in coping with the COVID-19 pandemic. While they have not matched the success of the Asia Pacific region, they have benefited from early action and from proactive coordination by the WHO regional office and the Africa Centres for Disease Control.

The United States, which lags the world in recognition of a universal right to health, needs to put its own house in order. But it also bears responsibility for paying its fair share in supporting public health in African and other developing countries. As COVID-19 makes clear, that is the prudent as well as moral thing to do.

Climate change: Africa is the continent most vulnerable to global climate change, though it has contributed the least to causing it. Many African countries depend on fossil fuel exports. Much of the rural population relies on charcoal for cooking, contributing to the loss of tree cover. Fiscal resources for both mitigation and adaptation fall far short of the need.

The U.S. return to the Paris climate agreement will be only a first step. Renewable energy is expanding rapidly in Africa and there is enormous potential for additional expansion, drawing private and public investment from the countries most responsible for the problem. There is room for both the United States and China if they are willing to work with African partners.

Tax justice: Tax evasion, tax avoidance, and illicit financial flows have eroded the fiscal capacity of African governments. African civil society as well as governments have called for international action. But success depends on action in the United States and other major financial centers, where global banks, accounting firms, and legal firms help secretive corporations and individuals hide financial assets.

Giant multinational corporations also avoid taxation by shifting assets to jurisdictions with lower tax rates. Internet giants Google, Facebook, and Microsoft, for example, avoided as much as $2.8 billion in taxes in 20 developing countries.

In the United States, legislative action is key to greater transparency, as advocated by the Financial Transparency and Corporate Accountability Coalition. But strong executive actions also have a role to play. Stemming illicit financial flows could have more impact on African countries' fiscal capacity to meet their own needs than either aid or trade.

It is likely that the Biden administration's Africa policy will largely reflect continuity with previous administrations. But Africa and the United States share common interests that are increasingly visible, and this gives some hope that, with creative diplomacy, greater humility, and attention to African concerns, policymakers can move closer to mutually beneficial engagement.

The bottom line is that U.S. Africa policy will be most productive if U.S. policymakers are willing to learn and collaborate rather than to preach or dictate.

The United States should strive to understand African realities and address problems in a spirit of collaboration and mutual learning.

CHAPTER ELEVEN

AFRICA/GLOBAL: "DAUGHTER OF AFRICA" STEPS UP TO LEAD ON GLOBAL CRISES

November 15, 2022

At the climate summit in Egypt last week, President Biden pledged that the United States would take the lead on the climate crisis. But his speech was eclipsed the same day by a powerful call to action by Prime Minister Mia Mottley of Barbados.

The next day Mottley delivered the 20th Nelson Mandela Lecture in Durban, South Africa, and was hailed by Mandela's widow Graça Machel as the new leader of the Global South, taking the baton from Mandela to confront this generation's polycrisis.

To his credit, President Biden at least showed up at the COP27 summit, in contrast to his geopolitical rivals in Moscow and Beijing. And he was able to point to significant action on the climate in the Inflation Reduction Act in August.

While that act was a significant step forward for the United States to reduce its own omissions, the central theme of the summit was payment of "loss and damage" to those countries most affected by climate change by those countries most responsible for the fossil fuel emissions causing it. Biden avoided that language entirely, instead pledging to ask Congress for $2 billion to assist developing countries in responding to climate change.

In Durban, Mottley put the case for loss and damages like this:

"If I lived next door to you, and every day I am dumping on your property, dumping on your property, and the money you had to send your children to school or to pay medical care for your wife all of a sudden, now has to be taken up to clean up the property because you can't sleep at night, you can't eat food in peace, then you would say that I should be sued and that I must stand responsibility for the fact that then causing you to spend the majority of your earnings on being able just to live."

Addressing the fears of rich countries about "open-ended liability," she added:

"As a former attorney-general I say we don't ask you for open-ended liability, but what we do ask you for is justice. And this is not a matter purely for the government or the state, but that there are non-state actors, multinational corporations whose balance sheets far exceed that of many countries of the world, and whose balance sheets get there by reason of the same pollution. Who have a responsibility to pay. The Bible talks about tithing and the Koran speaks to us about giving back to those in need. And we simply say that if you are going to make $200-billion in the last quarter alone, then you have a responsibility to put something on the table in a loss and damage fund for those who are now having to pay out and pay out."

Responding to Mottley's speech, Graça Machel praised her leadership and reminded her listeners of their own responsibility.

"It is an African child, a woman from a tiny country who rises in this global crisis of leadership. And she talks to the global community, to the human family and says, yes, there are many crises. But I'm here and ready to lead. Mia, you spoke to us, you reignite our agency, our responsibility for our own future. It's not that anyone else is going to build it for us. You need to count on every single one of us as we did in the past and to make a movement in which everyone will have to accept responsibility."

The quotes above give only a hint of the insight and passion Mottley shows in speaking, which you can sample below in two short videos. The first is her 13-minute speech at COP27, and the second is an excerpt from her full speech at the Nelson Mandela Memorial Lecture, followed by brief remarks by Graça Machel.

> [Mia Mottley] was hailed by Mandela's widow, Graça Machel, as the new leader of the Global South, taking the baton from Mandela to confront this generation's polycrisis.

It is particularly fitting that this new leader of the Global South comes from Barbados, which was, as Howard French details in his new book *Born in Blackness* (now available in paperback), the original source of the slave-produced sugar industry that fueled England's economy in the 17th century.

https://youtu.be/5J0egwAfO0w

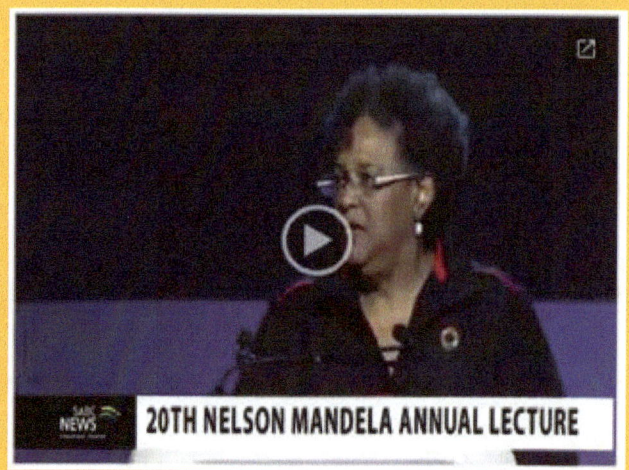

https://youtu.be/oHwpAPMJ23c

PART TWO
FROM GLOBAL APARTHEID TO GLOBAL SOLIDARITY

CHAPTER TWELVE

CONFRONTING GLOBAL APARTHEID DEMANDS GLOBAL SOLIDARITY

by Imani Countess and William Minter

Imani Countess is the project director for the US-Africa Bridge Building Project. William Minter is a consultant for the Project and the editor of AfricaFocus Bulletin.

April 2021

The COVID-19 pandemic has both revealed and deepened structural inequalities around the world. Nearly every country has been hit by economic downturn, but the impacts are unevenly felt. Within and across countries, the people who have suffered most are those already disadvantaged by race, class, gender, or place of birth, reflecting the harsh inequality that has characterized our world for centuries.

This deepening inequality haunts our global future. According to a report released by Oxfam in January 2021, "Billionaire fortunes returned to their pre-pandemic highs in just nine months, while recovery for the world's poorest people could take over a decade."

International scientific collaboration has yielded multiple vaccines against the novel coronavirus. But the most vulnerable people and countries have been last in line for doses, or are not in line at all, threatening a vaccine apartheid. If that continues, it will be impossible to end the pandemic, as the virus will continue to mutate and spread across borders.

"Global Apartheid" Is More Than a Metaphor

The term "apartheid" comes from South Africa, notorious in the 20th century as the last stronghold of white minority rule. Political apartheid in South Africa ended in 1994 with free elections open to South Africans of all races. But South Africa and the world are still embedded in an international system of inequality reflecting the history of European conquest and domination.

In this system, wealth and power are still structured by race and place, both within and between nations. Whether or not one labels it global apartheid, there are striking parallels with South African apartheid.

In July 2020, UN Secretary-General António Guterres, in the annual Nelson Mandela lecture, addressed what he called the "inequality pandemic" and called the world to a "new social contract." Such a contract, it is clear, will not happen quickly. But it will not happen at all unless millions around the world mobilize to make it happen.

South African Apartheid Was Part of a Global System of Unequal Rights

South Africa shares a history of white supremacy with other white settler states, including the United States, as Senator Robert Kennedy acknowledged in a speech to students in Cape Town in 1966. Its apartheid regime was part of a world order defined for centuries by hierarchies of racial privileges both between and within countries.

Since the discovery of diamonds and gold in the late 19th century, South Africa and its neighbors in the Southern African region had been linked closely to Western economies, particularly the United States, England, and continental Europe. Internally, apartheid in South Africa was a multilevel system of labor control and differential rights, paralleling the global hierarchy. There were gradations of privilege for whites, Asians, "Coloured," and "natives," as well as for "natives" in urban areas, those in rural "homelands," and "foreign natives."

Beginning in the 1960s, when independent African countries joined the United Nations, the end of political apartheid played out on a global stage. Exposure of the

South African regime's inhumanity, including forced labor, torture, and attacks on neighboring states, led the United Nations General Assembly in 1974 to designate apartheid as a crime against humanity.

Transnational Solidarity Was Essential to the Anti-Apartheid Movement

Over the next two decades, the regime maintained highly visible repression within its borders while also waging proxy wars that devastated the entire Southern African region. The human toll on South Africans and their neighbors mounted into millions of lives lost. South Africa's Western allies, despite growing willingness to speak against apartheid, stubbornly maintained their military and economic ties with the regime.

In opposing white minority rule, the South African liberation movements relied on mobilizing internal opposition, but they also issued appeals for support worldwide. They called for sanctions against the white minority regime and for direct support for South African liberation, including support for armed struggle. This outreach was essential because of the extent to which rich Western countries both profited from and sustained the South African economy and state.

Those calls were answered in different ways by governments, by multilateral bodies such as the Organization of African Unity and the United Nations, and by hundreds of solidarity organizations in almost every country of the world.

Solidarity Was Based on the Recognition of Common Humanity

By the 1980s it was possible to speak of a transnational anti-apartheid movement. But it was a movement that drew in many different constituencies, with varying connections to and understandings of the situation in South Africa. For people in Africa and other world regions who had themselves experienced European conquest and colonial rule, the connection was clear. In the United States, too, the long history of the Black freedom movement closely paralleled that in South Africa. And the entire world recalled the anti-fascist struggle of the mid-20th century and its promises of freedom. South Africans seeking solidarity understood that they were speaking to specific audiences, not to an undifferentiated global community, and they strove to meet people where they were.

The fundamental message of the transnational anti-apartheid movement was, and remains, equal rights for all, applicable not only in South Africa but around the world. We must learn to live and work together on the basis of our common humanity, as expressed in the African concept Ubuntu.

That does not mean calling for neutrality or covering up the realities of injustice and oppression. It does mean rejecting the principle of separation (the literal meaning of "apartheid") and bringing people into more inclusive communities with a common vision of justice for all.

Collective Action Relied on Diverse Strategies and Multiple Constituencies

In the 1980s, activists developed a range of collective action strategies to support South African calls for political liberation. These included divestment of corporate, pension, and municipal funds from institutions invested in apartheid, as well as protests, mobilizations, and campaigns. Local activists used their own experience and knowledge of specific places and specific institutions to craft appropriate strategies and tactics.

The movement drew in politicians and civil servants in national governments, staff of multilateral institutions, leaders of religious, student, trade union, professional, and social justice organizations, and grassroots leaders in local communities. These diverse actors built collective power and worked together for a common cause. In doing so, they had to look beyond racial and national divides, work through internal debates about strategy, and overcome conflicts driven by ideology and personal ambition.

The same general principles apply today to movements confronting a global pandemic, the climate crisis, and rising overt threats from authoritarianism, xenophobia, and racism. But today's global movements must also confront not only new global realities but also enduring injustices not addressed by the anti-apartheid movement or other national freedom struggles of the 20th century.

The Victory Against South African Apartheid Was Real But Incomplete

The victory we celebrated with the election of Nelson Mandela in 1994 was real, as were earlier victories in freedom struggles in other times and places. But that victory was by no means complete. Democratic political rights, in South Africa or any other country, are essential prerequisites for social and economic justice—but provide no guarantees. Indeed, the 21st century has brought steadily widening inequality and mounting threats to democracy, in South Africa and in countries around the world.

Today we have a new set of intersecting crises, with the authoritarian playbook of "divide and rule" gaining ground in many countries. In meeting this moment, we can take inspiration and guidance from the collective victories of earlier generations. We must take seriously the truth that none of us are free until all of us are free. This principle, voiced over the years by Emma Lazarus, Fannie Lou Hamer, and Martin Luther King Jr., must apply across all the intersecting divisions that separate us from each other, including national borders as well as the familiar triad of divisions by race, class, and gender.

The transnational anti-apartheid movement is one powerful illustration of how this principle can be applied. First, the movement built strong personal and organizational ties across borders in commitment to a common cause. Second, global leadership came from those most endangered by South Africa's apartheid regime, namely movements in South Africa and neighboring countries.

But that movement also had internal shortcomings. The greatest limitation, as in other movements targeting national, racial, or class injustice, was the failure to address gender injustice. Despite public celebration of women in the struggle, failure to listen to women's voices, and even tolerance of gender violence, was more the rule than the exception. That remains the case today worldwide, despite the profusion of pledges to address gender equity.

New Movements Give Hope for Global Solidarity

Over the past decade, as global inequalities have deepened, a wave of movements has been charting new strategies and paths forward. These movements include, to give just a few examples, Black Lives Matter, the climate justice movement, movements for women's rights and LGBTQ rights, and union organizing among care workers and those in the informal economy, who are disproportionately women and youth.

These emergent movements build on new understandings of history as well as on an analysis of the current moment. As Angela Davis noted in the Steve Biko Memorial Lecture in 2016, our work must be rooted in history yet must go beyond the limitations of the past. That means building structures that raise the voices of those who have been barred historically from leadership positions in social change movements. From the local to the global level, organizations and movements must feature "inclusiveness, interconnectedness, interdependency, intersectionality, and internationalism," Davis told the audience at the University of South Africa.

The obstacles may seem overwhelming. But we can redefine the possible, argues Varshini Prakash of the Sunrise Movement, the youth movement that has put the Green New Deal at the center of the political debate on climate change in the United States. "In your demands and your vision, don't lead with what is possible in today's reality but with what is necessary."

Whether on climate, on the COVID-19 pandemic, or on rising inequalities by race, gender, class, and place of birth, joining forces for justice across national boundaries is not a choice. It is a necessity.

The COVID-19 pandemic is an immediate critical test of whether we can put this principle into practice. It will not be the last.

A Movement, Not Just a Leader

Nelson Mandela, the imprisoned leader of the African National Congress, was the best-known face of the anti-apartheid movement. Millions around the world watched as Mandela was released from prison in February 1990.

Two months later, I sat in London's Wembley Stadium with 70,000 others celebrating Mandela's release and the start of a difficult but hopeful transition in the movement against political apartheid. Several Americans sat in front of me. It turned out they were from Pikesville, Maryland; I was born and raised in nearby Baltimore. Pikesville was a majority-white suburb of folks who fled the city in the 1960s and '70s in response to desegregation efforts. Nonetheless, there we were in London, joined together in celebrating the success of a transnational solidarity movement led by Black and Brown South Africans.

That movement included not only iconic leaders like Mandela, but also grassroots leaders not in the international public eye. Just as important, it included countless activists around the world—a complicated mix of campaigners, national liberation parties, political formations and organizations, UN agencies, faith-based organizations, unions, students, and scholars.

Such a coalition is just as essential in confronting today's global apartheid.

– Imani Countess

Selected Resources on the Transnational Anti-Apartheid Movement

Have You Heard from Johannesburg?
7-part video series on the transnational anti-apartheid movement, available as video-on-demand.

The Road to Democracy in South Africa: International Solidarity
Extensive studies by South African and other scholars from the South African Democracy Education Trust. Some chapters downloadable.

African Activist Archive Project
On-line digital documentation (more than 10,000 items) from national and local activist groups in the United States.

The Anti-Apartheid Movement
Brief summary and selected documents from South African History Online.

Walter Bgoya: From Tanzania to Kansas and Back Again
The key role of Tanzania in Southern African liberation struggles.

O.R. Tambo's forgotten speech at Chatham House
Speech by ANC President Oliver Tambo, 1985.

CHAPTER THIRTEEN

STEVE BIKO MEMORIAL LECTURE
BY ANGELA DAVIS

Through her activism and scholarship over more than five decades, Angela Davis has been deeply involved in the quest for social justice both in the United States and globally. Page includes excerpts from the 2016 lecture and a 23-minute embedded video.
April 2021

Through her activism and scholarship over more than five decades, Angela Davis has been deeply involved in the quest for social justice both in the United States and globally. Her work as an educator—both at the university level and in the larger public sphere—has always emphasized the importance of building communities of struggle for economic, racial, and gender justice.

On September 9, 2016, Davis delivered the 17th annual Steve Biko Memorial Lecture at the University of South Africa (UNISA) in Pretoria. The full hour-and-a-half ceremony as broadcast by SABC is available on YouTube.

For a 23-minute video clip from the lecture, view the embedded video below, used on this website with the permission of Dr. Davis. The following short excerpts come from that segment of the lecture.

Women in the Struggle in South Africa

We know that the first major protests, so to speak—the mother of all protests—had been the Women's March to Pretoria on August 9, 1956.

So I have kept in my mind the image of that monumental gathering—Lilian Ngoyi, Helen Joseph, Albertina Sisulu, Fatima Meer, Florence Maphosho, Ruth Mompati, Sophie Williams de Bruyn, and all of the 20,000 women staging a silent protest here in Pretoria in front of Union Buildings. Now, you have touched the women. You have struck a rock. You have dislodged a boulder. You will be crushed.

Women have always been at the heart of antiracist and progressive activism. We thus have to give ourselves permission to honor the women activists as we celebrate the legacies of the men who have come to represent the struggles of the past. And those men who most deserve to be celebrated, men like W. E. B. Du Bois, Martin Luther King, Malcolm X in the United States—in South Africa, men like Nelson Mandela, Chris Hani, and of course, Steve Biko—as influenced as they may have all been by ideologies of patriarchy, of heteropatriarchy, their work helped to create a discursive arena for the development of Black feminist consciousness. They were also aware that their leadership was precisely enabled by those with whom they struggled, and not only the men, but the women as well.

> Students are now recognizing that the legacies of past struggles are not static. If these legacies mean anything at all, they are mandates to develop new strategies, new technologies of struggle.

We are thankful, profoundly thankful, for these legacies, but we do not receive them uncritically. Our understandings of the past are very much determined by our positions in the present and by how we imagine the future. From the perspective of the present, we can apprehend what was hidden behind the restrictive discourses of the past. Steve Biko died so that we would be able to develop these perspectives today.

> The young activists of today stand on our shoulders. And precisely because they stand on our shoulders, they see something of what we have seen, but they also see and understand a great deal more. They are beginning to address unresolved questions and some of the erasures and foreclosures about which I spoke earlier. They stand on our shoulders, but we do not provide a steady foundation, precisely because our questions were questions of a different era.

Unfinished Activisms

Knowledge is useless unless it assists us to question habits—social practices, institutions, ideologies, the state. This questioning cannot end even when victories are won—even when victories are won.

Students are now recognizing that the legacies of past struggles are not static. If these legacies mean anything at all, they are mandates to develop new strategies, new technologies of struggle. And these legacies, when they are taken up by new generations, reveal unfulfilled promises of the past and therefore give rise to new activisms.

As an activist of Steve Biko's generation, I have to constantly remind myself that the struggles of our contemporary times should be thought of as productive contradictions, because they constitute a rupture with past struggles, but at the same time, they reside on a continuum with those struggles, and they have been enabled by activisms of the past. They are unfinished activisms. Activisms enabled by the Montgomery bus boycott in 1955, which was at its core a women's boycott. It was a women's boycott. By the August 9 Women's March 60 years ago. By the founding of the Black Panther Party 50 years ago, almost exactly 50 years ago. It will be 50 years in October. By the uprising in Soweto 40 years ago. By the struggles undertaken by Biko and his comrades to create the South African Students' Organization. By the struggles of Nelson Mandela and the heroic members of the ANC, by uMkhonto we Sizwe. This is the genealogy young activists share across oceans.

> There has been an uneasy relationship with the veterans of the movement that came before them. The uneasiness emanates from the fact that veterans often take themselves and their knowledges too seriously.

The young activists of today stand on our shoulders. And precisely because they stand on our shoulders, they see something of what we have seen, but they also see and understand a great deal more. They are beginning to address unresolved questions and some of the erasures and foreclosures about which I spoke earlier. They stand on our shoulders, but we do not provide a steady foundation, precisely because our questions were questions of a different era.

#FeesMustFall

One of the truly exciting dimensions about the activisms both here in South Africa and in the Black Lives Matter movement in the US is that they are being led by women. I had the honor of meeting Nompendulo Mkhatshwa who is the current president of the Student Representative Council at Wits, and Shaeera Kalla, who is the past president. Under their leadership, the contestation of the fee hikes—#Fees Must Fall—began to resonate across the country and around the world.

There are some who have said that the student de-

> One of the truly exciting dimensions about the activisms both here in South Africa and in the Black Lives Matter movement in the US is that they are being led by women.

mands are unrealistic, especially when students began to call for free education. But the demand for free education is only unrealistic because we continue to live with the mandates of capitalism, and we are compelled to think about education as a commodity. Especially in the aftermath of the global Occupy movement, the thoroughgoing commodification of education under the dictates of capitalism is increasingly viewed by progressive activists as an obscenity. This is not the way things should be. Freedom should mean in the very first place the freedom of education, the freedom to learn. And the prerequisite for enjoying freedom of education should not be the capacity to pay. It should not be the capacity to pay.

#BlackLivesMatter

The three young women in the US—Alicia Garza, Patrisse Cullors, and Opal Tometi—who first produced the hashtag #BlackLivesMatter in the aftermath of the vigilante, racist killing of Trayvon Martin and then went on to create the network Black Lives Matter as the Ferguson protest erupted two years ago—these young women are collectively striving to remind us of the revolution we need as they try to develop strategies for struggle today.

There has been an uneasy relationship with the veterans of the movement that came before them. The uneasiness emanates from the fact that veterans often take themselves and their knowledges too seriously. Sometimes, we assume that our questions and the tentative answers we provided to those questions deserve to be accorded a preeminence that silences future questions and answers. Sometimes, we look for leadership in the familiar guise—the charismatic male leader who in the US historically has emerged from church communities or religious circles. And when we cannot find that form of leadership, we say their movement has no leaders. But they answer back, our movement is full of leaders. We are not a leaderless movement. We are a leaderful movement.

The Black Lives Matter movement seeks to build new forms of leadership—feminist leadership, leadership whether of women or men, queer, trans, or straight, leadership that is collective, inclusive, and democratic. So perhaps we now need the leadership of those who have been historically barred from leadership positions, those who have been silenced. Perhaps we need leadership that will assist us to develop new vocabularies, vocabularies that encourage inclusiveness and interconnectedness, vocabularies that recognize interdependencies, intersectionalities, and internationalisms of our struggle—in other words, vocabularies that highlight the feminist dimensions of all of our social justice struggles.

Angela Davis Steve Biko Memorial Lecture, September 9, 2016

Full 44-minute lecture on YouTube

Watch 23-minute excerpt

https://youtu.be/waCMrb_xV7c

CHAPTER FOURTEEN

VARSHINI PRAKASH ON REDEFINING WHAT'S POSSIBLE

If we had based our goals on today's political possibilities, we would never have been successful.
By Varshini Prakash | Sunrise Movement | 2020
May 2021

This essay is adapted with permission from The New Possible: Visions of Our World Beyond Crisis (Cascade Books, January 2021). It appeared online originally in the Sierra Club magazine with the headline "Teach Your Elders Well." The book is available at a discount from the non-profit Bookshop.org.

We are young people who have witnessed a world in chaos careening toward climate catastrophe. We have watched and waited our entire lives for people much older and more powerful than us to take care of the crises that were emerging. Yet little has happened. Now our generation is standing up to say, "We are ready to be the adults in the room. We are ready to take the future into our own hands. We are ready to envision reality in a different way."

> Young people have historically played an important role in social movements and political change. I think that's one of the most unique things about young people: We're not jaded about what is or isn't possible. We just know what needs to happen, and we work like hell to make sure that it does.

A defining moment for me was December 2015, when a series of extremely strong floods deluged Tamil Nadu, the state in India that my dad (and a lot of my family) is from. It was amazing to me, looking at the images on my computer from half a world away, to be able to see the streets that I had walked on as a kid with my grandma or driven on with my grandfather in his little car. Suddenly I was seeing women and children who somehow looked very familiar to me walking waist-deep or chest-deep in water, traveling miles to sanctuary.

> What we found when we were creating Sunrise was that there was no political home for young people in America who were concerned about the climate crisis.

My grandparents were, fortunately, not in town at that time, but the water had come all the way up to their apartment floor. Hundreds of people died in that flood, and thousands were displaced. That was 2015, and it was a big wake-up call to me that the climate crisis was right now. The increase in the number and severity of flooding episodes—predicted as a result of climate change—was happening now, in the present, not in the future. That was the moment. I thought, What do I have to lose? This time it was someone else's grandmother; the next time, it could be mine. We didn't have time to waste.

If we had based our goals and our ambitions on the parameters of today's political possibilities, we would never have been successful.

That very same month, my friend Sarah and I decided we were going to start an environmental movement for young people. We needed a movement that could be powerful and could grow quickly—quick enough to respond to the climate crisis as it is worsening all around us. This was the beginning of the Sunrise Movement.

What we found when we were creating Sunrise was that there was no political home for young people in America who were concerned about the climate crisis. There was no political home for teenagers and twentysomethings who woke up every day horrified by the crisis and went to sleep imagining a chaotic, climate-disordered world. We realized that it would be absolutely game-changing if we could harness the power of young people—all their passion, optimism, and hope—and translate it into campaigns for long-lasting political change.

Young people have historically played an important role in social movements and political change. John Lewis was just a college student when he became a leader in some of the most intense protests of the civil rights movement. Then there was Diane Nash, whose youth campaigns were crucial to its success. James Lawson organized young people on campuses across the country in large part because he understood the role that young people played—in being willing to take risks and have courage, not living or being governed by the rules of yesterday. I think that's one of the most unique things about young people: We're not jaded about what is or isn't possible. We just know what needs to happen, and we work like hell to make sure that it does. That's how progress happens.

Youth movements have a particular approach to working for change, and we at Sunrise have been inspired by them. I think of four lessons in particular that we've learned from them.

One of the biggest and most important principles of effective protest is this: **In your demands and your vision, don't lead with what is possible in today's reality but with what is necessary**—for, say, the survival of humanity, or for achieving the ultimate goals of whatever campaign or issue you're working on. So often, I find that older generations are hindered by their view of what is possible or impossible right now. The most common things I hear are "It's not practical" and "It's not realistic, considering who's in office right now," and so on. Everything that Sunrise has achieved has been under a Trump administration. If we had been led by that more pragmatic doctrine, if we had based our goals and our ambitions on the parameters of today's political possibilities, we would never have been successful.

Second, we were unafraid to go after not just Republicans—who were denying the validity of climate science and supporting misinformation campaigns—but also Democrats. We said to them, "You, too, have not done enough on this issue. You have said you believe the science. You have voted the right way. But truly, we need champions. We need fighters. We need people who are ready to stick their necks out on issues, who will fight day in and day out, who will be the leaders that we so badly need on the critical issues and talk about them from racial and economic justice perspectives." **What's crucial is being willing to call for the level of action you want, no matter what your political affiliation is.**

Third, **storytelling is powerful**. When we went into Nancy Pelosi's office [during a protest in 2018], we didn't just deliver a petition with a bunch of numbers about parts per million or 2°C. We shared stories about what we had lost because of the climate crisis, or what we were afraid of losing. We told stories about what we

> One of the biggest and most important principles of effective protest is this: In your demands and your vision, don't lead with what is possible in today's reality but with what is necessary—for, say, the survival of humanity, or for achieving the ultimate goals of whatever campaign or issue you're working on.

hoped for our future. Some of the storytellers were in high school, not even able to vote yet, but were engaged in politics because of how much they cared for their future. People told stories about what it was like to live through hurricanes and come out the other end, about the trauma these experiences instill, and about their hope that such traumas don't have to be the story for future generations.

> The biggest thing that needs to happen for a better future is that ordinary people need to get more power. I don't expect power holders or people in office to make that happen. We have to build movements.

Fourth, young people are amazing these days at using all the tools at our disposal to reach other young people, sharing our ideals not just from a political perspective but also from a cultural perspective. We powerfully marry digital organizing with offline organizing, using humor, TikTok, Instagram, and other tools. We saturate culture with our ideas, reaching people through song, art, video, and graphics. Many people have told me they joined Sunrise because they really liked our logo. We thought a lot about our logo and its meaning; we also had a designer work carefully on it and come back to us with multiple iterations. Your visuals and communication, both digitally and offline, have to communicate something significant to people.

Right now, we are seeing an expansion of what is possible. Take, for example, someone like Joe Biden, the very definition of a moderate candidate, who at the beginning of 2020 had one of the weakest climate plans among all the Democratic candidates. The pandemic hit, and then a massive uprising around racial injustice took the country and the world by storm. **Biden has defined himself over his career largely as an incrementalist. Yet now, because of these huge systems-disrupting problems and the calls for transformative change, he's being forced to consider far bigger, broader, and more transformational solutions.** They might actually be systems-shifting reforms. For example, his climate plan grew from a $1.7 trillion green jobs and infrastructure plan over 10 years to a $2 trillion plan over four years, with 40 % of those investments going directly to frontline communities. It's hard to even fathom what that could do for communities of color and poor people around the nation. It's far more than any other president or president-elect has committed to on this issue.

The biggest thing that needs to happen for a better future is that **ordinary people need to get more power. I don't expect power holders or people in office to make that happen. We have to build movements. In particular, we need to rebuild youth movements and the labor movement. We have to have the discipline, strategic acumen, and intellect of the fighters who came before us. And we have to grow our ranks by orders of magnitude.**

The truth is that you can dream up all the white papers you want and create all the policy proposals you want, but we can't enact any of it into reality if we don't have power. That is the bottom line for me when answering almost any question about what is and isn't possible in the next few years. The road forward is uncertain. But the question of what's possible stretches us to open up our imagination and create new worlds in ways that we might never have dreamed of before.

About the Sunrise Movement

The Sunrise Movement first came to national prominence following the 2018 midterm election, when Sunrise activists staged a sit-in at the offices of House Speaker Nancy Pelosi, demanding a Green New Deal instead of the same old promises to study the climate issue and prepare recommendations. They were joined by newly elected Representative Alexandria Ocasio-Cortez.

The organization was founded in the summer of 2016, by activists who had previously been involved in student campaigns for universities and colleges to withdraw their investments in fossil fuel companies. Beginning in 2010, students at Swarthmore College began to build a campaign based on the 1970s and 1980s experience of the anti-apartheid divestment movement on the campus. They hosted a conference in 2013 leading to a national Fossil Fuel Divestment Student Network.

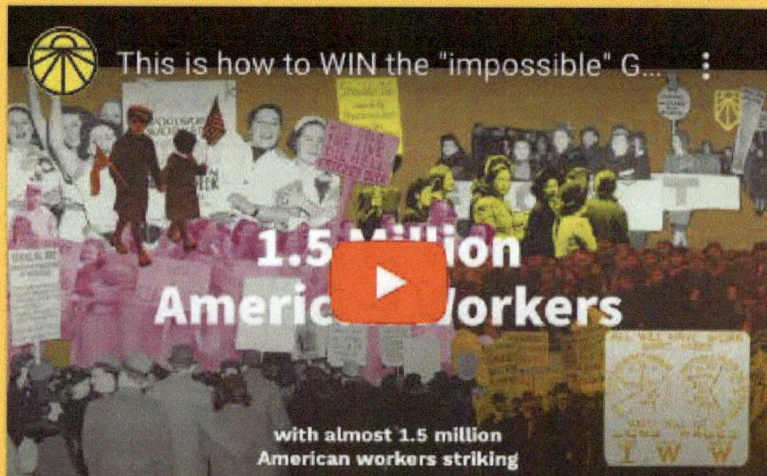

https://youtu.be/rJiiMz0CC5U

But in 2016, as Varshini Prakash explains in this 8-minute video below, many of them decided that action on campus was not enough.

This is how to WIN the "impossible" Green New Deal

Additional Resources on the Climate Justice Movement, Disinvestment, and Reinvestment

350.org and https://350africa.org
350.org was founded in 2008 with the goal of building a global climate movement. 350 was named after 350 parts per million—the safe concentration of carbon dioxide in the atmosphere.

deCOALonize
The deCOALonize campaign is a movement committed to stopping the development of coal and coal-related industries for a clean and sustainable energy future in Kenya and the region.

Carbon Tracker Initiative
Carbon Tracker is an independent financial think tank that carries out in-depth analysis on the impact of the energy transition on capital markets and the potential investment in high-cost, carbon-intensive fossil fuels.

What is Fossil Fuel Divestment
International network of campaigns working toward freeing communities from fossil fuels.

The Case for Fossil Fuel Divestment
Article in Forbes Magazine, February 2021.

Fossil Fuel Divestment
News and analysis from The Guardian on carbon and fossil fuel divestment.

Green New Deal Can and Must be Global
By Imani Countess and William Minter in AfricaFocus Bulletin, January 27, 2020.

The Powerful New Financial Argument for Fossil-Fuel Divestment
By Bill McKibben in The New Yorker, April 3, 2021.

CHAPTER FIFTEEN

FROM DISINVESTMENT TO REINVESTMENT

by Donna Katzin

Donna Katzin is the founding executive director of Shared Interest, which she led for 26 years, having previously directed the South Africa and International Justice Programs of the Interfaith Center on Corporate Responsibility. Having begun her work life as a community and labor organizer, she also serves as a member of the Board of Directors of Community Change.

May 2021

In today's global economy, the rallying cry "An injury to one is an injury to all" has become less a slogan than a statement of fact. Racism, poverty, climate change and pandemics know no borders.

International solidarity activists who helped bring South Africa's apartheid to its knees used multiple methods to exert economic pressure for peaceful change. These included familiar strategies of consumer boycotts and sanctions by governments. Particularly innovative and effective, however, were campaigns to pressure multinational corporations to withdraw their investments and sever economic ties to South Africa. These campaigns for *disinvestment* of resources, mobilizing massive support across the globe, set precedents and provide touchstones for today's solidarity movements.

In the United States alone, these campaigns galvanized hundreds of faith-based organizations and unions, 155 campuses, 90 cities, 22 counties and 26 states. Together they sparked the withdrawal of more than 200 multinational corporations and assets totaling over $1 billion in US direct investments. Internationally, by 1988, 445 companies had withdrawn or were withdrawing from South Africa and Namibia—87% of the total companies invested. Even when corporations did not disinvest, the campaigns imposed costs that moved them to exert pressures on the South African government, which felt the pinch. The international oil embargo of the 1980's, for example, which literally fueled the apartheid economy, more than doubled South Africa's oil import bill to between $15 billion and $20 billion—roughly equal to its gross foreign debt (Embargo: Apartheid's Oil Secrets Revealed, p. 343).

International solidarity activists who helped bring South Africa's apartheid to its knees used multiple methods to exert economic pressure for peaceful change. These included familiar strategies of consumer boycotts and sanctions by governments. Particularly innovative and effective, however, were campaigns to pressure multinational corporations to withdraw their investments and sever economic ties to South Africa.

The campaigns directed at international banks operating in South Africa were particularly instrumental. And many banks that did not withdraw or sever their ties, refused to roll over debts or renew credit for South Africa–precipitating a moratorium on international debt repayments. Together, economic pressure campaigns produced a toxic cocktail of a deteriorating currency, rising interest rates and import costs, double-digit inflation, capital flight, the specter of an international creditors' run on South Africa's banks, and declining tax revenues and resources for the apartheid state. Shortly after Nelson Mandela was elected, political power changed hands. Economic power did not. Archbishop Desmond Tutu challenged the international anti-apartheid movement, saying: "The end of apartheid was Part One of the struggle … Part Two is more difficult. To make the miracle endure. We asked you to disinvest. Now we say to you 'Invest. Make South Africa succeed–for the sake of the world.'"

> Reinvestment—not new to U.S. activists and values-driven investors—had been embedded in a racial and economic justice framework.

Shared Interest, a non-profit launched in 1994, took the Archbishop at his word. It pivoted to *reinvestment* by establishing a guarantee fund with investors' capital to unlock South African banks' credit for low-income Black entrepreneurs, farmers, and cooperatives. The strategy turned the anti-apartheid bank campaign on its head by moving the country's commercial lenders to extend credit to their own economically disenfranchised majority. Since 1994, Shared Interest has benefited more than 2.3 million people by issuing $30 million in guarantees unlocking more than $125 million in credit to South and Southern African borrowers who would otherwise be considered "unbankable."

Racial and Immigrant Justice

Reinvestment—not new to U.S. activists and values-driven investors—had been embedded in a racial and economic justice framework. Following the U.S. social upheaval of the 1960s, and confronting banks' blatant "redlining" of low-income communities of color, grassroots advocates called for reinvestment in capital-starved neighborhoods, which established their own community development loan funds, credit unions and banks. When the Community Reinvestment Act became law in 1977, it incentivized banks to invest in low-income neighborhoods, and to contribute to community development financial institutions (CDFIs) tailoring financial products and technical support to their communities.

The disinvestment-reinvestment strategy has since taken root in other movements. The Movement for Black Lives and their allies, for example, catalyze campaigns for housing, education, health and criminal justice in communities of color. They organize to defund entities that exploit, threaten and imprison Black, indigenous and people of color (BIPOC) communities, and reallocate funds to strategies that restore their power and address their priorities. Immigrants' rights groups have protested private prisons' incarceration of 73% of immigrant detainees (compared to 9% of the total prison population), and moved eight major banks to commit to discontinue loans to these facilities, which will reduce their financing by 87%. They have also launched the #DefundHate campaign for the U.S. government to disinvest the $25 billion it annually pays to identify, jail and deport immigrants, demanding the funds be reinvested in vital services for BIPOC communities.

For People and Planet

As climate change accelerates, many international environmental activists are demanding disinvestment from fossil fuels and reinvestment in renewable energy. Since 2012, their campaigns have pulled institutional investments totaling $11 trillion out of fossil fuels—more than 15% of all global equity funds, according to the World Bank. Recently the Rockefeller Foundation endowment, initially capitalized by oil refining and the Standard Oil Company, announced it is pulling $5 billion out of fossil fuels and focusing investment on renewable energy. Racial and economic justice lenses are key, as the communities hardest hit by climate change, whose members contribute least to the problem and have the fewest resources to combat it, are most often low-income and people of color.

> During apartheid, international activists challenged multinational corporations threatening South Africa's natural environment and the lives of its people..

During apartheid, international activists challenged multinational corporations threatening South Africa's natural environment and the lives of its people. They targeted companies like American Cyanamid, which leaked mercury into the Umgeni River, poisoning downstream drinking water. U.S. shareholders working through the Interfaith Center on Corporate Responsibilities (ICCR), with South African environmental and community groups and Cyanamid's workers, pressured the company to withdraw its toxic practices and presence from South Africa.

They also organized against oil companies with community and labor support. One spirited campaign—best known for its bumper sticker (Get the SHELL off the Turnpike)—lost Shell its $250 million New Jersey Turnpike franchise. Internationally, the Shell Boycott is estimated to have cost the company billions of dollars (Embargo, p. 336).

Today environmental justice advocates are also developing new reinvestment tools, such as the Climate Leadership and Community Protection Act, to wean New York state from fossil fuels by 2050, and require that 40% of state climate and energy funding be invested in environmental justice communities. The Climate and Community Investment Act (CCIA) pending before the NY State Senate, would fine corporate polluters $15 billion a year, and reinvest these funds in frontline communities to create more than 150,000 green jobs and help build a state economy powered by renewable energy.

Vaccine Apartheid

Moving profit-driven companies to reinvest may be a promising direction for health justice activists. Today "vaccine apartheid" is blatant in the U.S., where people of color are three times more likely than others to die from COVID and related illnesses. More starkly, 1.7% of the African continent has received a vaccine, while the U.S. government projects that by June, 70% of its people will be vaccinated. Global south groups like those of the African Coalition for Corporate Accountability, with less financial leverage and direct access to corporate leadership but more access to directly impacted communities, have largely focused on multilateral and national policies. Organizations such as ICCR are also waging corporate campaigns in the global north to influence shareholders and companies themselves.

Global "reinvestment" coalitions could coordinate campaigns to pressure companies that use public funds for the development, manufacturing and production of vaccines, but fail to make their vaccines accessible where they are needed most. They could further require them to "reinvest" by pricing vaccines affordably and delivering them equitably to low-income countries and communities.

Disinvestment to Reinvestment

In conclusion, disinvestment-to-reinvestment strategies highlight priorities for international solidarity work:

- Ensuring that frontline communities' interests and voices are integral to the work;
- Building vulnerable communities' and countries' self-sufficiency by unlocking their human, financial and natural resources for their own development;
- Rooting campaigns in social, economic and environmental rights and restorative justice;
- Addressing structural causes of poverty, racism, climate change and pandemics that know no borders by replacing exploitative, extractive systems with equitable, empowering and replenishing solutions, and reducing capital concentration in privileged hands;
- Sustaining international solidarity campaigns that may take decades; and
- Continuing struggles when the victories of a lifetime are only the beginning.

Key Definitions
by Project editor William Minter

Disinvestment-Reinvestment refers to the goal of shifting resources (by corporations, governments, or individuals who control significant investable wealth) out of a targeted country, geographical territory, economic sector, or government budget sector and into other places or sectors more beneficial to the public welfare.

The shorter terms "Divestment-Investment" or "Divest-Invest" are also commonly used to describe this goal. But strictly speaking divestment refers to only one of many strategies and tactics used to pressure corporations to change their use of resources, that is, by mobilizing shareholders to sell their shares in a targeted company and invest in a more acceptable alternative.

Strategies for economic pressure that may be used on their own or to incentivize corporations, governments or individuals to act are rapidly evolving, often employed simultaneously, and too many to list. Used both in domestic and transnational contexts, these include strikes by workers, sanctions by governments, and corporate campaigns against "bad actor" companies using multiple methods. Such campaigns may use not only divestment, but also public education, protests, "naming and shaming," and consumer boycotts. Governments at all levels can influence corporate behavior by regulations, subsidies, and/or penalties, such as selective purchasing agreements.

Individual or institutional investors in corporations can also screen their investment portfolios according to negative or positive environmental, social, and governance (ESG) criteria. Or they can engage in shareholder activism through such initiatives as corporate dialogues and filing shareholder resolutions. As scholars and activists have long noted, these initiatives alone, in the absence of continued direct strategies by social justice activists, may serve to deflect criticism rather than to promote real change. That was the case for the Sullivan Principles in South Africa, for example. For a more general analysis of transnational codes of conduct, based on cases in India and Guatemala as well, see the article and book by Gay Seidman.

Selected Resources on Disinvestment and Reinvestment
by Project editor William Minter

SharedInterest
Investing in Southern Africa's future by guaranteeing commercial loans to low-income communities and their own financial institutions.

Movement for Black Lives
The MBL works for investments in Black communities, determined by Black communities, and divestment from exploitative institutions (such as private prisons), practices (including police surveillance and suppression of workers' rights), and extractive industries (such as fossil fuels).

Green America
Guide to Socially Responsible Investing and Better Banking.

Investors for Human Rights
An initiative of the Interfaith Center for Investor Responsibility (ICCR), including asset management firms, trade union funds, public pension funds, foundations, endowments, faith-based organizations, and family funds.

BDS
The Boycott, Divestment, Sanctions (BDS) movement works to end international support for Israel's subjugation of Palestinians and pressure Israel to comply with international law.

New Israel Fund
The New Israel Fund works to and to achieve equality for all the citizens of the state regardless of religion, national origin, race, gender or sexual orientation and to safeguard human and civil rights – particularly in the occupied territories.

Go Fossil-Free
International network of campaigns working toward freeing communities from fossil fuels.

Fossil-Fuel Divestment
News and analysis on carbon and fossil fuel divestment

CHAPTER SIXTEEN

AFRICAN YOUNG WOMEN RESISTING BEYOND BORDERS

By Rosebell Kagumire
Rosebell Kagumire is a writer, award-winning blogger, pan-African feminist activist, and communications strategist. She is the current curator and editor of AfricanFeminism.com. *She is also a co-editor of the recent book on The Role of Patriarchy in the Roll-back of Democracy, focusing on countries in East Africa and the Horn of Africa (*available for free download*). Read more about her background in* this interview from March 2021.
June 2021

In early 2020, just before the pandemic became the word and the life, young Ugandan women took to Twitter to expose men they alleged had sexually harassed and in some cases sexually assaulted them. These Twitter threads sent ripples beyond the online world, breaking through the national silence about the pervasive sexual abuse in the country.

For the first time, young women were speaking out in unison, although for some only momentarily. They shared their lived experiences as survivors of sexual violence, and there was no doubt that many whom they outed as rapists had targeted several young women. This was Uganda's own #MeToo moment, although the push for accountability has been a long and difficult struggle. These young women were building on the bravery of women who had earlier told their stories despite the public wrath they faced.

Sheena Bageine took on the mantle for those who still couldn't speak publicly about their experience. She received their stories and posted them anonymously. Sheena was arrested, spent a night in a police cell, and was later charged with offensive communication and cyberstalking. This is how patriarchal power operates, from online silencing to state systems ready to "teach a lesson" to women who refuse to shut up.

Young Ugandan women responded, from lawyers to mental health specialists to social media warriors, and the #FreeSheena hashtag trended. Within a few hours, she had become a liability for compromised police who released her on bail. Sheena's case is still ongoing. But the actions of her peers and the solidarity she evoked show how agile young women's mobilization is in the digital age, despite the entrenched hegemonies that still prevail in daily life.

This courage has been inspired by the boldness of a long line of women organizers and resisters. In recent years, Dr. Stella Nyanzi, a poet and academic, has set the tone for how radical young women can be if they want to. She has tapped into old forms of refusing to accord civility when dealing with those abusing power. In a poem on Facebook, she defiantly described the

Millions of young women across the African continent have found a common voice for community building, organizing, and mobilization, taking advantage of the steady increase of internet penetration and the proliferation of cheaper smartphones.

president of Uganda as a pair of buttocks for failing to provide sanitary pads to adolescent girls who drop out of school. She was arrested, tried and imprisoned for more than a year.

Millions of young women across the African continent have found a common voice for community building, organizing, and mobilization, taking advantage of the steady increase of internet penetration and the proliferation of cheaper smartphones.

Though they are fewer than their male counterparts online, you can't miss young African women's bold outrage and organising. Access to information has always been key to any consciousness awakening. Members of this generation, despite economic and digital disparities that still remain, access information much more quickly than their own parents ever could.

Seeing other young women dare to cross the lines defining the civility expected of women, they too find their courage to join in small but growing communities. Online spaces have thus enabled pan-African organizing. A protest in Namibia or Sudan can quickly become known, within a matter of hours or days, in other countries, where others can find ways of showing solidarity.

According to a 2019 Afrobarometer report, the proportion of women who regularly use the internet had more than doubled over the preceding five years in 34 African countries, from 11% to 26%. But the report also showed a continuing gender gap of 8% to 11%. Women are less likely than men to own a mobile phone, use it every day, have a mobile phone with access to the internet, own a computer, access the internet regularly, and get their news from the internet or social media.

Women on these platforms face enormous challenges. They are often not considered as expert sources, even by their colleagues within progressive movement campaigns and even when the issues are about lived experiences of women. Or the voices of young women are pigeonholed and only allowed to be audible on "women's issues." The marginalization within public discourse extends into the online world, where hierarchies of who is heard are recreated and extended from offline. Many young women retreat from public platforms into smaller groups of trusted friends. This denies a public voice. And, like men, they must also navigate the growing trend of internet shutdowns and surveillance by governments.

Despite these obstacles, African feminist voices are making an impact both on and offline. As with men, those women with greatest access to the internet are disproportionately well-educated and affluent enough to pay the costs of internet access. But the growing number of feminist collectives, with commitment to collaboration and inclusiveness, attests to the potential for inclusive politics.

In some cases, issues that have been historically treated as simply "women's issues" are slowly making it to the center of political contestation. Younger people on the continent are pushing for changes which even their elders, including those who reject the status quo, aren't providing. Feminist voices are gaining prominence as a crucial part of this resistance.

Asking young women and queer Africans to put their own struggles aside, in deference to the argument that "national" liberation must come first, as our foremothers did again and again, is not acceptable.

For example, the Feminist Coalition in Nigeria mobilized to respond to the needs of protesters in the #EndSARS protests that rocked Nigeria in response to police brutality in October 2020. Around the same time in Namibia, youth-led #ShutitAllDown protesters demanded action to address femicide, rape, and sexual abuse.

Formed in 2019 during the popular uprising against the Omar al Bashir regime, the #SudanWomenProtest initiative brought together thousands of women to protest against "militarization, pervasive injustice against women and girls, gendered killings, and the normalization of sexual violence as the result of severe discriminatory laws that are still in effect in Sudan." Sudanese women had been resisting for decades. Their visibility in the 2019 revolution that overthrew Bashir came as a "shock" to the world, as a video of a woman on top of a car leading protest chants went viral. In March 2021, the initiative continued the pressure on Sudan's transitional government to remove all sexist and discriminatory policy.

Keenly aware of global campaigns such as #BlackLivesMatter, #SayHerName, and #IBelieveHer, young women around the continent have taken their own initiatives. And like their counterparts elsewhere, they have infused intersectional feminist perspectives into their organizing. In South Africa they have formed movements for gender justice, such as the #AmINext protests in response to the 2019 rape and murder of university student Uyinene Mrwetyana. But young women have also been key leaders in the non-gender-specific #RhodesMustFall and #FeesMustFall movements.

Offline, young feminist movements and collectives remain marginalized even in young people's movements pushing for political changes. Young people in Africa are increasingly organizing in search of radical change in the way African nations are governed, to deliver dignity and respect for citizens' voices. Without the equal participation and leadership of young feminists, however, such a social transformation will remain elusive.

Young African women are learning and teaching that struggles must be linked rather than seen as mutually exclusive alternatives. In Nigeria, for example, young activists in the middle of the #EndSars anti-police-brutality campaign also insist that #NigerianQueerLivesMatter.

Asking young women and queer Africans to put their own struggles aside, in deference to the argument that "national" liberation must come first, as our foremothers did again and again, is not acceptable.

Women were central to the movements for independence and everyday resistance to colonial rule. But often the movements themselves morphed into ruling political class hegemonies. While we have increased the number of women in parliaments in Africa to match the global average of 25%, actual power in government and society falls far short of that achievement. True liberation for women and minorities from shackles introduced by colonial subversion of gender remains elusive. From homes to bars to streets and workplaces, for all the strides made in "empowering women," we have yet to truly see the liberation of women, in the sense of being able to walk this world free in their own skin and their own bodies—free from violence.

> **From homes to bars to streets and workplaces, for all the strides made in "empowering women," we have yet to truly see the liberation of women, in the sense of being able to walk this world free in their own skin and their own bodies—free from violence.**

And often there's an expectation that oppressed people, in this case, African young women and gender-diverse people, should be civil in demanding that their full humanity be recognized. We hear condescending phrases such as "you are asking for too much."

But who defines what is "too much" for anyone's freedom and existence? For Sheena Bageine and Stella Nyanzi here in Uganda, and young women and queer Africans resisting dehumanization around the continent, the response is to be "too much." It is only when women are "too much" that new cracks in the wall of patriarchal dictatorships can emerge.

Selected Resources on African Feminism

AfricanFeminism is a pan-African feminists digital platform and collaborative writing project between African authors/writers with the long-term ambition of bringing on board at least one feminist voice from each country on the continent.

African Feminism Past and Present (AfricaFocus Bulletin, 2017) contains a compilation of short articles as well as links to other sources, including books.

Talking back: African Feminisms in Dialogue (Africa is a Country, 2020) is a series of articles edited by Senegalese scholar Rama Salla Dieng.

Feminist Africa provides a forum for progressive, cutting-edge gender research and feminist dialogue focused on the continent. Founded in 2002 in Cape Town, it has recently moved its headquarters to Ghana. See also a wide-ranging Zoom discussion in March 2021 including its founder Amina Mama and Rosebell Kagumire.

Building Feminist Practice: A Pocketbook for Human Rights Defenders (Civil Rights Defenders, updated version 2021) is intended as a practical and accessible resource that guides and supports human rights defenders in Africa in building a feminist practice.

NALA—Feminist Collective is a new organization launched in June 2021. It is led by a Council of 17 African women under 40. Its mission is to Foster, Enable and Mobilize (FEM) young women from Africa and the Diaspora, to bridge between policy and implementation, intergovernmental and grassroots spaces as well as generation gap.

Selected Resources on Black Feminism in the United States

The Activist Roots of Black Feminist Theory by Linda Burnham (Organizing Upgrade, December 2020) The idea that race, class and gender are interrelated dynamics of power and oppression has gained sufficient currency in the academic world to go by the shorthand "intersectionality." But the origins of contemporary Black feminist theory are not sufficiently known or acknowledged, and, given the invaluable work of university-based theorists, too many assume that the core concepts of Black feminism were born in the academy. In fact, much can be traced to activists in groups including the Student Non-Violent Coordinating Committee (SNCC), the Third World Women's Alliance, and the Combahee River Collective.

The Combahee River Collective Statement (April 1977) "The most general statement of our politics at the present time would be that we are actively committed to struggling against racial, sexual, heterosexual, and class oppression, and see as our particular task the development of integrated analysis and practice based upon the fact that the major systems of oppression are interlocking. The synthesis of these oppressions creates the conditions of our lives."

How We Get Free: Black Feminism and the Combahee River Collective by Keeanga-Yahmatta Taylor (2017)
A series of very enlightening recent interviews with both members of the Collective and current Black feminists associated with Black Lives Matter.

Making All Black Lives Matter by Barbara Ransby (2018) Both a history and a keen analysis of complexities by scholar/activist Barbara Ransby.

Movement For Black Lives
An umbrella organization for many of the diverse groups involved in #BlackLivesMatter organizing, with a focus on key policy issues and campaigns.

CHAPTER SEVENTEEN

AFRICAN FEMINIST CHARTER

By naming ourselves as Feminists we politicise the struggle for women's rights, we question the legitimacy of the structures that keep women subjugated, and we develop tools for transformatory analysis and action.

June 2021

Dr. Ayesha Imam

https://youtu.be/ZNn9zk0XVMg

Preface

Charter available in original formats in html and pdf. Formatting and additional links on this page are the responsibility of the US-Africa Bridge Building Project.

The African Feminist Forum is an independent feminist platform. It has been hosted since its inception by the African Women's Development Fund. The Fourth African Feminist Forum was held in 2016 in Harare, Zimbabwe. Although there has not been a forum since then, and this website has not been updated since 2017, it contains many useful resources, including a link to video interviews on its YouTube channel tagged KnowYourAfricanFeminists. Several of the interviews are embedded in the text below.

AFF Working Group Members in 2006

Ayesha Imam (Nigeria/Senegal), Bene Madunagu (Nigeria), Muthoni Wanyeki (Kenya), Sarah Mukasa (Uganda), Jessica Horn (Uganda/UK), Sylvia Tamale (Uganda), Codou Bop (Senegal), Everjoice Win (Zimbabwe), Demere Kitunga (Tanzania), Mary Rusimbi (Tanzania), Alice Karekezi (Rwanda), Bisi Adeleye-Fayemi (Nigeria/UK), Hope Chigudu (Zimbabwe), Shamillah Wilson (South Africa)

First published by African Women's Development Fund in 2007; Reprinted by African Women's Development Fund in 2016.

In this spirit of sharing feminist knowledge, this charter is distributed under a Creative Commons license that allows for non-commerical distribution in original form with full credit given to the authors.

Introduction

The African Feminist Forum took place from 15—19 November 2006 in Accra, Ghana. The meeting brought together over 100 feminist activists from all over the region and the diaspora. The space was crafted as an autonomous space in which African feminists from all walks of life at different levels of engagement within the feminist movement such as mobilizing at local levels for women's empowerment to academia, could reflect on a collective basis and chart ways to strengthen and grow the feminist movement on the continent.

With this Charter, we reaffirm our commitment to dismantling patriarchy in all its manifestations in Africa. We remind ourselves of our duty to defend and respect the rights of all women, without qualification.

We commit to protecting the legacy of our feminist ancestors who made numerous sacrifices, in order that we can exercise greater autonomy .

The Charter is an inspirational as well as an aspirational document. Mechanisms for operationalising it were also drawn up at the meeting.

A key outcome of the forum was the adoption of the Charter of Feminist Principles, which was agreed by the Regional Working group for the Forum, to be one of its principal aims. It was felt that we need something to help us define and affirm our commitment to feminist principles, which will guide our analysis, and practice.

As such the Charter sets out the collective values that we hold as key to our work and to our lives as African feminists. It charts the change we wish to see in our communities, and also how this change is to be achieved. In addition it spells out our individual and collective responsibilities to the movement and to one another within the movement.

Key recommendations were:
- The dissemination and popularization of the Charter as a critical movement building tool. This requires such inputs as, translation of the charter into as many languages as possible, communication of the charter through different mediums such as radio, websites, television, and so on.
- The Charter was viewed by many as an accountability mechanism for feminist organizing. As such it was recommended that it be developed into a tool that women's organizations can use for monitoring their own institutional development as well as peer review with other feminists.

Preamble: Naming Ourselves as Feminists

We define and name ourselves publicly as Feminists because we celebrate our feminist identities and politics. We recognize that the work of fighting for women's rights is deeply political,and the process of naming is political too. Choosing to name ourselves Feminist places us in a clear ideological position.

By naming ourselves as Feminists we politicise the struggle for women's rights, we question the legitimacy

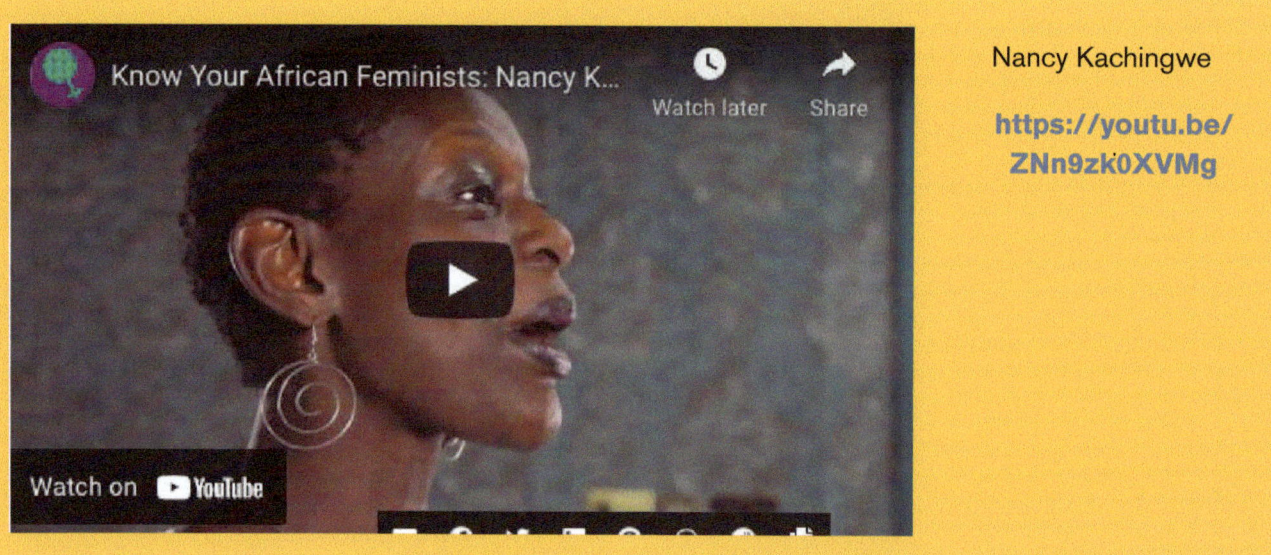

Nancy Kachingwe

https://youtu.be/ZNn9zk0XVMg

of the structures that keep women subjugated, and we develop tools for transformatory analysis and action.

We have multiple and varied identities as African Feminists. We are African women when we live here in Africa and even when we live elsewhere, our focus is on the lives of African women on the continent. Our feminist identity is not qualified with 'Ifs', 'Buts', or 'Howevers'. We are Feminists. Full stop.

We define and name ourselves publicly as Feminists because we celebrate our feminist identities and politics.

Our Understanding Of Feminism And Patriarchy

As African feminists our understanding of feminism places patriarchal social relations structures and systems which are embedded in other oppressive and exploitative structures at the center of our analysis.

Patriarchy is a system of male authority which legitimizes the oppression of women through political, social, economic, legal, cultural, religious and military institutions. Men's access to, and control over resources and rewards within the private and public sphere derives its legitimacy from the patriarchal ideology of male dominance. Patriarchy varies in time and space, meaning that it changes over time, and varies according to class, race, ethnic, religious and global imperial relationships and structures. Furthermore, in the current conjunctures, patriarchy does not simply change according to these factors, but is inter-related with and informs relationships of class, race, ethnic, religious, and global-imperialism. Thus to challenge patriarchy effectively also requires challenging other systems of oppression and exploitation, which frequently mutually support each other.

Our understanding of Patriarchy is crucial because it provides for us as feminists, a framework within which to express the totality of oppressive and exploitative relations which affect African women.

Patriarchal ideology enables and legitimizes the structuring of every aspect of our lives by establishing the framework within which society defines and views men and women and constructs male supremacy.

Our ideological task as feminists is to understand this system and our political task is to end it. Our focus is fighting against patriarchy as a system rather than fighting individual men or women. Therefore, as feminists, we define our work as investing individual and institutional energies in the struggle against all forms of patriarchal oppression and exploitation.

Our Identity as African Feminists

As Feminists who come from/work/live in Africa, we claim the right and the space to be Feminist and African. We recognize that we do not have a homogenous identity as feminists—we acknowledge and celebrate our diversities and our shared commitment to a transformatory agenda for African societies and African women in particular. This is what gives us our common feminist identity. Our current struggles as African Feminists are inextricably linked to our past as a continent, diverse pre-colonial contexts, slavery, colonization, liberation struggles, neocolonialism, globalization, etc. Modern African States were built off the backs of African Feminists who fought alongside men for the liberation of the continent. As we craft new African States in this new millennium, we also craft new identities for African women, identities as full citizens, free from patriarchal oppression, with rights of access, ownership and control over resources and our own bodies and utilizing positive aspects of our cultures in liberating and nurturing ways. We also recognize that our pre-colonial, colonial and post-colonial histories and herstories require special measures to be taken in favour of particular African women in different contexts.

As African feminists, we are also part of a global feminist movement against patriarchal oppression in all its manifestations. Our experiences are linked to that of women in other parts of the world with whom we have shared solidarity and support over the years.

As we assert our space as African feminists, we also draw inspiration from our feminist ancestors who blazed the trail and made it possible to affirm the rights of African women. As we invoke the memory of those

Dr. Amina Mama

https://youtu.be/77BUFAzo35U

women whose names are hardly ever recorded in any history books, we insist that it is a profound insult to claim that feminism was imported into Africa from the West. We reclaim and assert the long and rich tradition of African women's resistance to patriarchy in Africa.

We henceforth claim the right to theorize for ourselves, write for ourselves, strategise for ourselves and speak for ourselves as African feminists. We acknowledge the historical and significant gains that have been made by the African Women's Movement over the past forty years, and we make bold to lay claim to these gains as African feminists they happened because African Feminists led the way, from the grassroots level and up; they strategised, organized, networked, went on strike and marched in protest,and did the research, analysis, lobbying, institution building and all that it took for States, employers and institutions to acknowledge women's personhood.

Individual Ethics

As individual feminists, we are committed to and believe in gender equality based on feminist principles which are:

- The recognition and presentation of African women as the subjects not the objects of our work, and as agents in their lives and societies.
- The indivisibility, inalienability and universality of women's human rights.
- The right to healthy, mutually respectful and fulfilling personal relationships.
- The effective participation in building and strengthening progressive African feminist organizing and networking to bring about transformatory change.
- The right to express our spirituality within or outside of organized religions.
- The acknowledgment of the feminist agency of African women which has a rich Herstory that has been largely undocumented and ignored.
- A spirit of feminist solidarity and mutual respect based on frank, honest and open discussion of difference with each other.
- The support, nurture, and care of other African feminists, along with the care for our own well-being.
- The practice of non-violence and the achievement of non-violent societies.
- The right of all women to live free of patriarchal oppression, discrimination and violence.
- The right of all women to have access to sustainable and just livelihoods as well as welfare provision, including quality health care, education, water and sanitation.
- Freedom of choice and autonomy regarding bodily integrity issues, including reproductive rights, abortion, sexual identity and sexual orientation.

- A critical engagement with discourses of religion, culture, tradition and domesticity with a focus on the centrality of women's rights.

Institutional Ethics

As feminist organisations we commit to the following:
- Advocating for openness, transparency, equality and accountability in feminist-led institutions and organisations.
- Affirming that being a feminist institution is not incompatible with being professional, efficient, disciplined and accountable for all concerned. We believe that feminist spaces are created to empower and uplift women. At no time should we allow our institutional spaces to degenerate into sites of oppression and undermining of other women.
- Exercising responsible leadership and management of organisations whether in a paid or unpaid capacity and striving to uphold critical feminist values and principles at all times.
- Insisting on and supporting African women's labour rights, including egalitarian governance, fair and equal remuneration and maternity policies.
- Exercising accountable leadership in feminist organisations taking into consideration the needs of others for self- fulfillment and professional development. This includes creating spaces for power-sharing across-generations.
- Using power and authority responsibly, and managing institutional hierarchies with respect
- Striving to inform our activism with theoretical analysis and to connect the practice of activism to our theoretical understanding of African feminism.
- Creating and sustaining feminist organisations to foster women's leadership. Women's organizations and networks should be led and managed by women. It is a contradiction of feminist leadership principles to have men leading, managing and being spokespersons for women's organizations.
- Being open to critically assessing our impact as feminist organizations, and being honest and proactive with regards to our role in the movement.
- Feminist organisations as models of good practice in the community of civil society organizations, ensuring that the financial and material resources mobilised in the name of African women are put to the service of African women and not diverted to serve personal interests. Systems and structures with appropriate Codes of Conduct to prevent corruption and fraud, and to manage disputes and complaints fairly, are the means of ensuring institutionalized within our organizations.
- Opposing the subversion and/or hijacking of autonomous feminist spaces to serve right wing, conservative agendas.

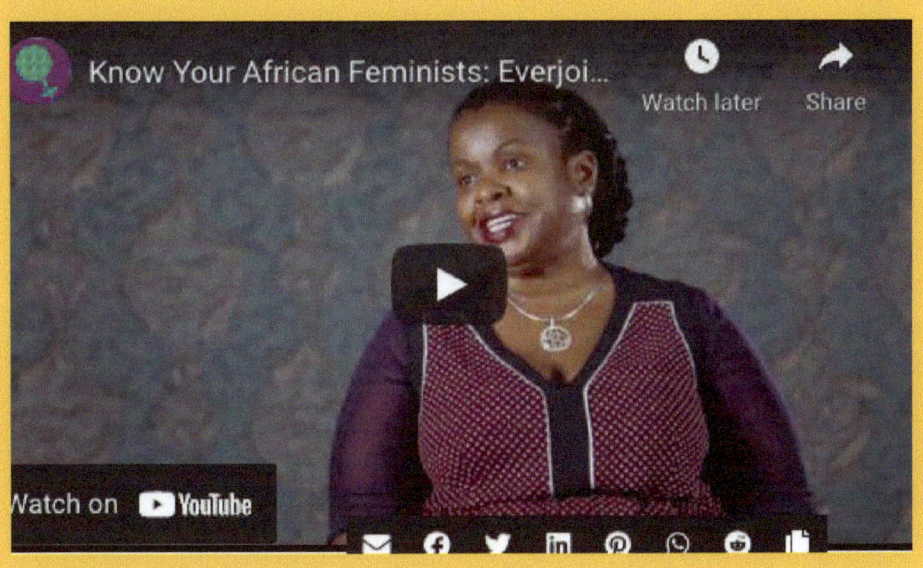

Everjoice Win

https://youtu.be/QoLeVH_zmLE

We acknowledge and celebrate our diversities and our shared commitment to a transformatory agenda for African societies and African women in particular.

- Ensuring that feminist non-governmental or mass organisations are created in response to real needs expressed by women that need to be met, and not to serve selfish interests, and unaccountable income-generating.

Feminist Leadership

As leaders in the feminist movement, we recognize that feminist agency has popularized the notion of women as leaders. As feminist leaders we are committed to making a critical difference in leadership, based on the understanding that the quality of women's leadership is even more important than the numbers of women in leadership. We believe in and commit ourselves to the following:

- Disciplined work ethics guided by integrity and accountability at all times.
- Expanding and strengthening a multi- generational network and pool of feminist leaders across the continent.
- Ensuring that the feminist movement is recognised as a legitimate constituency for women in leadership positions.
- Building and expanding our knowledge and information base on an ongoing basis, as the foundation for shaping our analysis and strategies and for championing a culture of learning, beginning with ourselves within the feminist movement.
- Nurturing, mentoring and providing opportunities for young feminists in a non-matronising manner.
- Crediting African women's labour, intellectual and otherwise in our work.
- Creating time to respond in a competent, credible and reliable manner to other feminists in need of solidarity and support whether political, practical or emotional.
- Being open to giving and receiving peer reviews and constructive feedback from other feminists.

Our feminist identity is not qualified with 'Ifs', 'Buts', or 'Howevers'.

We are Feminists. Full stop.

CHAPTER EIGHTEEN

LESSONS LEARNED IN TRANSNATIONAL SOLIDARITY: TOWARDS A PARTNERSHIP OF EQUALS

by Sahra Ryklief

Sahra Ryklief has worked on information provision and education for trade unions since 1990, beginning with what is now the Labour Research Service, *before taking on her current position as the General Secretary of the* International Federation of Workers Education Associations *(IFWEA) in 2007. August 2021*

Ten years ago, I sat in a coffee shop and listened to an influential member of a fraternal international organisation relate how an office bearer in my organisation had succeeded in persuading all the disenchanted key people in my organisation to rally, unite and contribute, thereby single-handedly, 'saving' the organisation. Having over 20 years in the South African labour movement and an additional 15 of international exposure at that point, it was not even an effort to keep my facial expression pleasantly blank, nod gently, and burble some noncommittal response to this utter nonsense.

Listening to my and several others' collective efforts being condensed into this messianic narrative, reducing my role as lead actor to that of passive beneficiary of someone's heroic largess, did not require much restraint, apart from a need to mask my internal amusement at the irony of the situation. No one thrives or even survives in international work by being overly sensitive. Dear reader, you may even be observant enough to notice that I avoided any national, racial or gender description of either the narrator, or the office bearer singled out for such distinction. For my message in this essay is about crafting a concerted response to the power relationship which invariably underlies all acts of solidarity, and I do not wish to distract you with how it is perceived when it manifests.

The vehicle for crafting this response is the organisational home for my wonderful adventure in international exchanges with the IFWEA. This transnational organization was founded in 1947 and I have had the privilege of being its General Secretary since December 2007. Prior to that, I served as a member of the IFWEA Executive Committee for a decade. My work with IFWEA has led me to develop a deep respect for the education organisations which make up its membership. I am continuously inspired by the resilience, dedication of service, comradeship and respect the people of my international 'tribe' display to one another. Together, we have agreed that crafting a 21st century model of international solidarity is fundamental to our education work with our partners in the labour movement, as the most pressing labour market and also social issues of our time are interconnected and global.

> Having over 20 years in the South African labour movement and an additional 15 of international exposure at that point, it was not even an effort to keep my facial expression pleasantly blank, nod gently, and burble some noncommittal response to this utter nonsense.

An essential testing ground for this work has been IFWEA's annual programme for young leaders called the Youth Globalisation Awareness Programme, which we have conducted since 2012. By 2020, 198 YGAP graduates from 33 countries had participated. YGAP targets young educators, trade union and youth leaders between the ages of 18 – 35 years. The YGAP curriculum changes annually and is designed by an international co-ordinating team. For two weeks, delegates participate in a curriculum of interactive activities designed to enhance their political understanding in a way that is inclusive, creative, diverse, respectful and, most importantly, fun. YGAP culminates in a few days of field placements in organisations working on labour, social justice and democracy issues, such as the Commercial, Stevedoring, Agricultural and Allied Workers Union. Delegates graduate with a renewed perspective of internationalism and are able to confidently design and deliver communication and/or education on global solidarity in their home countries.

One of the initial exercises is to ask participants to give us their personal understanding of what solidarity means, and also ask them what the word for solidarity is in their home language. By their responses, most have a self-defined view of themselves as social rather than personal. They see themselves as part of something larger than their immediate self, family and friends. This is a likely consequence of their organisational experience in their national labour movements or global trade union federations. Such membership is often grounded in a shared perspective of common humanity. They embrace the Southern African concept of ubuntu when it is introduced to them. Some go so far as to describe the personal value they have gained from human interaction across national/local and language divisions, their feelings of interconnectedness, of being part of a wider community, of needing to solve one another's problems together.

There is something very powerful in believing that humanity is one. It is but a short step to a perspective that the rights and resources you enjoy in your country or continent should belong to all who live in the world. To embrace people's struggle for economic and democratic freedom, equality and justice as your struggle as well. To feel their suffering as yours. To believe that until their battles are won, you cannot rest. It warms my and my colleague's hearts to hear this expressed every year by young leaders from diverse countries and organisations in the global labour movement.

So if I were asked, what my most important observation about international labour solidarity after more than three decades of international work, I can say with total conviction that it is powered by an immense faith in our common humanity, premised on a view that our world is changeable and a better one is possible, and executed by people with the best of intentions who want to be a part of this change.

> **One of the initial exercises is to ask participants to give us their personal understanding of what solidarity means, and also ask them what the word for solidarity is in their home language.**

The complications occur when we move from the realm of emotions and ideas into the act of solidarity and its results. It is here that the unravelling begins. Underlying the idea that we *should* all be equal, is the reality that we are not. Firstly, whilst solidarity's universal ideological premise decries fundamental differences, its actions are a response to the concrete reality that there are.

Secondly, solidarity is based on the premise that our world is changeable and that a better world is possible. However, despite 100 years of transnational labour solidarity, first pioneered, *inter alia*, by unions such as the IWW in the USA, the trade union federations in the Nordic countries, and the ICU in Southern Africa, conditions for vulnerable workers are degenerating from what they were only a few decades ago. Global inequality, while it appears in relative terms to be decreasing, has in actual fact been increasing in absolute terms, especially if applied to income averages and in-country differentials. Adding to this is the rapid digitization of multiple aspects of our working life, thereby reinforcing and intensifying existing social inequalities in our societies and between countries.

With these severe inequalities as the environmental context, to be a persistent proponent of transnational solidarity is to accept that our immediate acts of solidarity are not going to change the world any time soon. It is for this reason that we have to, at the very least, ensure that it changes us, the people and organisations involved in labour solidarity, in such a manner that we become better equipped and prepared to shape the longer term change we seek to achieve.

How then, can we forge transnational labour solidarity in a way that does this? I chose to advocate that we do this by paying close attention to the narrative which frames our approach. In crafting that narrative, we tell the story of what is wrong with the world, and what we would like to see. When confronting the profound structural changes to the forms of labour, we do not yet have all the answers to the big organizational challenges confronting us. So who is doing the telling of what the change should be?

To understand and appreciate the scale of informalisation in the south which drives non-wage economies; illegal migration; low union densities and weak political influence, is difficult from the well-resourced north. To those advocates of transnational solidarity shining the spotlight on those who are not being heard, who have been made invisible by being left out of the innovative solutions for economic development, often means that they call on their solidarity partners to give testimony as their only role in transnational exchanges.

I cannot begin to list the number of international conferences, seminars and workshops I have attended in Europe and North America, where the speakers' panel consists of Africans giving witness to their conditions, whilst the analysts and formulators of policies for change come from experts in the north. Can imported policies and structures and top-down approaches initiated by those in totally different conditions, inspire sufficient actors on the ground to change their socio-economic and political realities? A perfect example is the Pan African Parliament, which imploded recently and has been suspended until it seeks guidance from the EU, its main supporter, on how to proceed.

In recent years, we have witnessed the rise of the new movements, such as "Rhodes must fall"; "Black Lives Matter"; "Climate Justice" and "Me Too", who have and continue to challenge the prevailing structures and narratives of the day in our countries. They have energised the youth and influenced debates on multiple issues. It is not always possible to expect mainstream trade unions to connect with these movements in an organisational manner. Our most important connection could be by bringing that which is relevant and refreshing from these movements into the dialogue of ours.

> How then, can we forge transnational labour solidarity in a way that does this? I chose to advocate that we do this by paying close attention to the narrative which frames our approach.

One of the issues which has emerged, is a strong critique of the "saviour complex". I am disregarding the racial classification of "white saviour." I have seen too many of my fellow black South Africans portray a similar set of attitudes to Africans from other countries on the continent. It is the naming of the debilitating power relationship of well-resourced benefactors and poorly resourced beneficiaries that interests me. Solidarity has to have as its core the building a relational community, crafting the narrative collectively, solving our problems together. Collaborative effort provides motivation and builds the capacity of trade unions, NGOs and social organisations to work together. Unless we give due attention and significance to the role definition and relationship as partners in solidarity, we will not engender change.

As IFWEA, we argue that part of any improvement of our current approach is education that encourages collective empowerment towards global and transnational activism. This should not be interpreted that we are advocating eternal workshopping. You can start by listening before speaking, learning before acting and partnering instead of leading. You can trust that the leadership of the organisations you seek to support are bound to have a pretty solid vision of the solutions to their problems, and that they see your relationship as part of that solution. If that part is merely to provide resources, you can work to broaden it, to exchange ideas, methods, outcomes and learning experiences as an integral element of any and all transnational solidarity exchanges. You can make sure that you acknowledge and celebrate all who have contributed towards your collective partnership, and not only focus on those who provided the resources.

The way is now clear, thanks to these new movements, to confront the power issues openly. We should not lose this opportunity, or any possible regeneration of labour activism will be of short duration.
A Luta Continua!

> I cannot begin to list the number of international conferences, seminars and workshops I have attended in Europe and North America where the speakers' panel consists of Africans giving witness to their conditions, whilst the analysts and formulators of policies for change come from experts in the north. Can imported policies and structures and top-down approaches initiated by those in totally different conditions, inspire sufficient actors on the ground to change their socio-economic and political realities?

Selected Resources on Inequality and Transnational Solidarity

"Underlying the idea that we should all be equal, is the reality that we are not. Firstly, whilst solidarity's universal ideological premise decries fundamental differences, its actions are a response to the concrete reality that there are." – Sahra Ryklief

As Ryklief notes in this essay, unequal power relations are pervasive. They can and must be overcome to build a better world, whatever the causes of those inequalities.

Much of the debate to date has focused on racial division and the "white savior" complex. That debate was sharply focused by the Kony 2012 campaign by the U.S.-based group Invisible Children, calling for U.S. intervention to stop the Lord's Resistance Army led by Joseph Kony in central Africa. African critical response to this campaign was both immediate and eloquent, as illustrated in this widely distributed video by Ugandan blogger Rosebell Kagumire (transcript and more background on African criticism). The critique was amplified by Nigerian American novelist and literary critic Teju Cole in a twitter thread and an article in the Atlantic entitled the White Savior Industrial Complex.

On the wider power issues, and possibilities for addressing them, in addition to Ryklief's essay, two recent background resources, focused on the United Nations and on religious institutions respectively, are the story of former UN under secretary-general Noeleen Heyzer, from Singapore, and a study-guide for the Unitarian Universalist College of Social Justice.

For a hilarious take on celebrity fundraising in Western countries for Africa, see the video and website Radi-Aid: Africa for Norway.

For resources on education for solidarity, see Education for Empowerment and Identity Change and Popular Education, forthcoming papers by Sahra Ryklief and colleagues.

Selected Resources on Transnational Trade Union Movements and Workers' Rights

IFWEA
The International Federation of Workers' Education Associations (IFWEA) is a global federation of worker educators. We focus on adult education opportunities for workers and their communities.

ITUC-Africa
The African Regional Organisation of the International Trade Union Confederation (ITUC-Africa) is a pan-African trade union organisation created in November 2007 following the merger of two former African trade union organisations, namely ICFTU-Afro and DOAWTU.

WIEGO
Women in Informal Employment: Globalizing and Organizing (WIEGO) is a global network focused on empowering the working poor, especially women, in the informal economy to secure their livelihoods.

Public Services International
Our global union federation, our movement, our members: together we make society happen. Public service workers run hospitals and emergency services, schools and universities, public administrations and local governments, water and electricity utilities. Imagine a world without us.

International Labour Organization (ILO) Resources on Decent Work
Productive employment and decent work are key elements to achieving a fair globalization and poverty reduction. The ILO has developed an agenda for the community of work looking at job creation, rights at work, social protection and social dialogue, with gender equality as a crosscutting objective.

Solidarity Divided: An Interview with Bill Fletcher, Jr.
"The South African comment [at a meeting in 2010 in Johannesburg] went way beyond the parameters of what the SEIU folks identified as progressive trade unionism. For example, let's just take the issue of unemployment. The union movement in the United States, by and large, ignores the unemployed as a sector of the working class, and ignores the unemployed from their own sectors, after a few months, upon layoffs."

AFRICAN TRADE UNIONS AND AFRICA'S FUTURE

This report was written in 2014, based on extensive research done by Solidarity Center Africa Region staff and consultants in 2013.
August 30, 2021

This report was written in 2014, based on extensive research done by Solidarity Center Africa Region staff and consultants in 2013, including interviews with trade unionists in nine African countries.

As noted in the foreword below by Kwasi Adu-Amankwah, "An array of conventions at the international level and laws at the national level offer potential for protecting the rights and interests of workers. All too often, however, these legal instruments are not utilized for the benefit of workers, largely because of unwillingness or inability of governments to enforce them and the failure of trade unions to ensure compliance."

Unfortunately, this and other major conclusions of the report remain true today, even as the COVID-19 pandemic continues to spread. Workers, governments, and trade unions alike are stretched to the limits by the economic fallout of the pandemic, as well as by multiple other preexisting stresses and crises.

Global solidarity, as outlined in the original essay by Sahra Ryklief which this web page accompanies, has never been more urgent.

— *Imani Countess, Project Director*

> Genuine leadership is needed to steer Africa out of its difficulties and enable Africa and its people to progress.

African Trade Unions and Africa's Future: Strategic Choices in a Changing World

Solidarity Center
April 2014
https://www.solidaritycenter.org/wp-content/uploads/2014/11/Africa.Trade-Union-report-.6.14.pdf

Foreword

by Kwasi Adu-Amankwah

Kwasi Adu-Amankwah is General Secretary of the African Regional Organization of the International Trade Union Confederation (ITUC-Africa), based in Lomé, Togo. He was elected to that post in 2007. He previously served in several positions in the Ghana Trades Union Congress, most recently as its Secretary General from 2000 to 2007.

The Solidarity Center report titled *African Trade Unions and Africa's Future: Strategic Choices in a Changing World* is a valuable document that provides useful reflection and insight on the African labor market and trade union situation. The report is based mainly on a survey of nine countries, eight with English as the official language, one with Portuguese. Five of the countries are in Southern Africa, namely, Mozambique, South Africa, Swaziland, Zambia and Zimbabwe; three in West Africa, namely, Ghana, Liberia and Nigeria; and one in East Africa, Kenya. The report highlights the overall preoccupation of governments with macroeconomic stability and Gross Domestic Product (GDP) growth, which are not necessarily related to expanded employment and job creation nor

Firestone Agricultural Workers Union of Liberia (FAWUL) members, Liberia. Photo credit: Imani Countess.

to improved incomes and livelihoods. Reports by international agencies celebrate high rates of growth in a range of African countries and an inflow of investments, including from new partners such as China and Arabian Gulf States. But as this survey shows, such growth has not automatically translated into better well-being for the people. More striking, as the result of economic growth, are new trends in the labor market such as outsourcing, subcontracting, growing informality and the rise of precarious jobs—all of which have had consequences for trade unions.

The survey shows that trade unions have played a significant part in the political and economic lives of their countries. Among other things, unions have played key roles in:

- The decolonization and national liberation struggles;
- Promoting and defending democratic institutions after the formal achievement of political rights;
- Participating in organized structures for social dialogue or administration of public benefits, which require specialized personnel knowledgeable about these areas;
- Mobilizing on policy issues of particular interest to workers, such as minimum wage legislation and the scope of coverage of social insurance; and
- Participating in debates about the economic policy strategies of government.

An array of conventions at the international level and laws at the national level offer potential for protecting the rights and interests of workers. All too often, however, these legal instruments are not utilized for the benefit of workers, largely because of unwillingness or inability of governments to enforce them and the failure of trade unions to ensure compliance.

This in turn relates to the capacity of trade unions to function as solid organizations that can defend, protect and advance the interests of workers and meet their expectations. Issues of concern include the shrinking traditional base of trade unions in the formal sector, lack of resources from inadequate subscriptions and other sources, inadequate research capacity and insufficient specialized personnel and skills for negotiations with employers and governments.

As part of the response to their changing fortunes, the survey shows, most unions now attach considerable importance to organizing in the informal economy. Unions have also, over more than a decade, paid increasing attention to enhancing the participation of women in the trade union movement and in union leadership, a theme well developed in the report.

Given that it is based on a single survey covering a limited sample of nine countries, the report does not and cannot provide a comprehensive picture of trade unionism across Africa. In particular, it does not include insights from the trade union movement in the French-speaking countries of West and Central Africa, most notably the Democratic Republic of the Congo. A trend mentioned in the report that merits further research, and which is especially notable in the French-speaking countries, is the fragmentation of unions. This results in multiple national trade union centers, most of them unsustainable on their own, competing for the loyalties of a formal-sector labor force that is a relatively small proportion of the labor force in the country.

The report also does not address the particularly difficult environments for unions in countries such as those in North Africa, where unions must navigate between powerful governments on the one hand and the threats of fundamentalism and terrorism on the other.

> **In the modern history of Africa, the union movement has emerged as an important source of countervailing power for securing short-to medium-term benefits for workers directly and for pushing the frontiers of politics and policy in the direction of social transformation for the benefit of the people as a whole.**

More generally, it is essential that African trade unions consider not only the particular issues raised by this report but also the wider framework for trade union intervention in policy. This in turn must be linked to a class and nationalist perspective and analysis. Such analysis must be appropriate for each country while also addressing broad issues of industrialization, regional integration, domestic control over policy and reclaiming cultural heritage: in sum, an alternative paradigm for development in Africa.

The trade union movement in Africa faces enormous challenges arising from the critical situation that confronts Africa and its people. The African people have been losers in their encounters with other civilizations over several centuries, with negative consequences for the material well-being of the majority of Africans. In the development of the modern state, from the colonial era into what can be described today as the neocolonial era, the systems of governance and institutions of public authority that have emerged often do not serve the interests of the people. Genuine leadership is needed to steer Africa out of its difficulties and enable Africa and its people to progress.

Since pre-colonial times, popular organization and mass mobilization have been central to advancing the interests of the African people. Trade unions across large parts of Africa marshaled popular forces and played significant roles in the anti-colonial struggle. In the post-colonial era, unions have continued, albeit with varying degrees of success, to play crucial roles in protecting the economic and social rights of workers and in securing benefits for them in the midst of the overall difficulties facing the African masses. In the modern history of Africa, therefore, the union movement has emerged as an important source of countervailing power for securing short to medium-term benefits for workers directly and for pushing the frontiers of politics and policy in the direction of social transformation for the benefit of the people as a whole.

Neoliberal globalization has brought growing poverty and misery to the world's working poor and unemployed, as well as rising inequalities within countries and between regions of the world. Against this backdrop, there is an urgent need for trade union renewal. African trade unions need to get more workers organized and mobilized to secure day-today collective interests and to struggle for changes in the currently dominant paradigm of development.

Unions must reach workers in the traditional formal sector to reawaken their interest in unionism and in the struggle for achievement of worker rights. At the same time unions must rise to the challenge of organizing workers in the informal economy, enabling these workers to secure rights and social benefits as well as achieve self-help.

As part of this renewed commitment to rebuilding, unions must develop their capacity not only to negotiate benefits in the world of work, but also to exert political and policy influence on national development strategies. This can help ensure that the imprint of African workers is brought to bear on the imperatives of industrialization, African regional integration and the resurgence of culture that allows Africa to make its own creative contribution to modern development.

Unions must organize and mobilize workers to secure short- to medium-term benefits while simultaneously joining with other progressive forces for transformation and development.

Renewed commitment to building unions should also be linked consciously to efforts to reduce the dependence of trade unions, particularly financial dependence. While solidarity may always be an essential ingredient in the mix of resources on which trade unions draw, trade union dependence on donors, whether external or internal, is certain to compromise union ideals and undermine the growth of sustainable unions that serve their members in the best traditions of the trade union movement. Solidarity support to African trade unions, particularly of a financial and logistical kind, should thus be fashioned in a manner that helps unions move toward independence and self-reliance. Efforts that promote trade union unity, especially at national level, can make an important contribution to achieving such independence and sustainability.

Everything needs to be done to rebuild trade unions in Africa to ensure they can make their due contribution toward salvaging the blighted continent from the depths to which it has sunk. Unions must organize and mobilize workers to secure short- to medium-term benefits while simultaneously joining with other progressive forces for transformation and development. Failure to take on both tasks will condemn Africa to continuing crises and social explosions, betraying the hopes and aspirations of the continent's peoples.

CHAPTER TWENTY

LAWYERS CROSSING BORDERS

In the 20th century, as the Pan-African struggle advanced across the continent, lawyers across the diaspora and in imperial capitals found ways to join hands in solidarity across borders.
September 2021

Pan-Africanism and Global Solidarity

Of all the transnational movements first identified with the prefix "pan" in the late 19th and early 20th century, the Pan-African movement has been the one with the greatest impact and the greatest staying power. While the term dates to the Pan-African Conference of 1900 in London, the history it represents dates back to the slave trade and the global racial order established more than 500 years ago.

Within that still-existing order, people of African descent have ranked at or near the bottom in hierarchies of access to human rights, both within borders and across borders. That common fate has inspired common identities. But it has also fostered commitment to universal values of social justice, embodied in the saying "none of us is free until all of us are free."

This original essay by Meredith Terretta (below), accompanied by an excerpt from a review by Adom Getachew of the recent history of Pan-Africanism by Hakim Adi, well illustrates the richness of the Pan-African movement.

So does the global impact of music from the diaspora and the African continent, such as Bob Marley's Redemption Song and Manu Dibango's Soul Makossa.

– *William Minter*

Lawyers Crossing Borders: From Anti-Colonialism to Anti-Apartheid

Meredith Terretta, Professor of History, University of Ottawa. Dr. Terretta is the author of Nation of Outlaws, State of Violence: Nationalism, Grassfields Tradition, and State Building in Cameroon. *Her other publications cover a wide range including the history of Cameroon, human rights, the role of lawyers in African rights claims in the 20th century, and current issues of refugee rights.*

In the 20th century, as the Pan-African struggle advanced across the continent, lawyers across the diaspora and in imperial capitals found ways to join hands in solidarity across borders. Victories were limited at the height of colonialism. These long-distance solidarities were not only transnational but also transimperial. They connected people not only across territorial boundaries, but across imperial and linguistic boundaries.

One of the pioneers was Trinidad-born Henry Sylvester Williams. was most famous for being the organizer of the first Pan-African Congress in 1900. He also was trained as a barrister at Gray's Inn, London. Concerned about the conditions of Black South Africans, he moved to Cape Town in 1903 and became the first Black person to practice as an advocate for the Supreme Court in the Cape Colony, from 1903 to 1905. In *The Land is Ours: South Africa's First Black Lawyers and the Birth of Constitutionalism*, South African lawyer Tembeka Ngcukaitobi recounts how Williams represented Black Africans, particularly on land cases.

Anti-Colonial Strategies

Elsewhere in Africa, activist lawyers recognized that in colonial territories, the law was neither neutral nor equal. It served to elevate the rights of European citizens and white settlers, at the expense of African inhabitants' rights. Anti-colonial lawyers, in solidarity with African political elites, pursued two alternate pathways to promote more equitable rights, with reformist or revolutionary goals.

The first of these pathways led to equal rights via citizenship—imperial citizenship akin to that of white colonial officials and settlers whose metropolitan citizenship afforded them their higher legal status in colonial settings. Following this pathway, the law would be reformed to confer rights of European citizenship to Africans, placing them on par with white settlers in colonial territories. The second pathway aimed at liberation from white rule. In this second, visionary pathway, law would tear down the colonial legal structure and build it anew.

Activist lawyers and political actors drew on legal pluralism in colonial settings to wield the law for reform or for revolution, depending on the time and place. Cause lawyers traveled across territories, joining with African actors to expose race-based judicial irregularities that advantaged white settlers, the colonial state, and extractive corporations in mining and agriculture. The cases were diverse, but there were also common elements. Lawyers—usually from afar—represented political defendants in claiming rights before judicial bodies, and very often mobilized public opinion and policy.

After World War II

These long-distance advocacy connections persisted and expanded after the upheavals of WWII. One prominent case from that period was recently documented by Lessie B. Tate and Jackson de Carvalho, faculty members at Prairie View A & M University in Texas, an historically Black university founded in 1876. In 1948, two graduates of Howard University (see sidebar), African American Alberta Seaton and British Bermudan Earle Seaton, met East African students in London. The couple later traveled to East Africa where they made further links with African nationalists, and Earle established a law practice at Moshi in northern Tanganyika (now Tanzania). In 1950, Seaton became lead counsel on a land case brought by some three thousand African farmers displaced from their farms by thirteen white planters. Seaton took the case to the United Nations in 1952, where it was heard before the Trusteeship Council of the United Nations. Kirilo Japhet, Secretary of the Arusha Branch of the Tanganyika African Association provided oral testimony.

Seaton's efforts signaled the widening reach of cause lawyers in the international arena. Like Seaton, other lawyers from across the African diaspora set up law offices in African countries, using their legal knowledge and international contacts to advance the anti-colonial cause. One prominent example was Richard Danglemont, from Guadeloupe in the French Antilles, who practiced in Cameroon from 1953 to 1974.

After World War II, white lawyers joined the ranks of advocate lawyers who defended political actors and trade unionists in African territories. The French Communist Jewish lawyer, Pierre Kaldor, himself imprisoned under German occupation of France, chaired the Democratic Liberties Defense Committee of Black Africa, which defended African rights throughout French Africa. From February 1949 to October 1950, Henry Douzon and colleagues represented the leaders of the Democratic Party of Côte d'Ivoire, who were arrested on charges of "accessory to organized violence and looting" after popular uprisings and strikes in Grand Bassam.

In 1948, in neighboring Gold Coast, Ralph Millner, senior advocate of the British Haldane Society, defended Kwame Nkrumah and five of his colleagues for their alleged instigation of protests throughout the colony. In preparing for Ghana's independence, Nkrumah hired British senior advocate Geoffrey Bing to provide legal counsel, and Bing served as Attorney General from 1957-1961.

In Kenya, during the revolt from 1952-1956, called "Mau Mau" by white settlers, the British detained over a million Kikuyu in camps or resettled them in "emergency villages." Official records showed only 32 white civilians were killed, as well as 1,819 Africans loyal to the government and 63 whites and 101 Africans in the counterinsurgency forces. The government recorded 11,503 insurgents killed, as well as 1,015 legally executed under Emergency regulations, 432 for unlawful possession of arms and ammunition and 222 for "consorting with terrorists."

British trial lawyer Denis Nowell Pritt represented the Kenya African Union leadership as well as Kikuyu suspected of leading the revolt in appealing their death sentences. African barristers from Gold Coast, Nigeria, and India, including the diplomat Diwan Chaman Lall, joined the defense team of arrested political leaders.

After Independence

After independence, African lawyers continued to cross borders to represent oppositionists and defend their rights. In 1958, E.N.P. Sowah of Ghana was declared a prohibited immigrant when he attempted to enter Kenya, still a British colony, to join the legal defense of labor leader Tom Mboya and six African legislators accused of conspiracy. The denial of entry to the foreign lawyers of political defendants became common practice across late colonial African territories. It also became commonplace in a majority of post-independence African states, revealing how colonial the law remained after political independence.

In December 1970, Fadilou Diop, president of the Senegalese Bar Association, parliamentarian, and human rights lawyer in Dakar, was deported from Cameroon where he had traveled to represent the detained revolutionary, Ernest Ouandié, slated for trial before the Military Tribunal. After Diop's expulsion, in violation of a bilateral judicial agreement between Cameroon and Senegal that authorized Diop to practice there, in the absence of his choice of legal counsel, Ouandié was condemned to death and executed on 15 January 1971.

In the second half of the 20th century, support for African rights, through legal channels at both national and international levels, expanded dramatically with a focus on the white-minority-ruled and colonial states in Southern Africa. Liberation movements built linkages to the United Nations, to governments in Africa and around the world, and to global solidarity movements. That history, with ramifications in almost every country around the world, is far too rich to summarize in this short essay. It includes individual lawyers (such as Elizabeth Landis, who advised the UN Commission on Namibia) as well as specialist legal organizations, such as the International Defense and Aid Fund (which defended Nelson Mandela and his colleagues in the Treason Trial in South Africa) and the Southern Africa Project of the Lawyers' Committee for Civil Rights under Law (which played a key role from its founding in 1967 to the end of political apartheid in the 1990s). [See sidebar for a sample of sources to begin with.]

An Unfinished Journey

Decolonization and the end of legalized white-minority rule, however, did not overturn the fundamental order of colonial law. Emergency legislation, justified as a way to "maintain public order," or "keep the peace" allowed states to circumvent regular judicial processes, enabling them to target oppositionists, trade unionists, and their legal advocates. In some countries, there have been closed-door military tribunals, off limits to trial observers. African governments often invoked state sovereignty to reject foreign observers at political trials.

Legal systems, in Africa as around the world, have thus left fundamental issues of democracy and human rights unresolved, including land distribution and labor rights. While international human rights agreements have proliferated, so have multilateral agreements that privilege the rights of corporations and foster economic inequality.

Howard University

Since its founding in 1867, Howard University in Washington, DC has **served as an incubator of Pan-African connections**. Faculty, students, and graduates come not only from the United States but from the Caribbean, Africa, and around the world.

Prominent Pan-African scholar and activist C.L.R. James, although not officially on the faculty, had **major influence on Howard students and other activists** while living in Washington in the 1960s and 1970s. So did Caribbean political leader and scholar Eric Williams, who taught political science at Howard University before returning to Trinidad in 1948. The 6th Pan-African Congress in Tanzania in 1974 **emerged in this milieu from dialogue with Tanzanian diplomats**.

In addition to the Meru Land Case described in this essay, Howard connections included faculty who played prominent roles in U.S. Africa policy, such as Law School Dean **C. Clyde Ferguson**. Particularly prominent for their direct links to African freedom struggles were Goler Butcher, Pauli Murray, and Leslie Rubin.

Both in her capacity as professor in international law and on the staff of the House Subcommittee on Africa, **Goler Butcher** played a leading role in the campaign against apartheid in South Africa.

Pauli Murray, whose central role in legal progress against both racial and gender injustice is only now beginning to be acknowledged, also taught law in Ghana in the early 1960s, co-authoring a book on the constitution of Ghana with exiled white South African lawyer Leslie Rubin.

Rubin himself later moved to Washington **to take up a post at Howard Law School**, where he continued active in the campaign against apartheid both in the USA and at the United Nations.

Thanks to Myra Ann Houser and Lisa Crooms Robinson for contributing background for this sidebar.

Selected Background Readings

For additional contextual background, readers may find these diverse sources of interest:

On the independence of Ghana: **a paper based on oral sources by an exchange student in Ghana from the United States.**

On the independence of Cameroon: **article by Meredith Terretta on the concept of human rights and the failures of the United Nations.**

On the independence of Guinea (Conakry): **review of books by Elizabeth Schmidt**

Kenya – **a brief summary of British counter-insurgency in Kenya against "Mau Mau".**

Also the book by Caroline Elkins: Imperial Reckoning.

Namibia – **an analysis by Elizabeth Landis from 1971 of the legal status of Namibia.**

Southern Africa – **South Africa History Online article on the International Defence and Aid Fund.**

Southern Africa – **Gay McDougall and the Lawyers' Committee for Civil Rights under Law.**

Also the book by Myra Ann Houser: Bureaucrats of Liberation.

CHAPTER TWENTY ONE

A FULLER FREEDOM:
THE LOST PROMISE OF PAN-AFRICANISM

Hakim Adi's recent book situates the tragedies of mid-20th-century Pan-Africanism in a longer history.
September 2021

Pan-Africanism and Global Solidarity

Of all the transnational movements first identified with the prefix "pan" in the late 19th and early 20th century, the Pan-African movement has been the one with the greatest impact and the greatest staying power. While the term dates to the Pan-African Conference of 1900 in London, the history it represents dates back to the slave trade and the global racial order established more than 500 years ago.

Within that still-existing order, people of African descent have ranked at or near the bottom in hierarchies of access to human rights, both within borders and across borders. That common fate has inspired common identities. But it has also fostered commitment to universal values of social justice, embodied in the saying "none of us is free until all of us are free."

This excerpt from a book review by Adom Getachew, on the recent history of Pan-Africanism by Hakim Adi , well illustrates the richness of the Pan-African movement. It accompanies an original essay by Meredith Terretta on the role of solidarity by lawyers from around the African world in anticolonial struggles in the 20th century.

The wide scope of Pan-Africanism is also illustrated by the global impact of music from the diaspora and the African continent, such as Bob Marley's Redemption Song and Manu Dibango's Soul Makossa.

— *William Minter*

A Fuller Freedom:
The Lost Promise of Pan-Africanism

By Adom Getachew
October 29, 2019
Review of Pan-Africanism: A History, *by Hakim Adi*
https://www.thenation.com/article/archive/pan-africanism-history-hakim-adi-review/
[Excerpt reproduced with permission from
The Nation.*]*
Adom Getachew is an Assistant Professor of Political Science at the University of Chicago. *Her work focuses on the intellectual and political histories of Africa and the Caribbean. Her first book,* Worldmaking After Empire, *has won multiple awards.*

Had Peter Abrahams, the South African—born novelist, journalist, and Pan-Africanist, not been killed tragically in his Jamaican home in January 2017, he would have celebrated his 100th birthday this year. Born in 1919 on the outskirts of Johannesburg to an Ethiopian father and a "colored" (in the parlance of apartheid) mother, Abrahams lived his life along the winding paths of Pan-Africanism in the 20th century. In the same year that Abrahams was born, W.E.B. Du Bois helped organize the First Pan-African Congress to lay out a vision of what the end of the "war to end all wars" might mean for the colonized and Jim Crowed, who had long been subjugated by empire and white supremacy. When the end of another world war spurred the creation of the United Nations in 1945, Abrahams was old enough to join in the Pan-Africanists' Fifth Congress, serving as its secretary of publicity.

By that time, he had escaped South Africa after being accused of treason for criticizing his country's inequalities and had established himself as a writer with the publication of the short story collection Dark Testament and the novel Song of the City. At the Fifth Congress, he was joined by a cohort of black intellectuals—Amy Ashwood Garvey, Jomo Kenyatta, Kwame Nkrumah, George Padmore—who would soon define the coming postcolonial era. "The struggle for political power by Colonial and subject peoples," the congress declared, "is the first step towards, and the necessary prerequisite to, complete social, economic and political emancipation."

Reflecting on the proceedings, Abrahams identified this call with a new "militant phase" of the struggle against colonialism. "Forward to the Socialist United States of Africa! Long live Pan-Africanism!" he exhorted after the congress's closing. To Du Bois's 1900 declaration that "the problem of the 20th century is the problem of the color line," Abrahams and his generation answered with a vision of an independent and united Africa that could finally secure racial equality across the globe.

However, Abrahams's story also mirrored the swift disillusion that followed with the emergence of neocolonialism and the fractures within the Pan-Africanist movement. In his prescient 1956 novel *A Wreath for Udomo*, he depicted the unraveling of Pan-Africanism just as it was becoming a wide-ranging movement. The book's main character, Michael Udomo, is a composite figure (based on Nkrumah and Padmore) who moves from organizing for African independence in London to becoming the prime minister of a fictional "Panafrica." Narrated in two parts, "The Dream" and "The Reality," the novel tracks the exhilarating promise of national liberation, the hopes of a militant generation of Pan-Africanists, and the tragic choice that follows as Udomo weighs the costs of betraying the cause by accepting aid from a white settler nation or risking the ire of powerful states by supporting a fellow revolutionary. His dilemmas culminate in his destruction at the hands of his domestic opposition.

In the years to come, numerous anticolonial activists—from Nkrumah in Ghana to Ahmed Ben Bella in Algeria and Patrice Lumumba in Congo—would meet a similar fate, witnessing their hopes for independence dashed in the face of domestic dissension, Cold War interventions, and persistent economic dependence. In an age of decolonization, the Pan-Africanist wager was premised on the view that nationalism and internationalism must go hand in hand, that national independence could be secured only within regional and international institutions. As a result, the early postcolonial constitutions of Ghana, Guinea, and Mali, for instance, included clauses that authorized the delegation of sovereignty to a Union of African States when such an entity came into being. Yet over the three decades that followed World War II, internationalism and nationalism gradually came apart. While the sovereign state proved to be a limited vehicle for realizing independence and equality, its rights of nonintervention and territorial integrity emerged as powerful tools, especially against domestic critics and subnational challenges to state authority. In this context, committed Pan-Africanists and internationalists soon became wedded to the sovereign nation-state and its capacity to discipline newly independent and fragile societies.

"The one-man leadership thing I never condoned," Abrahams later recalled, but even in the face of such thwarted hopes, he remained loyal to the cause of Pan-African liberation for the rest of his life. A chance meeting in 1955 with Norman Manley, who was then leading Jamaica's anticolonial struggle, prompted Abrahams to move to the island, where he participated in its transition to independence and later supported the social transformation inaugurated by Norman Manley's son Michael Manley, the democratic socialist prime minister who swept into office in 1972. Abrahams worked as the chairman of Radio Jamaica and hoped that the Caribbean might realize the democratic, egalitarian, and internationalist vision of society that he had long fought for. From his home in the mountains of Jamaica, Abrahams set his sights across the Atlantic, critically assessing the failures of the postcolonial African states and especially the rise of authoritarian regimes. But as he declared near the end of his long life, "Jamaica is Africa to me."

Driven by a similar impulse toward historical recovery, Hakim Adi's recent book *Pan-Africanism: A History* situates the tragedies of mid-20th-century

Pan-Africanism in a longer and more capacious history. Pan-Africanism, he shows, began in the 18th century with the struggle against slavery and has persisted well into the 21st century with, among other movements, contemporary reparations activism. Rather than a crashing wave, Adi argues, Pan-Africanism "might be more usefully viewed as one river with many streams and currents." It flowed and ebbed and then flowed (and ebbed) again, helping to shape much of the 20th century in the process and continuing to leave a deep imprint on the 21st. ...

Adi opens his book with the history of the transatlantic slave trade and the black struggles for emancipation that arose from it. The forced migration of 12 million people across the Atlantic as chattel, he argues, created the conditions in which "Africa" became a transnational marker—an idea as much as a place. In this context, Olaudah Equiano, born in what is now the Igbo region of Nigeria in 1745 and enslaved at a young age, styled himself the "African" in his 1789 Interesting Narrative of the Life of Olaudah Equiano. With fellow freedman Ottobah Cugoano he organized the Sons of Africa, a group that agitated for the end of the slave trade. From the communities of escaped slaves that dotted the Americas and the early repatriation movements to the emergence of a "black empire" in the Haitian Revolution, the image of Pan-Africa began to take shape.

But as Adi shows, if Pan-Africa was born out of the experience of diasporic bondage, it was not a unidirectional transmission from the enslaved and the colonized in the Americas to Africa. The transatlantic idea of Africa also took inspiration from the connections formed between these communities and the Africans still on the continent. ... For instance, the vision of "African regeneration" articulated by Edward Blyden, the Caribbean author of 1857's *A Vindication of the Negro Race*, who eventually settled in Liberia, inspired a whole cohort of West African intellectuals. ... Reversing this trajectory of influence, the writings of James Africanus Horton, a Sierra Leonean doctor who supported and extended Blyden's vision, proved an important source for the Jamaican Marcus Garvey, whose group the Universal Negro Improvement Association would become the largest black mass movement in the world. ...

The tensions inaugurated in the age of decolonization—between a black politics conscripted into a defense of the nation-state and one that aspired to succeed or transcend it—are with us today.

Throughout the late 19th and 20th centuries, black people moved around the world in search of work and greater freedom, and through this they generated solidarities out of the collective experience of racialized slavery and colonialism, turning forced displacement and exile into political possibility. Meetings like the 1900 Pan-African Conference and its successors might suggest that these forms of mobility were limited to a small male elite. But as Adi highlights, the official spaces of Pan-Africanism relied on women's labor, even if women were marginalized. The 1900 conference, best remembered for Du Bois's evocative formulation of the global color line, was in fact co-organized by Alice Victoria Kinloch of South Africa, who emerged as a critic of black oppression in her homeland before moving to Britain in 1896. ...

Outside the rarefied conferences and chance meetings in imperial metropoles like London and Paris, the vision of a global Africa was lived and enacted in everyday life and culture by millions who remain anonymous to history. The idea of African freedom and unity traveled with the Caribbean workers who dug the Panama Canal. It was carried with the African Americans who escaped north in the Great Migration, and it traversed the African continent with figures like Abrahams's father, who traveled from his native Ethiopia to South Africa in order to find work in the mines and plantations of a voracious new imperialism. Black sailors and migrant workers in the circum-Caribbean and in southern Africa clandestinely distributed UNIA's newspaper, Negro World. The Comintern-funded Negro Worker, the Paris-based Le Cri des Nègres, and countless other black newspapers and magazines carried news of a global Africa along similar networks. After formal decolonization was achieved, the message of Pan-Africanism lived on in the vernaculars of Rastafarianism and reggae music, the aesthetics of the Afro, and the global reverberations of "Black is beautiful."

Weaving together the institutional high politics of Pan-Africanism with its popular and cultural iterations, Adi presents his readers with a wide tapestry of black freedom dreams that challenges many of the neat divisions imposed on black intellectual and political life by historians and scholars. ...

The shift of Pan-African activity from imperial metropoles to the African continent and from international networks to postcolonial nation-states is perhaps Pan-Africanism's most contentious and uncertain moment—one that exposed the fragile suturing of difference and unity. The emergence of independent states like Ghana and Tanzania—led by two advocates of African socialism, Nkrumah and Julius Nyerere—created institutional and ideological openings to realize African unity. Yet the achievement of state sovereignty also worked to stymie more radical visions of Pan-Africanism. ...

The tensions inaugurated in the age of decolonization—between a black politics conscripted into a defense of the nation-state and one that aspired to succeed or transcend it—are with us today. Adi points to the OAU-sponsored First Pan-African Conference on Reparations for Slavery, Colonization and Neocolonization, which took place in 1993 in Abuja, Nigeria, as one of the starting points of a new Pan-African politics. The Abuja proclamation declared that "the damage sustained by the African peoples is not a 'thing of the past' but is painfully manifest in the damaged lives of contemporary Africans from Harlem to Harare, in the damaged economies of the Black World from Guinea to Guyana, from Somalia to Suriname." Yet at the 2001 World Conference Against Racism, Racial Discrimination and Xenophobia in Durban, South Africa, the geopolitical fractures of the black world frustrated a collective call for reparations. While Nigeria's then-President Olusegun Obasanjo told the conference that an apology from the European states that had imposed slavery and colonialism would suffice, Nigerian activists and civil society organizations joined the Caribbean states in demanding a more expansive program of repair.

Despite the differences that have undermined Pan-Africanism throughout its existence, Adi is right to reject accounts that reduce its staying power to "a matter of hazy vague emotions—a vision or a dream." The promise of Pan-Africanism was always much more than that. Like most political ideals, it helped galvanize generations into taking action. But as much as Pan-Africanism was an organized movement, it was also a sensibility, a culture, and a lived experience—guises in which it continues to shape contemporary life. Out of forced exile and dispersal, it built a Black World, and from the depths of slavery, it limned the outlines of a fuller freedom in its songs of redemption.

Selected Resources on Pan-Africanism

Among the thousands of books on Pan-Africanism, two recent books by Adom Getachew and Hakim Adi can be highly recommended as starting points. There are too many classic works to list, but two authors with wide influence across the Pan-African world who should be noted are C. L. R. James and Walter Rodney.

Adom Getachew, *Worldmaking After Empire: The Rise and Fall of Self-Determination*, 2020.

Hakim Adi, *Pan-Africanism: A History*, 2018.

C. L. R James, *A History of Pan African Revolt*, with a new introduction by Robin D. G. Kelley, 1938, 2012.

Walter Rodney, *How Europe Underdeveloped Africa*, with an introduction by Angela Davis, 1972, 2018.

Recent videos on Pan-Africanism available online include a *webinar on Pan-Africanism in the 21st Century* hosted by Africans Rising on May 24, 2021 and a YouTube video by Brian Kagoro from *March 1, 2019*.

CHAPTER TWENTY TWO

FROM STANDING ROCK TO LINE 3: INDIGENOUS ACTION TO SAVE THE PLANET

In this report, we demonstrate the tangible impact these Indigenous campaigns of resistance have had in the fight against fossil fuel expansion across what is currently called Canada and the United States of America.
October 2021

In an earlier essay in this series, Donna Katzin stressed that the goal of *disinvestment* of resources from harmful activities must go together with *reinvestment* of resources in activities that have beneficial results for the future. This is crystal clear in the urgent need for transition from fossil fuels to renewable energy. The cost of letting promises and belated minimal policy shifts substitute for significant action will be high.

In mid-October Indigenous climate justice advocates led a broad coalition in week-long demonstrations in Washington, DC to urge President Biden to take executive actions within his power to stop ongoing new fossil-fuel production projects. Although thousands participated, 655 were arrested, and the Bureau of Indian Affairs occupied by Indigenous protesters for the first time since 1972, the event was hardly covered in national news outlets.

That's why Indigenous activists are not only protesting, petitioning, and fighting in the courts. They are also taking direct action to stop fossil fuel projects (see below) and building a new global vision based on care-giving rather than limitless extraction of resources for short-term profit for a few.

— *William Minter*

Adding up the total, indigenous resistance has stopped or delayed greenhouse gas pollution equivalent to at least 1/4 of annual U.S. and Canadian emissions.

Indigenous Resistance Against Carbon
August 2021
Indigenous Environmental Network
https://www.ienearth.org/
Oil Change International
http://priceofoil.org/
[Excerpts from executive summary below. Full report available at links above]

Indigenous Resistance Against Carbon seeks to uplift the work of countless Tribal Nations, Indigenous water protectors, land defenders, pipeline fighters, and many other grassroots formations who have dedicated their lives to defending the sacredness of Mother Earth and protecting their inherent rights of Indigenous sovereignty and self determination. In this effort, Indigenous Peoples have developed highly effective campaigns that utilize a blended mix of non-violent direct action, political lobbying, multimedia, divestment, and other tactics to accomplish victories in the fight against neoliberal projects that seek to destroy our world via extraction.

In this report, we demonstrate the tangible impact these Indigenous campaigns of resistance have had in the fight against fossil fuel expansion across what is currently called Canada and the United States of America. More specifically, we quantify the metric tons of carbon dioxide equivalent (CO_2e) emissions that have either been stopped or delayed in the past decade due to the brave actions of Indigenous land defenders. Adding up the total, indigenous resistance has stopped or delayed greenhouse gas pollution equivalent to at least one-quarter of annual U.S. and Canadian emissions.

Our aim is two-fold: First, that Indigenous land defenders are emboldened to see the collective results of their efforts and utilize this information as a resource to garner further support. Second, that settler nation-state representatives, organizations, institutions, and individuals recognize the impact of Indigenous leadership in confronting climate chaos and its primary drivers. We hope that such settlers, allies or not, come to stand with Indigenous Peoples and honor the inherent rights of the first peoples of Turtle Island—the land currently called North America—by implementing clear policies and procedures grounded in Free, Prior and Informed Consent, and by ending fossil fuel expansion once and for all. . . .

Indigenous Rights and Responsibilities Framework

Indigenous social movements across Turtle Island have been pivotal in the fight for climate justice. From the struggle against the Cherry Point coal export terminal in Lummi territory to the fights against pipelines crossing critical waterways, Indigenous land defenders have exercised their rights and responsibilities to not only stop fossil fuel projects in their tracks, but establish precedents to build successful social justice movements. The essential backbone of these movements is grounded in an Indigenous Rights framework.

This Indigenous Rights and Responsibilities approach is based upon the concepts of Indigenous Sovereignty, which exist regardless of the actions of settler nation-states. Indigenous Sovereignty endures as long as Indigenous Peoples endure, and understanding these concepts illuminates why advocacy to prevent the extraction, production, processing, and release of carbon is based not solely on the notion of inherent rights, but on the responsibility and obligations of Indigenous Peoples and Tribal Nations to the land itself. . . .

Destructive actions like fossil fuel extraction and the construction of fossil fuel infrastructure on Indigenous territories, lands, and waterways directly attack traditional Indigenous knowledge by seeking to untether spiritual ways, languages, cultural practices, legal systems, and social, economic, and legal systems from relationship with those lands and water. An Indigenous Rights and Responsibilities framework links the struggle to protect the land with the ever present struggle to resist settler nation state acts of violence and colonization fueled by an extractive economic system.

By resisting such acts, Indigenous land defenders and Nations disrupt the goals of the world's most powerful institutions—nation-states and multinational corporations. This is done with a strategic framework that protects the land, builds collective power, confronts white supremacy, and challenges tenets of capitalism and Eurocentric materialism. These fights demonstrate how a movement built upon an Indigenous Rights framework far exceeds the goals of environmental protection and provides a road map to decolonizing our current economic paradigm.

Whether by physically disrupting construction, legally challenging projects, or effecting procedural delays, Indigenous land defenders and Nations utilize a multi-tiered approach to resist fossil fuel projects. These tactics demonstrate that Indigenous Rights and Responsibilities are far more than rhetorical devices—they are tangible structures impacting the viability of fossil fuel expansion. . . .

Due to the unique histories of Indigenous Peoples' interactions with the United States and Canada, Tribal Nations and First Nations have a wide range of reserved rights that have been recognized and upheld within the eyes of nation-state court systems. These legal battles, coupled with grassroots expressions of self-determination, have stopped and delayed the expansion of fossil fuels, and also exposed the financial liabilities of such expansion when Indigenous Rights are violated. . . .

Free, Prior and Informed Consent

When challenging fossil fuel projects and confronting polluting industries, the international standard of Free, Prior and Informed Consent (FPIC) is a key process through which Indigenous peoples assert their sovereignty and self-determination. This right is recognized in the United Nations Declaration on the Rights of Indigenous Peoples (UNDRIP) and—when implemented properly by nation states—allows Indigenous people to grant or withhold permission to projects that may affect them or their territories. . . .

> Destructive actions like fossil fuel extraction and the construction of fossil fuel infrastructure on Indigenous territories, lands, and waterways directly attack traditional Indigenous knowledge by seeking to untether spiritual ways, languages, cultural practices, legal systems, and social, economic, and legal systems from relationship with those lands and water.

Canada and the United States acknowledge UNDRIP on premise alone, but both nation-states have refused to adopt its text without qualifications. Due to this refusal, while these nations acknowledge the tenets of Indigenous Rights, they have consistently chosen to define these rights in a way that does not ultimately threaten control over lands, natural resources, and development plans that may affect Indigenous people and territories.

In both the United States and Canada, the current modus operandi to engage Indigenous Peoples on extractive projects is a process of consultation. Under this process, federal governments consult with Tribes and First Nations, seeking their input on planned projects. Such input and consultation does not guarantee outcomes in line with the wishes of those Nations; this consultation is crucially distinct from consent.

Furthermore, there are many examples of projects well underway before this so-called 'consultation' even begins with Tribes—effectively nullifying the intention of the process and exposing its severe inadequacies. Free, Prior and Informed Consent constitutes a much more rigorous standard than consultation, and it is a bare minimum standard needed to uphold the rights of Indigenous Peoples. . . .

Criminalization of Defenders: Standing Rock and Beyond

This report on Indigenous resistance to fossil fuel projects would be incomplete without attention to severe threats faced by frontline leaders and communities when they speak out and take action. The fight against the Dakota Access Pipeline is a notable example of these threats—what happened in Standing Rock should not be seen as an anomalous incident, but rather a disturbing commonality across Indigenous resistance efforts worldwide.

The grassroots fight against Energy Transfer Partners' Dakota Access Pipeline began in early 2016. The Bakken oil pipeline was expected to transport crude oil from the traditional lands of the Three Affiliated Tribes of the Mandan, Hidatsa, and Arikara Nations to an oil terminal in southern Illinois. The Dakota Access route crossed the treaty territories of the Oceti Sakowin people near the reservation boundaries of the Standing Rock Sioux Tribe, and crossed beneath the Missouri River on the Tribe's northern border. The Tribes and their citizens saw the pipeline as a serious threat to water resources, treaty rights, and sacred cultural sites, and mobilized one of the largest sustained Indigenous-led protests in the living memory of the United States.

In response to the mobilization against Dakota Access, local and state officials used military tactics to suppress public protest and intimidate water protectors. In May 2017, The Intercept reported on the activities of TigerSwan, a "mercenary" private contractor hired by Energy Transfer Partners to quell the efforts of water defenders at Oceti Sakowin, Standing Rock, North Dakota. . . . [The report] described illegal actions taken against peaceful Indigenous defenders and misinformation given to local police forces to attack thousands of people encamped near the Dakota Access Pipeline's Missouri River crossing. TigerSwan communications described the peaceful gathering as "jihadist" and "terrorist," and the private contractor used military-grade weapons and tactics to undercut, discredit, and punish the defenders. Tactics included infiltration, provocation, disruption of communications, aerial surveillance, and radio eavesdropping. Intimidation involved the use of large and visible forces of heavily armed personnel and personnel carriers, as well as drones and air surveillance.

The "task force" arrayed against the defender included agents from the U.S. Federal Bureau of Investigation, U.S. Department of Homeland Security, U.S. Justice Department and Marshals Service, and U.S. Bureau of Indian Affairs, as well as state and local law enforcement and police. TigerSwan transmitted daily reports "from the battlefield" to Energy Transfer Partners.

Local authorities arbitrarily arrested and harassed water protectors, and both local and TigerSwan forces used aggressive attack dogs and other forms of physical violence, including water cannons in freezing conditions. Despite later vindication by courts, thousands of victims of these abuses—the vast majority of whom were Indigenous—remain scarred by these clubs and beatings. . . .

In addition to physical violence, the Standing Rock Reservation was punished economically by the U.S. State of North Dakota, and the hard-won victories of Indigenous resistance were overturned when newly inaugurated U.S. President Donald Trump overruled President Barack Obama's denial of key permits and facilitated the completion of the Dakota Access Pipeline. During the height of the Dakota Access resistance, United Nations (UN) Special Rapporteur on the Rights of Indigenous Peoples Victoria Tauli-Corpuz and UN Permanent Forum on Indigenous Issues Expert Member Edward John visited Oceti Sakowin and condemned the violation of human and Indigenous rights by Energy Transfer Partners, TigerSwan and federal, state, and local security forces. Tauli-Corpuz specifically decried the company and government's violation of the Standing Rock Sioux Tribe's right to land.

In her 2018 report to the UN Human Rights Council, Tauli-Corpuz presented a thematic study on the criminalization of and attacks against Indigenous human rights defenders. Citing her own investigations and those of other Special Rapporteurs and the Organization of American States, she identified numerous rights

> **In response to the mobilization against Dakota Access, local and state officials used military tactics to suppress public protest and intimidate water protectors.**

violated at Standing Rock, including that of Self-Determination and the right to lands and territories. . . .

Counting Up the Impact

To assess the scale of Indigenous resistance against carbon, we begin by calculating the amount of greenhouse gas pollution each project would create. Most of these assessments were conducted by Oil Change International, with certain exceptions drawn from other sources (*see Appendix for details*).

We examined only the reported climate impact of specific pipelines, tar sands mines, and the Arctic National Wildlife Refuge. . . . For scale, we compare the climate impacts of projects facing Indigenous resistance over the last decade to 2019 estimates of total combined greenhouse gas pollution from the United States and Canada—6.56 billion metric tons of carbon dioxide equivalent (CO_2e). . . .

Victories in infrastructure fights alone represent the carbon equivalent of 12 % of annual U.S. and Canadian pollution, or 779 million metric tons CO_2e. Ongoing struggles equal 12 % of these nations' annual pollution, or 808 million metric tons CO_2e. If these struggles prove successful, this would mean Indigenous resistance will have stopped greenhouse gas pollution equivalent to nearly one-quarter (24 %) of annual total U.S. and Canadian emissions.

That 24 %, equaling 1.587 billion metric tons CO_2e, is the equivalent pollution of approximately 400 new coal-fired power plants—more than are still operating in the United States and Canada—or roughly 345 million passenger vehicles—more than all vehicles on the road in these countries.

If Not Us Then Who?

https://youtu.be/
0mbI-RIqtJU

Watch powerful 8.32 minute film on Standing Rock. Vicky Tauli-Corpuz, then the UN Special Rapporteur on the Rights of Indigenous Peoples, meets with Standing Rock leaders in 2017.

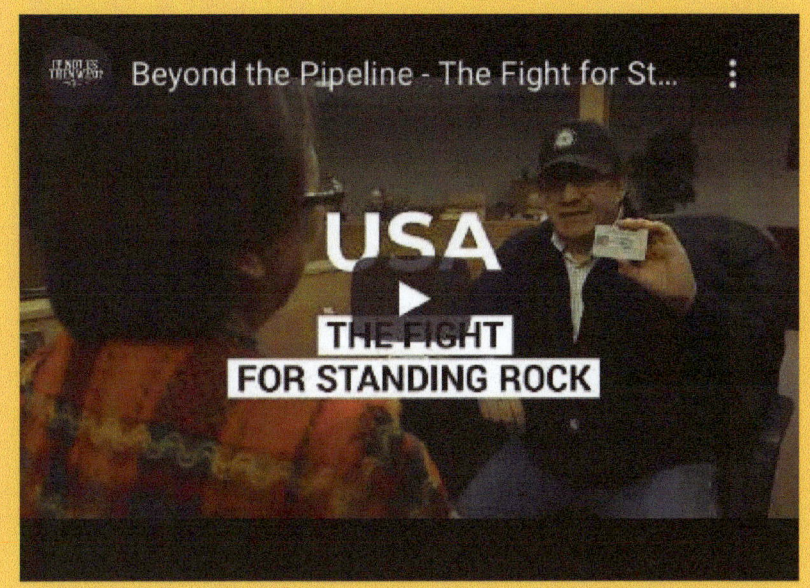

Selected Resources on Standing Rock and Beyond

The Standing Rock Sioux Tribe's Litigation on the Dakota Access Pipeline
https://earthjustice.org/features/faq-standing-rock-litigation

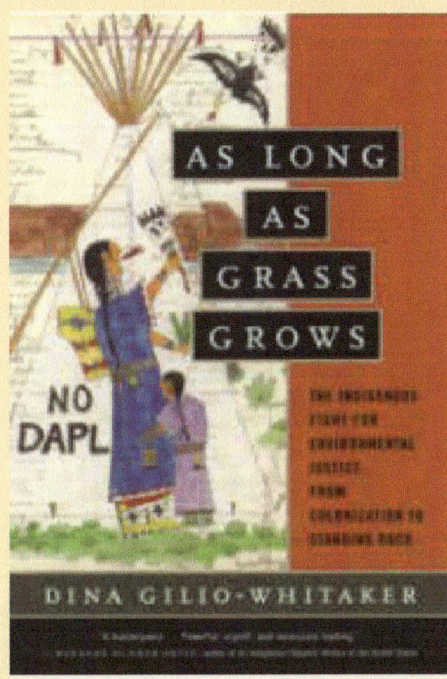

Dina Gilio-Whitaker, *As Long as Grass Grows*   Nick Estes, *Our History is the Future*

More books on Indigenous Resistance on Turtle Island
https://bookshop.org/lists/indigenous-resistance-on-turtle-island-standing-rock-beyond

Winona LaDuke on Line 3 Pipeline

"In one narrative, the Canadian corporation won. Columbus conquered anew, proof that might and money remain the rulers.

Then, there's another. That's the Ballad of the Water Protectors—a movement born in the battles in northern Minnesota and North Dakota, a movement that will grow and transform the economy of the future . . .

The Canadian oil industry estimated that a lack of pipeline capacity reduced the industry's income by tens of billions of dollars before the pandemic started… Uncertainty about Line 3 caused by Indigenous people and water protectors encouraged massive divestment from the tar sands by non-Canadian investors."

Source: https://fpif.org/indigenous-movements-are-key-to-the-fight-against-fossil-fuels

CHAPTER TWENTY THREE

THE RED DEAL: MOVING BEYOND THE GREEN NEW DEAL

Indigenous activists are not only protesting, petitioning, and fighting in the courts. They are also taking direct action to stop fossil fuel projects and building a new global vision based on caregiving.
October 2021

In an earlier essay in this series, Donna Katzin stressed that the goal of *disinvestment* of resources from harmful activities must go together with **reinvestment** of resources in activities that have beneficial results for the future. This is crystal clear in the urgent need for transition from fossil fuels to renewable energy. The cost of letting promises and belated minimal policy shifts substitute for significant action will be high.

In mid-October Indigenous climate justice advocates led a broad coalition in week-long demonstrations in Washington, DC to urge President Biden to take executive actions within his power to stop ongoing new fossil-fuel production projects. Although thousands participated, 655 were arrested, and the Bureau of Indian Affairs occupied by Indigenous protesters for the first time since 1972, the event was hardly covered in national news outlets.

That's why Indigenous activists are not only protesting, petitioning, and fighting in the courts. They are also taking direct action to stop fossil fuel projects and building a new global vision based on caregiving rather than limitless extraction of resources for short-term profit for a few (see below).

– William Minter

Create Jobs: Heal Our Planet

Excerpted from The Red Deal: Heal Our Planet *(PDF available for download)*

There is no hope for restoring the planet's fragile and dying ecosystems without Indigenous liberation. This isn't an exaggeration; it's simply the truth. Indigenous people understand the choice that confronts us: decolonization or extinction. We have unapologetically renewed our bonds with the earth by implementing our intellectual traditions in our movements for decolonization. There is no turning back; these bonds are sacred and will never be broken. This is why Indigenous water protectors and land defenders throughout the world are criminalized and assassinated on a daily basis. We have chosen life, therefore we've been marked for death.

Healing the planet is ultimately about creating infrastructures of caretaking that will replace infrastructures of capitalism.

Despite this grim reality, Indigenous people continue to caretake the land even under threat of daily attack. Like mothers, nurses, and educators, Indigenous water protectors and land defenders perform one of the most important types of labor we depend upon as a species for social and biological reproduction: caretaking. Humanity would not exist without caretakers. But caretaking is labor. It takes work to plant crops. It takes work to hunt. It takes work to raise children. It takes work to clean homes. It takes work to break down a buffalo. It takes work to learn the properties of medicines.

Healing the planet is ultimately about creating infrastructures of caretaking that will replace infrastructures of capitalism. Capitalism is contrary to life. Caretaking promotes life. As we note throughout the Red Deal, caretaking is at the center of contemporary Indigenous movements for decolonization and liberation. We therefore look to these movements for guidance on building infrastructures of caretaking that have the potential to produce caretaking economies and caretaking jobs now and in the future.

We also look to the infrastructure of caretaking that is currently emerging where capitalist nation-states have failed to save lives from COVID-19. Under the current system of global capitalism, caretaking is undervalued and often unrecognized as a form of labor. Caretakers like mothers and water protectors make up a huge %age of workers who produce the social and material means by which we live, yet they're not paid. In a world shaped by pandemic, caretakers have become the most important sector of workers, saving people's lives and keeping whole families and communities afloat.

Mutual aid networks populated by caretakers are proliferating, providing relief to the most vulnerable and paving the way for robust caretaking economies to potentially replace the crumbling system of global capitalism. Current mutual aid efforts are neither state sanctioned nor state-funded; they are entirely people-led and the result of working class solidarity between nurses, service providers, students, domestic workers, migrant farmers, and families. Mutual aid networks affirm life by caretaking humanity rather than denying life by abandoning and exploiting humanity. However, the monumental challenge that confronts us is how to turn caretaking labor into life-affirming mass movements that can topple global capitalism once the emergency conditions of the pandemic lift. Only when we are able to mount a real threat to the hegemony of global capitalism through such movements will we be able to heal the planet.

Like the development of mass movements, restoring our relationship with the land is not optional if we wish to avoid extinction. But this isn't some mystical vision where we go out and hug trees. This is a serious agenda for decolonization that requires comprehensive land return programs and funding for mass Indigenous-led land restoration projects. Healthy reciprocity with the environment also depends upon Indigenous peoples having unrestricted access to land, unencumbered by colonial borders and free of harassment from agents of the state. We understand that the land is our means of production as Indigenous people; this is why decolonization and land return are not metaphors. Land is also the means of production for settler economies, which require property as a basic building block (often called primitive accumulation by Marxists) for the accumulation of capital and power. We cannot successfully wage class war until Indigenous land repatriation is taken seriously as a precursor to seizing the means of production more broadly. And US imperialism—the greatest threat to the future of the planet—will never end if land remains in the hands of First World settler capitalists. The collective future of us all depends upon the ability of Indigenous caretakers to work with the land, restore its health, and re-establish balance with our relations.

With threats like radioactive contamination, wildfires, chemical pollution, and biodiversity loss, we will also need to seek new and alternative technologies, something Native people embrace because we have always been technological innovators, scientists and engineers. But as we know, capitalists have a monopoly on technology, with the majority of the most advanced technology being used for war efforts. Scientists are denied funding for projects that are not considered profitable or that directly disrupt the flow of capital to the already-wealthy. What if technology was created for the benefit of all life on Earth? In order to answer this question, we must turn to Indigenous knowledge. The following pages prove that our traditions of science, technology, and diplomacy are key to ensuring a future for all living beings on this planet. . . .

Area 1: Clean Sustainable Energy: Why is This important?

The world is transitioning from fossil fuels to clean and renewable energies, but not fast enough. Resource extraction is still ravaging Indigenous, Black, migrant, and other-than-human communities. The Amazon forest fire of 2019 resulted in the burning of over 2,000,000 acres and the assassination of Guajajara Indigenous leader and land defender, Paulo Paulino, all in the name of mining and logging. In early 2020 Canada invaded sovereign Wet'suwet'en territory to remove Unist'ot'en land defenders who had successfully stopped construction of the Coastal GasLink Pipeline for close to a decade. And the Navajo Nation is still one of largest resource colonies in the United States, supplying energy through coal and natural gas conversion to some of the largest cities in the American West while many of its own citizens live without basic infrastructure like clean water and electricity.

For Indigenous and poor communities throughout Turtle Island, the fracking revolution of the past decade has been particularly violent. Fracking is a type of drilling that injects chemicals and water into the ground to break up underlying shale rock, releasing the oil and natural gas contained within it. Fracking produces more natural gas than crude oil for the US economy; two-thirds of natural gas in the United States comes from fracking, while approximately fifty % of the nation's crude oil is procured through the same method. Corporations like TC Energy—formerly TransCanada, the corporation that built the Dakota Access Pipeline—claim that natural gas is one of the world's cleanest and safest energy sources. Natural gas is often called 'clean' because it emits 50 % less carbon than coal when you burn it.

Governments like the state of New Mexico have partnered with fracking corporations to create shiny PR campaigns about the benefits of natural gas as a bridge fuel that will help the planet transition from dirty fuel sources like coal into zero-net carbon renewables like solar. Native people know the truth about this so called 'clean' energy source. While the natural gas boom has created billions in profits for extractive corporations, governments, and investors, the fracking required to extract natural gas from below the earth's surface has devastated Indigenous communities in eastern Navajo. Infrastructure like the Coastal GasLink Pipeline that carries natural gas from fracking fields to ports for sale violate Wet'suwet'en sovereignty. And the explosion of temporary fracking labor in the Bakken Oil Shale region

> Governments like the state of New Mexico have partnered with fracking corporations to create shiny PR campaigns about the benefits of natural gas as a bridge fuel that will help the planet transition from dirty fuel sources like coal into zero-net carbon renewables like solar. Native people know the truth about this so called 'clean' energy source.

has increased rape and human trafficking by oil workers of Indigenous women and girls from nations like the Mandan, Hidatsa, and Arikara.

Meanwhile, extractive corporations are investing billions in renewable energy technologies to ensure they have a new source of profit once 'dirty' energy is phased out in favor of 'clean' sources. Renewable energy corporations and start-ups proliferate, creating a new class of millionaires and billionaires who invest in green technology to make a buck and proclaim they are saving the planet. The United States backs right-wing coups in Indigenous nations like Bolivia to access green energy sources like lithium. Whether extractive capitalism or green capitalism, profit is all the ruling class cares about. Not the future of humanity. Not Indigenous sovereignty. Not the health of the earth.

It is thus crucial that we imagine and organize for new sustainable energy alternatives led by Indigenous people. Indigenous people have lived sustainably since time immemorial, and can continue to live in reciprocity with all those we share the earth with. But sustainable does not mean primitive. We must reclaim Indigenous intellectual traditions of the Western Hemisphere, which have some of the most advanced technology in human history. We have millennia-old mathematical and scientific theories that allow us to track the movement of the solar system, map out stars and galaxies, and create functional plumbing and aqueduct systems. We had these technologies long before Europeans discovered such things. Science and technology have never been at odds with Indigenous lifeways; it is only because of capitalism's monopoly on technology that science is used to destroy the planet. Today the most advanced technology in the world is used to create military weapons that kill millions rather than harnessed to save life. Because of their total control by private corporations, the health sciences are incapable of saving human lives during the COVID-19 pandemic. Imagine if technology was developed by the humble people of the earth for the humble people of the earth? Capitalism can never be compatible with clean, sustainable energy. Capitalism kills the earth. For the earth to live, capitalism must die.

What Needs Our Urgent Attention?

Green energy jobs are often touted as the rationale for promoting renewable energy projects. However, if we look at renewable energy projects like Kayenta Solar Project, Moapa Southern Paiute Solar Project, and the Tsilhqot'in Solar Farm, the majority of employment for tribal members is temporary and only comes from construction and planning. The maintenance is done by outside contractors. From vision to completion, solar jobs are not a sustainable source of jobs for local communities unless maintenance, monitoring, and remediation are taken into account. Saying that renewable energy will "create more jobs" simply isn't enough. We must have a clear understanding of the spectrum of labor that goes into green energy and demand that local communities—not private contractors- -work these jobs.

The materials that are used in solar panel systems are extremely important to consider. Lithium-ion batteries, according to the US Department of Energy, are and will be the main storage of renewable energies. Lithium-ion batteries are made from two main minerals, cobalt and lithium. The Democratic Republic of Congo holds 60% of the world's cobalt, while Bolivia holds 70% of the world's lithium. Both countries face heavy exploitation from the world's economic powers like the US, China, Canada, France, and India. While these countries are supplying the Global North with green energy for the future, they remain some of the poorest nations in the world. We must not replicate the injustices and inequalities between the Global North and Global South that exist under our current structure of global capitalism by simply replacing fossil fuel extraction with renewable energy extraction. Even with the transition to green energy, the capitalist (and colonial) relation remains intact. This is called imperialism, whereby the wealth and power of Global North nations depends entirely upon the poverty and exploitation of Global South nations. We must fight against a system that deems the world's poor and Indigenous expendable for the sake of progress and profit.

What Can You Do About It?

We demand that all corporate polluters be held accountable and pay for full remediation of the land and reparations to the people who have felt the impacts of extraction for generations. This can look like boycotts and divestment campaigns, or urging tribal leaders to break contracts with corporate polluters. Educate tribal communities on the histories of resource extraction. Regardless of how clean and green the technology is, the process by which corporations extract value from Indigenous life for the benefit of settler colonialism remains the same. Organize to stop all forms of energy extraction from Native communities and lands, whether it is coal mining, fracking, or solar farms. Now more than ever we need people to understand that we have to actively create the world we want to live in. Man-made disasters like climate change and the unnecessary spread of COVID-19 are not manifestations of "the earth healing itself." Such deadly events are a direct result of the actions of those who pillage the earth: the ruling class. These capitalists view the earth as a resource to be exploited instead of a relative to be protected.

Wherever you are, create campaigns that pinpoint the central role of capitalism in creating this suffering, and the need to dismantle capitalism for the sake of our common future.

The Red Nation Authors Interviewed

https://youtu.be/_UIQ1qPzvRY

Selected Resources on Indigenous People and the Environment

The Red Nation, **The Red Deal; Indigenous Action to Save Our Earth**, 2021.

Roxanne Dunbar-Ortiz, **Not a Nation of Immigrants: Settler Colonialism, White Supremacy, and a History of Erasure and Exclusion**, 2021.

Quito J. Swan, **Pauulu's Diaspora: Black Internationalism and Environmental Justice**, 2020.

More **books on Indigenous People and the Environment.**

Selected Resources on Caretaking in the Global Economy

"The Care Economy," International Labour Organization

"Why Women's Time and Work Must Be Part of Future Policy Choices," Hewlett Foundation

"Women Took on Three Times as Much Child Care as Men During the Pandemic," Fortune

And for science-fiction fans
Kim Stanley Robinson, **The Ministry for the Future**, 2020.

Review of Ministry for the Future, Los Angeles Review of Books, 2020.

Interview with Kim Stanley Robinson, Jacobin, 2020.

CHAPTER TWENTY FOUR

PAN-AFRICANIST, CHRISTIAN, AND QUEER

By Bishop Joseph W. Tolton
November 2021

Bishop Tolton is the Founder and President of Interconnected Justice. The strategic intent of the organization is to be a force uniting global racial justice movements in which the continent of Africa and its diaspora build an ecosystem of self-defined and determined advocacy. As an LGBT Global faith leader Bishop Tolton continues to serve as the Bishop of Global Ministries for The Fellowship of Affirming Ministries.

This essay is adapted from an interview with Bishop Tolton by Imani Countess on September 21, 2021. The full transcript of the interview, which is available here, was condensed into this essay by Zeb Larson in collaboration with Bishop Tolton.

My name is Joseph W. Tolton and I was raised in the cradle of the Pentecostal Church. I would put the Bible on my windowsill as a young kid. We lived in a building where two buildings faced each other in an alleyway. My room was at the corner of the alleyway and my neighbors would tell my mother and grandmother, "Do you hear him in there preaching?" and they would say, "Yes, we do." The windowsill was my first pulpit.

Being raised Pentecostal is also very relevant to my sense of transnational curiosity. The whole idea of being Pentecostal is that we believe in what happened in the early church where people from every background came together to find the Disciples of Christ after the Christ had died.

My mom was also very committed to making sure that I got the best possible education, and I went to predominantly Jewish schools. I lift that up because one of the points that really led me to transnational work was being raised among the Jewish Community. That informed my sensibilities by being in a community who were so very intentional about being a community.

I am also gay. Growing up as a closeted being created a certain sense of restlessness around reconciliation and a sense of restlessness around finding my place in the world. This journey for acceptance and establishing a sense of belonging was definitely the result of growing up in this closeted way. This influences my transnational sensibilities because I was in a church that did not fully accept me and my journey became about finding a place where I fully belonged.

> My mom was also very committed to making sure that I got the best possible education, and I went to predominantly Jewish schools. I lift that up because one of the points that really led me to transnational work was being raised among the Jewish Community.

There was an exodus out of the black church in the late 1980s and early 1990s because of HIV and AIDS. I graduated from high school in 1985 and was asking all of the questions that an eighteen-year-old asks, knowing secretly that I am attracted to men and that men like me are coming down with this terrible disease. I thought that this was God's curse. My peers were dying, and I got a whiff of the church's response. It was ugly, it was nasty, it was vindictive, it was full of betrayal, and they were violently embarrassed by our presence.

That led to the growth of other services for Black people who were LGBTQ. I ultimately became a part of that movement of Black Pentecostals, Baptists, and Methodists who realized that we actually could start a new Reformation that married the chemistry of that worship with the theology that was much more open and inquisitive. I started a church in Harlem in 2006 called Rehoboth Temple for everyone but targeted to the LGBTQ community. We began to embrace the term "Queer" as an umbrella term that covers all that is not hetero-normative.

In 2009 when the anti-gay bill was tabled in Uganda, we all learned about it watching Rachel Maddow, a host on MSNBC in the U.S. In Uganda before the bill, LGBTQ people had a social zone carved out for themselves. LGBTQ people were crafty about creating an underground social culture so they could breathe without society having to deal with them. But forces elsewhere in the world had been undermining that for some time.

U.S. Christian Right Targets Africa

My personal reality was not just the result of domestic factors, but was very much the result of what was happening on a global scale. What I learned through investigation was that there was this deep relationship between the white conservative evangelical community in America and their global outposts. Conservative Christians went into these countries under the idea that they were going to help plant churches, dig wells, and build orphanages. But that was not their real agenda.

In the 1970s, the Christian Right understood that the world was globalizing. Domestically, they were losing a culture war, and they decided to change the playing field. Instead of domestic culture wars, they could do it globally. Newly-independent African states were very pliable in many ways. Conservative Christians understood that if they were pumped full of money and supported by ecclesiastical structures in the West, they would not pivot toward democracy. The impact is that the church at large in Africa is now conscripted into this very conservative scheme to make the continent the base of conservative Christian thought. By the early 2000s, they had infrastructure and human capital that African Americans or the progressive left was unaware of. That is what led to the shock of the anti-gay bill.

> **I ultimately became a part of that movement of Black Pentecostals, Baptists, and Methodists who realized that we actually could start a new Reformation that married the chemistry of that worship with the theology that was much more open and inquisitive. I started a church in Harlem in 2006 called Rehoboth Temple for everyone but targeted to the LGBTQ community.**

When the issue broke out in Uganda, there was an Episcopal priest, Bishop Dr. Christopher Senyonjo. He began to meet young LGBTQ people who were coming to him because they were homeless. His center became a place where young LGBTQ people in Uganda knew they could go for counseling. Once the bill was passed he was the only priest, the only person of faith, and he was 80 at the time, who stood up and said, "No, this is wrong. No, I cannot accept this and I will stand with this community."

Eventually, he was brought to the United States, where I met Dr. Senyonjo. He said "We have to not only have a message that is transformative, but we have to build the infrastructure for institutions that can hold that transformation." Not missing a beat, he then said "I find it interesting that you're a preacher who has an MBA and that, that's the way your head thinks. I think you would do well in Uganda. I think you should come to Uganda."

I went to Uganda in September of 2010 and my life has completely changed ever since that trip. When I met my Queer brothers and sisters, I was not only connecting with them around our Queer reality but also as people of African descent who had been separated. We found ourselves having an incredible conversation about not just the future for Queer people, but the ways in which this relationship between the religious right and ecclesiastical leaders on the continent and relationships between America's aid and the ways in which that propped up autocratic regimes.

Most of the white, Evangelical leaders who came to Uganda had no relationship with Black people in their backyard. These were pastors and leaders for whom the only Black people you would see in their church were somebody singing or directing the choir or playing the organ. In fact, these were conservative Christians who opposed policies that protect the health and well-being of African Americans and supported the brutal policing of black bodies.

Violence in Uganda

Things were very hot on the ground in Uganda and so SMUG, or Sexual Minorities Uganda began to get a lot more notice. David Kato had been one of the founders of SMUG and the Queer movement in East Africa. What David understood was that somebody in Uganda was going to die. He understood that the climate of vitriol was turning very violent as it fed a moral panic.

Unfortunately, he was the person who became a victim of that violence. He was killed in January of 2011 by an anti-gay person in his community who learned what he was doing. That was a Kairos moment (a moment of perfect opportunity) for Queer organizing throughout the continent. Working with Frank Mugisha, the Executive Director of SMUG, we were able to mobilize African American clergy and African American civil rights community to focus on this issue.

This changed things in the Black Church in America. You've got people like Reverend Al Sharpton who are coming around, you have the NAACP that are beginning to come out in support of marriage equality. When David was murdered in the context of the anti-gay bill, that changed the dynamic among African Americans.

> Most of the white, Evangelical leaders who came to Uganda had no relationship with Black people in their backyard. These were pastors and leaders for whom the only Black people you would see in their church were somebody singing or directing the choir or playing the organ.

Now it wasn't just condemning homosexuality from a faith-based perspective, it was about unleashing murderous possibilities. Among many blacks, it conjured up the thoughts of a lynching. Calvin Butts opened up the Abyssinian Baptist Church to the LGBTQ community to have a memorial for David. That changed organizing here in the United States too.

In Maryland in 2012 we invested as a Queer community a lot of money and attention and focus because we knew that the Maryland ballot initiative for marriage equality could win and be the first state to win if African Americans supported it at a rate of 45% and above. We only had about 29% to 30% of African Americans in support of marriage equality so we had a gap that we had to make up. Young preachers turned out for us. Everything changed. 47.5% of Blacks in Maryland voted for marriage equality. It signaled that the religious right had lost its stranglehold on the Black Church and could no longer manipulate the Black Church to fracture the progressive base.

In turn, we continue our work building solidarity in Africa. We have been able to build five churches in East Africa that are for LGBTQ people that are a part of the Fellowship of Affirming Ministries. You have this Pan-African transnational faith built by Queer people of African descent where we are united in our work together.

These churches were built to provide spiritual nourishment, but they were also to be advocacy-based ministries. We leverage the church's systems and structures and human capital for justice work. They have a task force to approach civil society, academia, government, the media, and engage sectors driving cultural influence. Our media presence in East Africa is incredibly strong. It's out and proud and on the television and in the newspaper. In Rwanda, we produced a national pride attended by government officials. In the DRC Congo, we invite in traditional organizations, even those a part of the AME church, but in Goma DRC, they're welcoming.

Pan-Africanist and Queer

Africa is experiencing a tremendous youth bulge and surge. By 2100 one out of every three people on the planet may be of African descent because of the demographic shifts that are happening. We have got to mobilize these young people on the continent and elsewhere to change their lived reality. I believe that this path is the unpaved road of Pan-Africanism. And that we must connect the movements that young people are building on the ground in Africa with movements in Brazil, Colombia, throughout the Caribbean, and certainly here in the United States. That is the work of interconnected justice, bringing together and building a unified web between nationally based Pan-African movements powered by young people.

The thing that has held us together has been our realization that I am you and you are me. That is the substance that binds us together. I am them and they are me. And I think that that's an incredible gift. That's a gift that we have to offer to the more mainstream Pan-African movement.

I'm incredibly excited to be venturing out in this way. I believe that we will continue to do the work of influencing the Christian church in Africa through indigenous spirituality and curiosity about the divine feminine. Healing will come when we do that. That fusion allows us to have more ownership of the faith and customize the faith as opposed to importing the faith that has come from the west. Work has got to turn to Pan-Africanist movements inspired by work over the continent. There is a cry for democracy and participatory government that can only be ushered in by a revival of Pan-Africanism. Lastly, partnerships with feminist and female-identifying groups must happen in concert with a full redefinition of what African masculinity is all about.

About Defining Identities

Excerpted from interview with Bishop Tolton by Imani Countess, September 21, 2021

IC: I really want to ask a question about definitions, because within some sectors, Queer is a frequently used word to describe non-heteronormative sexualities, right? I'm not really clear to what extent Queer is sort of an overarching term in Africa or even to what extent here in the US. Is it viewed as an inclusive term? You've given me permission to use the term, right, in previous conversations. I really would like for everyone else, to sort of be able to hear your thoughts on this as well.

JT: It's such an interesting term, it can be explosive and very incendiary. And it's generational. If you were to ask somebody 53 or possibly 10 years older or more, you know, there's a lot of, "No no, no, I am not Queer" because certainly in the 60s and 70s Queer was a derogatory term. It was almost like calling somebody, a bull dagger or a faggot and the LGBTIQQ community fought very hard for nomenclature that we felt was was sanctified and empowering. We wanted to be gay and lesbian, you know, bisexual or person of trans experience.

It is really the generation that comes under me. The older millennials who are in their late 30s now who really began to embrace, and I think many of the intellectuals, began to push back and embrace this term of Queer. Interestingly, I think that embracing the term Queer as kind of an umbrella term that covers as you said, all that is not a hetero-normative. I think that on many levels that was a bit in rebuke to the marriage equality movement, because of course, the marriage equality movement suggested that we as gay people were on many levels nothing more than a reflection of straight people. The difference, of course, is that our call for love was to the same sex as opposed to someone of the opposite sex. And that is what distinguished us.

And that kind of created the road to marriage equality. We are acceptable. We are normalized. We pick up our children, just like you do. We take care of our aging parents just like you do. We fuss and fight about, you know, you left the cap off the toothpaste, just like you do. And such a drive and push to be accepted, kind of like the politics of respectability for Black people.

In response to that and I think in rebuke to that, younger Queer activists really pushed to have this term, Queer mean, no, we are different. We are not just the reflection of straight people who are called to same-sex love but that we are a great variety. There are some that are going to have the 2.5 kids and the white picket fence, but then there are others who are going to be polyamorous and some are going to have all sorts of other situations, whereby which they express their love and their affection.

So I think now we've come full circle. Queer does cover the full spectrum of our garden of those of us that are not hetero-normative and then you'll have some who will default and use LGBTIQ or prefer gay or lesbian, because they think it just imposes a bit more dignity on the community.

General Background References

Globalizing The Culture Wars: U.S. Conservatives, African Churches, And Homophobia
Kapya Kaoma, Political Research Associates, December 1, 2009

A groundbreaking investigation by Political Research Associates discovered that sexual minorities in Africa have become collateral damage to our domestic conflicts and culture wars. U.S. conservative evangelicals are promoting an agenda in Africa that aims to criminalize homosexuality and otherwise infringe upon the human rights of LGBT people while also mobilizing African clerics in U.S. culture war battles.

Queer Pan-Africanism
Adriaan van Klinken, Leeds African Studies Bulletin, January 31, 2020

This article maps the emergence of an LGBT-affirming, or queer, pan-Africanist discourse which counter-balances popular, conservative pan-Africanist narratives that advocate against LGBT and queer identities and rights.

Ghana 2021

Ghana Gets Its Wake-up Call: Will it Be Answered?
Adotei Akwei, Amnesty International, October 15, 2021

In March 2021, the "Promotion of Proper Human Sexual Rights and Ghanaian Family Values Bill" was introduced in the Ghanaian parliament. In addition to criminalizing and imposing jail sentences of up to five years for being a member of the LGBTIQ+ community, supporting a member of the community, or discussing issues related to the community, the proposed bill also supports "conversion therapy," a practice that has been condemned globally, including by the UN Committee Against Torture. If passed, the proposed legislation would violate regional and international human rights obligations that Ghana has signed.

I Don't Recognize My Own Country Anymore in Ghana's New Anti-gay Bill
Arthur Musah, Quartz, October 18, 2021

I am a gay Ghanaian. I make this statement publicly because an emergency in Ghana has made it necessary for me to come out as loudly as possible. That emergency also requires everyone to come out as an ally of LGBTQ+ Ghanaians. I don't want to paint a false picture of a childhood Ghana that was fully accepting of my sexuality, but I want to talk about the drastic rise in homophobia that has gotten us to this place and the forces behind it.

African Indigenous Religions and Queer Dignity
David Tonghou Ngong, November 9, 2021

Ghana has become just the latest African country to confirm the fact that there are widespread anti-queer attitudes on the continent. Crucial to debates about this widespread anti-queer attitude is the question, what could be the source? In other words, why does the continent appear to be so anti-queer?

Colonialism should take a lot of blame for anti-queer attitudes in Africa. But missing is a frank engagement with how African indigenous cultures also fuel anti-queer attitudes.

CHAPTER TWENTY FIVE

WE MUST FREE OUR IMAGINATIONS

We stand for an African revolution which encompasses the demand for a re-imagination of our lives outside neo-colonial categories of identity and power.
November 2021

Queer African Manifesto/Declaration
April 18, 2010, Nairobi, Kenya

As Africans, we all have infinite potential. We stand for an African revolution which encompasses the demand for a re-imagination of our lives outside neo-colonial categories of identity and power. For centuries, we have faced control through structures, systems and individuals who disappear our existence as people with agency, courage, creativity, and economic and political authority.

As Africans, we stand for the celebration of our complexities and we are committed to ways of being which allow for self-determination at all levels of our sexual, social, political and economic lives. The possibilities are endless. We need economic justice; we need to claim and redistribute power; we need to eradicate violence; we need to redistribute land; we need gender justice; we need environmental justice; we need erotic justice; we need racial and ethnic justice; we need rightful access to affirming and responsive institutions, services and spaces; overall we need total liberation.

We are specifically committed to the transformation of the politics of sexuality in our contexts. As long as African LGBTI people are oppressed, the whole of Africa is oppressed.

This vision demands that we commit ourselves to:
- Reclaiming and sharing our stories (past and present), our lived realities, our contributions to society and our hopes for the future;
- Strengthening ourselves and our organizations, deepening our links and understanding of our communities, building principled alliances, and actively contributing towards the revolution.
- Challenging all legal systems and practices which either currently criminalize or seek to reinforce the criminalization of LGBTI people, organizations, knowledge creation, sexual self expression, and movement building.
- Challenging state support for oppressive sexual, gendered, discriminatory norms, legal and political structures and cultural systems.
- Strengthening the bonds of respect, cooperation, passion, and solidarity between LGBTI people, in our complexities, differences and diverse contexts. This includes respecting and celebrating our multiple ways of being, self expression, and languages.
- Contributing to the social and political recognition that sexuality, pleasure, and the erotic are part of our common humanity.
- Placing ourselves proactively within all movement building supportive of our vision.

I Am a Homosexual, Mum
By Binyavanga Wainaina
https://africasacountry.com/2014/01/i-am-a-homosexual-mum
January 19, 2014
The writer imagines coming out to his late mother.
A lost chapter from One Day I Will Write About This Place.

11 July, 2000.
This is not the right version of events.

Hey mum. I was putting my head on her shoulder, that last afternoon before she died. She was lying on her hospital bed. Kenyatta. Intensive Care. Critical Care.

There. Because this time I will not be away in South Africa, fucking things up in that chaotic way of mine. I will arrive on time, and be there when she dies. My heart arrives on time. I am holding my dying mother's hand. I am lifting her hand. Her hand will be swollen with diabetes. Her organs are failing. Hey mum. Ooooh. My mind sighs. My heart! I am whispering in her ear. She is awake, listening, soft calm loving, with my head right inside in her breathspace. She is so big—my mother, in this world, near the next world, each breath slow, but steady, as it should be. Inhale. She can carry everything. I will whisper, louder, in my minds-breath. To hers. She will listen, even if she doesn't hear. Can she?

Mum. I will say. Muum? I will say. It grooves so easy, a breath, a noise out of my mouth, mixed up with her breath, and she exhales. My heart gasps sharp and now my mind screams, sharp, so so hurt so so angry.

"I have never thrown my heart at you mum. You have never asked me to."

Only my mind says. This. Not my mouth. But surely the jerk of my breath and heart, there next to hers, has been registered? Is she letting me in?

Nobody, nobody, ever in my life has heard this. Never, mum. I did not trust you, mum. And. I. Pulled air hard and balled it down into my navel, and let it out slow and firm, clean and without bumps out of my mouth, loud and clear over a shoulder, into her ear.

"I am a homosexual, mum."

July, 2000.
This is the right version of events.

I am living in South Africa, without having seen my mother for five years, even though she is sick, because I am afraid and ashamed, and because I will be thirty years old and possibly without a visa to return here if I leave. I am hurricaning to move my life so I can see her. But she is in Nakuru, collapsing, and they will be rushing her kidneys to Kenyatta Hospital in Nairobi, where there will be a dialysis machine and a tropical storm of experts awaiting her.

Relatives will rush to see her and, organs will collapse, and machines will kick into action. I am rushing, winding up everything to leave South Africa. It will take two more days for me to leave, to fly out, when, in the morning of 11 July 2000, my uncle calls me to ask if I am sitting down.

"She's gone, Ken."

I will call my Auntie Grace in that family gathering nanosecond to find a way to cry urgently inside Baba, but they say he is crying and thundering and lightning in his 505 car around Nairobi because his wife is dead and nobody can find him for hours. Three days ago, he told me it was too late to come to see her. He told me to not risk losing my ability to return to South Africa by coming home for the funeral. I should not be travelling carelessly in that artist way of mine, without papers. Kenneth! He frowns on the phone. I cannot risk illegal deportation, he says, and losing everything. But it is my mother.

I am twenty nine. It is 11 July, 2000. I, Binyavanga Wainaina, quite honestly swear I have known I am a homosexual since I was five. I have never touched a man sexually. I have slept with three women in my life. One woman, successfully. Only once with her. It was amazing. But the next day, I was not able to.

It will take me five years after my mother's death to find a man who will give me a massage and some brief, paid-for love. In Earl's Court, London. And I will be freed, and tell my best friend, who will surprise me by understanding, without understanding. I will tell him what I did, but not tell him I am gay. I cannot say the word gay until I am thirty nine, four years after that brief massage encounter. Today, it is 18 January 2013, and I am forty three.

Anyway. It will not be a hurricane of diabetes that kills mum inside Kenyatta Hospital Critical Care, before I have taken four steps to get on a plane to sit by her side.

Somebody.
Nurse?
Will leave a small window open the night before she dies, in the July Kenyatta Hospital cold.

It is my birthday today. 18 January 2013. Two years ago, on 11 July 2011, my father had a massive stroke and was brain dead in minutes. Exactly eleven years to the day my mother died. His heart beat for four days, but there was nothing to tell him.

I am five years old.

He stood there, in overalls, awkward, his chest a railway track of sweaty bumps, and little hard beads of hair. Everything about him is smooth-slow. Bits of brown on a cracked tooth, that endless long smile. A good thing for me the slow way he moves, because I am transparent to people's patterns, and can trip so easily and fall into snarls and fear with jerky people. A long easy smile, he lifts me in the air and swings. He smells of diesel, and the world of all other people's movements has disappeared. I am away from everybody for the first time in my life, and it is glorious, and then it is a tunnel of fear. There are no creaks in him, like a tractor he will climb any hill, steadily. If he walks away, now, with me, I will go with him forever. I know if he puts me down my legs will not move again. I am so ashamed, I stop myself from clinging. I jump away from him and avoid him forever. For twentysomething years, I even hug men awkwardly.

There will be this feeling again. Stronger, firmer now. Aged maybe seven. Once with another slow easy golfer at Nakuru Golf Club, and I am shaking because he shook my hand. Then I am crying alone in the toilet because the repeat of this feeling has made me suddenly ripped apart and lonely. The feeling is not sexual. It is certain. It is overwhelming. It wants to make a home. It comes every few months like a bout of malaria and leaves me shaken for days, and confused for months. I do nothing about it.

I am five when I close my self into a vague happiness that asks for nothing much from anybody. Absent-minded. Sweet. I am grateful for all love. I give it more than I receive it, often. I can be selfish. I masturbate a lot, and never allow myself to crack and grow my heart. I touch no men. I read books. I love my dad so much, my heart is learning to stretch.

I am a homosexual.

Kenyan, Christian, Queer

Kenyan, Christian, Queer was produced in 2020 and released in October 2021. It is 20 minutes long.

https://youtu.be/bsU6QR0lfzs

We Must Free Our Imaginations

Bisi Alimi (Nigeria/UK), "If you say being gay is not African, you don't know your history"
The Guardian, September 9, 2015

The idea that homosexuality is 'western' is based on another western import—Christianity. True African culture celebrates diversity and promotes acceptance.

Binyavanga Wainaina (Kenya), **"We Must Free Our Imaginations"**
YouTube short video series, 2014
[Suggestion for non-Kenyans: turn on closed captioning]

One of Africa's best-known authors and gay rights activists, **Wainaina died in 2019 at the age of 48.** Wainaina was also known for his biting satirical essay **How to Write About Africa**.

Sylvia Tamale (Uganda), *Decolonization and Afro-Feminism*, 2020.
PDF available from publisher **Daraja Press**.

"In this boldly argued and well-written book, the seasoned intellectual/teacher/activist Sylvia Tamale presents Africa as an urgent decolonial Pan-African project. Using an Afro-feminist lens, she gives us a roadmap as she deconstructs gender, sexuality, the law, family and even Pan-Africanism."—Oyeronke Oyewumi

Sokari Ekine (Nigeria/UK/USA/Haiti), "The Persistence of Blackness"
Website with writings and photography.

Sokari Ekine is a Nigerian Black British genderqueer feminist who has lived and worked in Africa, Europe, the Caribbean, and the United States. Their aim as a photographer is to shift the gaze from denigrating representations of African sacred traditions and instead present a narrative in which we as a people engage with a planetary consciousness that celebrates black humanity.

Mercy Amba Oduyoye (Ghana, Nigeria, Switzerland)

Mercy Amba Oduyoye is the Director of the Institute of Women in Religion and Culture at Trinity Theological Seminary in Legon. She is affectionately known as the "mother of African women's theologies." She has been a life-long leader in the ecumenical movement and the World Council of Churches, and in her 1995 book *Daughters of Anowa: African Women and Patriarchy* provided an in-depth look at how **both African culture and Christianity** reinforced patriarchal understandings of society.

CHAPTER TWENTY SIX

KUMI NAIDOO AND WINONA LADUKE (PART 1)

Naidoo and LaDuke focused on the need and the potential for grassroots activists to step up when governments are failing to address the crisis.
March 2022

In December 2021, the month after the UN Climate Conference concluded in Glasgow, Al Jazeera featured Kumi Naidoo and Winona LaDuke in two inspiring conversations in London focused on the need and the potential for grassroots activists to step up when governments are failing to address the crisis.

The seven days beginning with the anniversary of the Sharpeville Massacre in South Africa on March 21, 1960 end on Sunday with the anniversary of the Battle of Horseshoe Bend on March 27, 1814, in which future president Andrew Jackson led his troops against the Creek nation in what is now Alabama.

These dates make this a very appropriate time to be reminded of the central role of anti-racist and indigenous activists in global struggles for climate justice.

At Sharpeville the dead were peaceful demonstrators. At Horseshoe Bend they were elite Creek warriors.

In each case, however, they were mowed down mercilessly by superior firepower.

This post contains a transcript and the streaming video of the first conversation.

From the front lines of the anti-apartheid and environmental justice movements, this episode of Studio B: Unscripted features two lifelong activists.

Author, economist and two-time vice presidential candidate of the US Green Party, Winona LaDuke, is co-founder of Honor the Earth, a non-profit organization dedicated to environmental and Indigenous rights.

An anti-apartheid activist from age 15, Kumi Naidoo later helped with South Africa's inaugural democratic election. He went on to head Greenpeace and Amnesty International, and is currently Global Ambassador for Africans Rising.

LaDUKE: It's a great opportunity and a privilege to be here with you. We are in a very colonial city, and we're a couple of anti-colonialists. We both come from long histories of British colonization, I would say. And here we are to talk about the future in some times—times of tremendous change. And I think that we've just had the big conference in Glasgow.

NAIDOO: So wonderful to be with you, Winona. I think that what the COP26 has just shown us recently is that we are so stuck in fundamentally a colonial mindset and in terms of colonial power dynamics, because what we had out of COP26 was basically a sentiment that says the lives of people in the Pacific and other small island states don't matter, and the least-developed countries don't matter.

The difficulty, it seems, is that those with the largest amount of power in the conversation are not willing to recognize that the mistake they made after the global financial crisis, which was—their approach was system recovery, system protection, and system maintenance. But what should have been done then and what is even more urgently needed now is system innovation, system redesign, and system transformation.

I should just say none of us should be too surprised, though, by what happened in the negotiations in Glasgow, because the shocking truth is do you know which was the largest delegation that attended?

LaDUKE: No. I have no idea.

NAIDOO: It was the fossil fuel industry.

LaDUKE: Oh, wow.

NAIDOO: They had 503 lobbyists.

LaDUKE: You should always have the dealer at the table. I feel like what we're talking about is late-stage addiction behavior, frankly. I've lived, as you have, in a fossil fuel era my entire life, and I'm looking for a graceful transition out of it. I don't want to crash my way out, where I can't drink the water, and I can't breathe the air, and everything is a toxic mess. What we want is a transition out. But what we have is an addicted society. And the fossil fuel industry continues to push those addictions.

I heard someone talk about the colonial imagination versus the Indigenous imagination. The colonial imagination can only figure out like within this box, and it can't get to the place where we need to get to, where it's more than just the rights of corporations, and it's more than just the rights of first-world people, but it's also like, what about the rest of the world, and what about the relatives, whether they have wings or fins or roots or paws? That's how you survive. Maybe Jeff Bezos and Elon Musk think they can make it without the rest of us, but the rest of us know that we are part of this world and that opportunity is here to make a change. No time like the present. That's what I figure.

NAIDOO: Absolutely.

LaDUKE: And it appears that Glasgow did not bring the change.

NAIDOO: Imagine Alcoholics Anonymous having a global conference, and the biggest delegation to the conference was the alcohol industry. Or in the past, a big antislavery conference, and the biggest delegation was slave owners. By the way, that's what it was. That's why slave owners got compensation and those who were slaves got no compensation. This is how the climate negotiations are going.

And now, people like myself, when we look at where we get inspiration from, I think that the inspiration right now is coming from young people, but it's also—when you're looking at bodies of knowledge, Indigenous wisdom teaches us the way out of this mess. Because unless humanity can learn to coexist with nature in a mutually interdependent relationship—you know, we're not going to be around for that much longer, and I always like to tell people, don't worry about saving the planet, because actually, if we continue on the suicidal path we're on, we will destroy our soil, destroy our water, warm up the planet. The end result is we will be gone as a species.

LaDUKE: Yeah, the plants will be back.

NAIDOO: And once we become extinct, the oceans will recover, the forests will grow back, and so on. This struggle, therefore, has to be understood as saving our children and their children's futures.

LaDUKE: Every living being had some original instructions. We would say (Ojibwe phrase)—take only what you need. Leave the rest. Be mindful—all your relatives. Understand the Creator's law is higher than the laws of nation-states or municipalities. Even the participants in COPs—you could say whatever you want, but in the end, we all got to drink the water. We all got to breathe the air. We all had those instructions.

Indigenous people—we're 4% of the world's population, and we're 75% of the world's biodiversity. What we need is to return to some instructions that say this is how you live. You live being mindful. You live being conscious. And you protect Mother Earth and not the rights of corporations. This is why you need things like the rights of nature over the rights of corporations.

My observation—I don't know if you see, but I see catastrophes of biblical proportions. There's fires and hurricanes and tornadoes, and the oceans are rising, and then a pandemic. In the history of the world, pandemics have always forced societies to change. This one is no different. What Arundhati Roy says—it's a portal between one world and the next. And inasmuch as the financial crisis of 2008 was a pretty clear opportunity to acknowledge that the economic systems are made up and are failing, this moment is certainly a time when we can, and in many ways, many of us have reset.

NAIDOO: I think we're facing a worse disease than COVID-19, and that disease is a disease we could call affluenza.

LaDUKE: (laughter) That is true.

NAIDOO: This is a disease where people have been led to believe that a good, meaningful, decent, happy life comes from more and more and more material acquisitions. I think that unless we look at bodies of wisdom, including—I think, again, this is something we learn from Indigenous culture—is that a good, meaningful, decent life comes from how we engage with nature, how we engage with our families, the quality of our relationships with our friends and neighbors, all of which aggressive casino capitalism has actually decimated. Does this resonate with you?

LaDUKE: Oh, entirely. Our teachings as Anishinaabe people are (speaks Ojibwe), which means the

> "Probably there are more people that are more comfortable with imagining the end of the world as we know it and all of us disappearing off this planet than to imagine the end of capitalism, because that's the power of the narratives we've been fed, like that's the only system that works, when clearly it's not working for the overwhelming majority."

good life. It doesn't mean how much stuff you have. (laughter) But there's this constant barrage that you need more. You need more. You need more, and you'll feel better. The fact is that people don't feel better. Americans are pretty unhappy overall. And getting more stuff just means you have to pay money to store it, from what I could figure.

NAIDOO: Now, people who don't necessarily think like you and I do will listen to us speaking and say, oh, this vision is so far from what the mainstream vision of society is. OK, you and I have been around for more than four decades in the struggle for justice. Sometimes, I don't know, I feel given how much effort one put in that we should have made much, much more progress, but the forces of resistance to change are so powerful. But there's something I feel in this moment that I've never felt before. Bad as things are now—and things actually are looking much worse in terms of extreme weather events, deepening inequality, rise of fascism, and so on—and failure of democracy.

But there's something very optimistic for me in this moment, and I want to see how you feel about it. That is, I don't remember any time in my history of trying to work for justice—is that there are so many people who believe that there's a possibility this time round for major structural and systemic change. Not simply what our governments do all the time, which is rearranging the deck chairs on the Titanic while humanity sinks, and baby steps in the right direction when what is needed is big change. Does that resonate with what you're hearing with people in your circles?

LaDUKE: Yeah, the fact is that the systems are failing. If you look around the United States, which is the country that levied itself upon me, you're looking over there, and you have a political crisis of pretty big proportions. You had an insurrection in January, right? And then you have economic systems that fail. You have judicial and legal systems that failed us—have failed us consistently. And you have food systems and energy systems that fail in climate change. What is clear is that if you want to survive, you need local energy. If you're expecting the grid is going to protect you, the big disasters of climate change-related disasters are going to take down your grid.

NAIDOO: So that's a message of the power—in planning moving forward, we need to go to a more decentralized approach in the way we put capability and control with local communities, because that's the only way we can guarantee —

LaDUKE: I'm going to say something to you that you know, which is: empire is overrated.

NAIDOO: Yeah. (laughter)

LaDUKE: You know what I'm saying? The bigger you get, that's great. But you know what? At the local level is where you got to eat. At the local level is where you're going to need your solar garden that is owned collectively. At the local level is where you're going to need some essential manufacturing with just and fair trade relations between—because an Indigenous model is a model of biodiversity—is a model of agrobiodiversity. Because Indigenous people's 5,000 languages are not about building empire. They're about reaffirming relationships in place. And that is what is missing with this industrial society is there is no relationship and reciprocity with the world that created us, you know?

NAIDOO: The other problem we have is the information environment within which we are operating.

Because I would put it to you that probably there are more people that are more comfortable with imagining the end of the world as we know it and all of us disappearing off this planet than to imagine the end of capitalism, because that's the power of the narratives we've been fed, like that's the only system that works, when clearly it's not working for the overwhelming majority.

For me, activism is primarily an act of love and courage. Activism is about saying we look at the world, and we refuse to accept that this is the best that humanity can create for itself. One of the anxieties I have about activism today is that far too often, our energies are going towards just surviving, because the repression is becoming so heavy against us and so on, and consolidating the people that already support the need for decency and the need for sustainability and respecting human rights.

But I think that we don't have a choice today if we are going to make sure that we secure this planet for future generations to also say we need to learn to, for example, love the people who voted for Trump or love the people who voted for Brexit or love the people who voted for things that we might disagree with. Because I think that we need to also recognize that they are also victims, that they have been victims of lies, deceit, misinformation, and so on. And we have to build a bridge. So in any case, shall we wrap it up there and go and take some questions from the audience?

Q: Hi, Kumi and Winona. I'm joining you from Fiji in the Pacific. My question is: Pacific Indigenous peoples are bearing the brunt of the impacts of climate change. We are experiencing displacement of our homes and our livelihoods and our knowledge and support systems. Our kinship ties to the land and ocean are under threat. But the current discourse on climate change impact doesn't give voice to our cultural identity and the relationship we have with nature that is being threatened by this climate emergency. How can we center this within the global climate change discourse that seems to be dominated by financial and corporate posturing?

NAIDOO: I had the opportunity to be in Kiribati, Fiji, and Vanuatu in 2015 and definitely felt what you said in a very deep, personal way. It's stayed with me since. And I want to be blunt about it. The way we center this is first about naming the problem that we

> "We would say (Ojibwe phrase)—take only what you need. Leave the rest. Be mindful—all your relatives. Understand the Creator's law is higher than the laws of nation-states or municipalities."

have—climate apartheid—right? Because those parts of the world that contributed the greatest to the problem are not those parts of the world, like the Pacific, that are suffering the first and the most brutal impacts of climate change. We need to recognize, therefore, that the conversation around what happened at COP26, how we understand it—we have to understand that, in fact, it's been a complete betrayal of small island states, for the folks in the Pacific, for people in coastal regions, least-developed countries, and so on.

Your question was how do we center it? I think that Winona implied that actually we cannot solely rely on the current systems that exist, which are broken in multiple ways. We can actually now start building new systems from below and start creating ways of doing agriculture, protecting our water sources, how we relate to each other, and so on in a much more decentralized, bottom-up way. And I think because those in power know that the systems that they are defending are indefensible, that if we can organize better amongst ourselves and generate examples of how we can do things better, I think that eventually that message is going to permeate in a context where the dominant leaders and political formations and in the dominant business community actually know that what they are speaking is completely bankrupt.

LaDUKE: I would agree. I think that they know. And I also say I just want to give my heart out to Pacific Islanders. We know that you are entirely reliant on your Mother Earth and your ocean for your life. A lot of what we do is in recognizing the situation that you are in is the same situation we are in. The better we can do to stop the tar sands pipelines, the better for you. That is my goal. I spent eight years fighting a pipeline that they just put in. It's a crime against Mother Earth. It's a crime. You can't bring more oil out and pretend that it's going to work out. You bring it out in Canada. You burn it in the United States. It's going to show up in the Pacific. So all we do is knowing that our community is related to your community. Good prayers for your and your community.

Q: Hi, I'm (inaudible). I'm actually from Pakistan and studying in the United States. You were saying that inequality, consumerism, neoliberalism, and all these have led to the climate crisis. So how do we reimagine a different future without all these aspects of our daily lives?

LaDUKE: Just remember that the world we live in now is not the world that we had all this time. This is like the past—I think of 200 years of very bad decisions. Past 100 years, very bad. The advent of fossil fuels acceleration, the rise of fossil fuels, the agriculture system, and the toxic militarization—it's kind of like being on steroids. Fossil fuels puts you on steroids—makes you a lot bigger and a lot faster. If you can get rid of some of the amnesia that you get from a massive fossil fuels injection and remember that there's a way to live that is a little bit more simple, that has more relations with your relatives that are close, then you have a better shot. Because the fact is that a globalized economy is predicated on a lot of fossil fuels. I can get a shrimp that was raised in Scotland, deveined in China, and arrives at a Walmart near me. You know what I'm saying? That's too far for a shrimp to travel. Maybe we rebuild things that are a little more local. There's many tools ahead. I don't know, Kumi might have a better answer for this. I just think shrimp shouldn't travel.

NAIDOO: Well, I think the issue of how far food travels is part of the kind of change that we need to make—not only because of carbon, but because of quality, because of freshness, because of health. I'm impressed that there are many young people, and some older people in the global north, who are beginning to recognize that actually the 200 years of so-called civilization that was pushed on us actually turns out to be pretty uncivilized. The changes that we are seeking to make—I don't think they are sacrifices. Sacrifice is the fact that people are working 20-hour days. Sacrifice is the idea that people are working three jobs just to put food on the table.

But what you're seeing is that all over the world today, people are actually co-creating from bottom up real solutions to real problems, from providing energy to rethinking agriculture and so on. And the challenge for us right now is how do we pick up those examples? Because the problem we have is we've got an ideological state apparatus, almost, that is against us. By that, I mean the framework for education, framework for religion, social norms and customs, how we fund arts and culture, but most critically, the framework for communications and media. So today, even being able to project new models and new ways of doing things is a challenge, because we don't have enough capability to do that.

So we have our next question already? Over to you.

Q: Hello. I'm based in the Bronx, New York, and heritage-wise, I'm part of the Fulani tribe of west Africa. And I really want to know, are we saving the planet, or are we saving the economy? What is meant by this in relation to polluting countries, and would new climate justice acts and policies allow for both?

LaDUKE: I call this economy the wendigo economy, the economy of a cannibal. It's a cannibal economy, because it consumes its life force. It consumes everything which is around and turns it into products that are then sold for some profit. I heard someone say that colonialism has the same root as the word colon, which is to digest. And I believe it. It's the digestion of the entire world.

So now, we're Planet Stuff. That's what someone said. We got more stuff that's human in the world than all of the biosphere, like all the elephants and all the trees and the coral reefs. You just got to change your alliance from what you shopped for in a bottle to how you rebuild a place to relocalize. On a worldwide scale, there is this resurgence and continuation of local farming, of local health, of local energy. And in this moment, we see that it's better to survive if you are counting on something coming in from China—probably have a better shot. That's the real economy, and that's the one that we actually all rely on. Because as much as Jeff Bezos wants to shop in space, there's no food or water. So best just make things good here, Jeff.

NAIDOO: Winona, I think it's a good point to wrap up this conversation by bringing in Martin Luther King. Martin Luther King speaking when I think I was a four-month-old baby, said, my friends, as I conclude my speech, I want to note that in the field of modern child psychology, there's a very dominant term called maladjusted. Now, all of us want to be well adjusted and not suffer from schizophrenia or other mental illnesses. But my friends, I say to you, there are certain things in this world that are so unjust and immoral that good, decent people should refuse to adjust to. He goes on to say I never intend to adjust myself to religious bigotry, racial discrimination, mindless expenditure on military weapons when people don't have food to eat. But on the economy, he says, I never intend to adjust myself to economic conditions that will take necessities from the many to give luxuries to the few when millions of God's children are smothering in an airtight cage of poverty in an affluent society.

If that was relevant in the mid-'60s in the US, it's a thousand times more relevant today, and sadly, it's relevant across the world. But on an inspirational note, he called on the world to set up a movement that never was set up. He said, I call upon decent men and women around the world to set up a new international organization to be known as the International Association for the Advancement of Creative Maladjustment. (laughter)

To those folks that think maybe some of the things that Winona and I are saying are too out there, this is what this moment calls for. This is a moment for us not to adjust to things that are so fundamentally unjust, right? And I think this is a moment for fresh thinking, creative ideas, and so on, and we should make no apologies for putting forward ideas that sound different, transformative, and so on, when in fact, the current systems are failing in every possible way.

(applause)

LaDUKE: I was charged with a thousand other people. I spent three days in jail fighting a Canadian multinational and watched Biden turn his back on us.

NAIDOO: How do you think we deal with the challenge of winning over people who have been led to believe that the current system serves them?

Kumi Naidoo & Winona LaDuke (Part 1), December 19, 2021
https://youtu.be/bPgle3gx_Sk

CHAPTER TWENTY SEVEN

KUMI NAIDOO & WINONA LADUKE (PART 2)

March 2022
In December 2021, the month after the UN Climate Conference concluded in Glasgow, Al Jazeera featured Kumi Naidoo and Winona LaDuke in two inspiring conversations in London.

In December 2021, the month after the UN Climate Conference concluded in Glasgow, Al Jazeera featured Kumi Naidoo and Winona LaDuke in two inspiring conversations in London. Naidoo and LaDuke focused on the need and the potential for grassroots activists to step up when governments are failing to address the crisis.

The seven days beginning with the anniversary of the Sharpeville Massacre in South Africa on March 21, 1960 end Sunday with the anniversary of the Battle of Horseshoe Bend on March 27, 1814, in which future president Andrew Jackson led his troops against the Creek nation in what is now Alabama.

These dates make this a very appropriate time to be reminded of the central role of anti-racist and indigenous activists in global struggles for climate justice.

At Sharpeville the dead were peaceful demonstrators. At Horseshoe Bend they were elite Creek warriors.

In each case, however, they were mowed down mercilessly by superior firepower.

This post contains a transcript and the streaming video of the second conversation.

> "The just transition, the rebuilding, the restoration economy, will take a lot of work. That opportunity is the opportunity to build an economy that makes sense."

NAIDOO: This is a moment for us not to adjust to things that are so fundamentally unjust.

LaDUKE: Since fleeing South Africa's apartheid, Kumi has scaled oil rigs and protested from the Arctic Ocean to the Alberta tar sands.

NAIDOO: The time of playing political poker with our planet has to be over right now.

LaDUKE: Everything is a toxic mess. What we want is a transition out. But what we have is an addicted society, and the fossil fuel industry continues to push those addictions.

NAIDOO: Winona has stood in opposition against coal and uranium mines, dam projects, and oil pipelines.

LaDUKE: It's not like I'm standing here as a matter of choice. I'm standing here as a matter of necessity.

NAIDOO: One of the challenges we face is how do we keep engaged in struggle for such a long time, when quite often, we're winning battles, but losing the overall war for justice? I draw my inspiration from a true story that I experienced as a young activist, when a friend of mine, Lenny Naidoo, was killed together with three young women from my home city, Durban. And I had to think about the last conversation I had with him when we were fleeing into exile in different directions, where he asked me the question, Kumi, what is the biggest contribution you can make to the cause of justice? I said giving your life. And he said, you mean going, getting shot and killed, and becoming a martyr? I said, I guess so. That was what was happening in South Africa in the '80s when he asked me that question. And then he said, no, that's the wrong answer. He said, it's not giving your life, but giving the rest of your life.

When he died, I had to think about that. In that is a wisdom that says the struggle for justice is a marathon and not a sprint. People might forget that when

Nelson Mandela was fighting the good fight, he was reviled. When Martin Luther King, Rosa Parks, Mahatma Gandhi, many others—at the time they stood up for justice, they were reviled. But history then records that in fact, they were precious assets that humanity created.

So I was curious to know, Winona, what gives you the courage to wake up day after day after day to say even though the cards are stacked against us, I'm still going to stand up for justice?

LaDUKE: First, I live in the most beautiful place the Creator could have been. So every day I look out and there was trumpeter swans before I left. The wild swans—they live with me. And I was like, that's who I work for, you know? I work for the swans, and I work for the horses, and I work for Mother Earth. I don't work for the state. I don't work for the—you know? I think that that in itself is pretty much a good reward.

But I just spent the last eight years trying to protect my territory from a Canadian multinational named Enbridge that just put in a tar sands pipeline, Line 3. Now, a $9 billion tar sands pipeline at the end of the fossil fuel era—you don't get a tiara for that one. You don't get a crown. Everybody is divesting from oil. Even Harvard, my alma mater, finally started its divestment policy. The Saudi sovereign fund divested. So you're at the end of the era, and this last dinosaur has got to shove a pipeline down your throat.

Every day, I stood up—I lived on the river. A thousand people were arrested fighting this pipeline, a lot of Indigenous women. They put the pipeline in during the pandemic. And I can see, as your brother who passed away in the 1990s can see, that the systems are not working. But the longer that you fight them, the more that things change.

As I look out there, I see that other pipelines did not get through. The Keystone XL pipeline was canceled. The Constitution pipeline was canceled.

NAIDOO: And many of those pipelines were spoken about as if it was a fait accompli, it was definitely going to go —

LaDUKE: That's right.

NAIDOO:—and people stopped it.

LaDUKE: But the little people like us that keep standing up. And our battle is long from over with Enbridge. Time will tell how the deconstruction of this industrial system occurs. We hope it occurs in a way that provides a lot of jobs for a lot of people, because taking out pipelines is a lot of labor. The just transition, or however we call it—the rebuilding, the restoration economy, will take a lot of work. That opportunity is the opportunity to build an economy that makes sense.

NAIDOO: That's very optimistic, in the sense that you're saying the mountain is steep, and it has to be climbed, but we're going to climb it, however difficult it is, right? This decade is the most consequential decade in humanity's history. What in struggle we are able to achieve over the next 10 years will determine what kind of future we have, particularly for people in small island states, the least-developed countries, and so on.

So I believe that if we're going to win right now in a short time space, there are far too many companies that are doing bad things in the front end, and we probably don't have time to go after each of them separately. I think what we need to do is follow the money and shut the flow of capital at source so that as many bad, polluting projects that are taking us to the climate cliff is stopped. Does that resonate with you at all?

LaDUKE: No, I think that that is a strategy. I mean, I was arrested. I was charged with a thousand other people. I spent three days in jail fighting a Canadian multinational and watched Biden turn his back on us. What we need to do definitely is go to the financial institutions. We fight them on the ground, because $2 billion in cost overruns is not good for your investors. The longer you fight them, the more expensive the project gets. But what we need is the people—the 1% that are making all the money, they have children, too. They have grandchildren, too. And the divestment movement is growing. That is one thing that we are grateful for—to keep divesting. Don't put your money there, but make the future instead.

NAIDOO: I feel that one of the challenges we have is we have to get better at communicating. How can we communicate in ways that much larger numbers of people can easily understand that we are destroying ourselves? We are shooting ourselves every day and killing the possibilities for our children to be able to prosper in the future.

I'm curious to know about—within Indigenous culture itself, what we can learn. Because what I feel is that

> "I think what we need to do is follow the money and shut the flow of capital at source so that as many bad, polluting projects that are taking us to the climate cliff is stopped."

right now, we need to use arts and culture, for example, much more as a way to communicate what is happening, rather than long documents and complicated policy statements.

LaDUKE: I agree. This month in my language is called Gashkadino-giizis, which means the freezing-over moon. It turns out that there is no moon in Ojibwe language that is named after a Roman emperor. We don't have a July, don't have an August, don't have that. So if you have a worldview that doesn't have to do with empire, which a lot of the world does, you can think a little differently than if you're preoccupied with the maintaining of empire.

In our prophecies—Anishinaabe people, they talk about this as the time of the seventh fire. And in our prophecies, we're told that we have a choice between two paths. A long time ago, they said one path is well worn, but scorched. The other path is not well worn, and it's green. And it would be our choice upon which path to embark. That's our instructions. Almost every Indigenous society has exactly the same teachings.

The other thing that my society or my Indigenous teachings don't have is we don't have armageddon. What we have is birth, death, and rebirth, just like a cyclical world. It is fall—dagwaagin. It is fall. The leaves are falling outside. Then they go down, we get snow, and it is quiet. It is quiet. Then we think, we remember, and then it is reborn in the spring. It is reborn.

In many of our teachings, we say this is the fourth world or the fifth world that we have to remake because humans make a mess. That's what we do. And then we remake. This is our time to remake. Get over it. Change is inevitable. It's a question of who controls the change. We want to be the ones that are the agents of change.

Now, we've got to put our minds together. A great leader, Sitting Bull—great political leader—he said, let us put our minds together to see what kind of future we can make for our children. The answers are people like you, me, many more, not some guy over there at COP—big guy in the government. The minds together is all of us.

NAIDOO: But the difficulty we have is while we need to put our minds together, colonialism's biggest trait was divide and rule, right? So we are sitting with a situation right now, and you know this as well as I do, that people have been divided by false promises. Even Indigenous communities have been divided, as you know, where companies come in and sell a false prosperity and so on.

Because one of the things that we have to figure out right now, I think, is for example, people who work for oil, coal, and gas companies—they are our kin. They are our brothers and sisters. They didn't say, we want to work in oil, coal, and gas, right? They were told that that's the way you deliver energy. Now, when we say that we need to make the transition, there are people within those industries who feel threatened. That's why you and I are advocates for a just transition, so that people will either be retrained for the renewable energy industry, or if they're close to retirement, they should be able to retire with dignity and so on. But how do you think we deal with the challenge of winning people over who have been led to believe that the current system serves them, even though it certainly doesn't?

LaDUKE: Well, I think the pandemic is a pretty good wake-up for everybody, and the fact that people don't want to go back to business as usual is quite clear in the United States. So in that, there's this opportunity to kind of liberate yourself from all of that other thinking and figure out what you want to do. I think a lot of people are doing that.

In North America, I see North Dakota—oil, oil, oil state. What are they training their people for? Wind turbines. Why? Because North Dakota is the windiest state. Why are you doing oil, North Dakota, when you could be doing wind? You could be doing hemp—hemp and linen. There's talk about that. The solutions are there.

NAIDOO: Talk a little bit about hemp.

LaDUKE: This is the thing. I've been growing hemp for six years. I have a permit from the State of Minnesota and a permit from the federal government. I grow fiber hemp. I call this the new green revolution, because you could replace the materials economy with hemp. You could sequester carbon with hemp. All that cement out there, if it was a country, it would the third-largest country in terms of CO_2 emissions in the world would be cement. If you went to hempcrete—what if you used building systems that stored carbon instead of were carbon-intensive, like the landscape or the cityscape that we have? So I'm saying the answers are there, and it is not necessarily new. It's the good thinking that we need.

Oh, I see a question that looks as if —

Q: Hi, my name is Sara (sp?). I'm calling in from Wiyot territory in northern California. My question has to do with youth. A recent survey of 10,000 youth across the globe reported that 77% feel that the future is frightening. Kumi talked about the next 10 years being very important. I'm thinking about the youth climate movement. I'm curious what advice you have for them, given that the burden has been handed down to them?

NAIDOO: Firstly, I would say young people and the youth movement have kept people like me going over the past couple of years. It's been a source of tremendous inspiration. In fact, I did a tweet after the declaration of COP26 came out. I said, it's OK. Take the night and cry that we have been criminally betrayed by the climate negotiators. But on Monday, the fight continues.

The other thing I would say to young people is they have to resist this so-called wisdom when we say young people are the leaders of tomorrow. Because if young people wait until they take leadership tomorrow, there might not be a tomorrow for young people to be able to exercise that leadership. The one thing young people have is freshness of perspective. Their lenses can look at old problems and look at it in a different way. I think that is what is critically needed right now. We need a new sense of imagination.

But the most important message I have for young people is do not let those who have been climate denialists, those that are speaking lies, those that have driven us to this point of distraction have the benefit of thinking that they have destroyed your spirit. The way we do our activism should be a source of energy, because we're going to need a lot of inspiration and energy on a daily basis if we're going to turn things around.

LaDUKE: Hello.

Q: Hi. I'm currently in South Africa. I am South African. And I always wonder about how environmentalism is a space of privilege at the moment. So my question is are there current examples of how marginalized populations are included and informed on the conversation and in actioning climate justice?

LaDUKE: From my perspective, I live on a reservation in northern Minnesota called White Earth. I'm Ojibwe or Anishinaabe. And we're looking out there and looking like, looks like you all don't have it together, so we're going to rebuild our local food system, because your food system doesn't work. And then we're going to make solar thermal panels so that poor people who live in a cold place can get heat in a really efficient way. So making sure that what the changes that are needed are accessible to the people who need them the most has to be paramount in a just transition. It's not about just making sure that the top guys get everything. The justice is in the rest of us who are feeling the impacts of climate change also have that. And the thing is—is that the next economy is not about competition. It's about cooperation.

NAIDOO: The one only thing I'd add to it is the question of how do those with privilege handle their privilege? And I think that it's important that even within civil society, within our movement, we need to address the questions of power imbalances that exist. So I just put up my hand and say that even—it's not just a question of government and business shutting out the most marginalized, but even those of us that seek to serve, and that work needs to be done.

LaDUKE: The other thing I just want to say is the 1% got to do their part. If you're in the 1%, stand up for the rest of us, because your kids are with us. There's privilege and then there's the responsibility of privilege. So stand up for your responsibility.

Hello, my friend.

Q: Thank you so much for this enlightened discussion. What lessons could the youth climate movement take from the anti-apartheid movement, and how could those lessons then help us pressure the governments to stick to their 1.5 Celsius pledge? Thank you.

NAIDOO: By the way, where are you speaking from?

Q: Santo Domingo, Dominican Republic—Caribbean.

NAIDOO: Oh, wonderful. Right now, we've got a crazy situation. There are even foundations and universities and even some religious institutions who say they're all opposed to climate change, but actually, some of their own investments are still sitting in fossil fuels. It's changing fast. But I think one of the things that helped us in South Africa to make the system delegitimized was by people who had money—and that's why Winona is so right. The people at the top who have serious money—if they were to step forward and say we're shifting every cent of ours away from dirty energy investment, but then make sure you shift it into something positive. Because also, I think the people who have made money from an unjust system that has driven us to this point of destruction also have an obligation now to use their money and resources in ways that are genuinely positive. So investing in innovation, in young people, and so on—that's one.

The second lesson, I think, that we can draw on is the importance of civil disobedience. If history has taught us anything, when humanity has faced a major injustice or a major struggle or major challenge, those struggles only move forward when decent women and men step up and say enough is enough and no more. We're prepared to put our life on the line if necessary. We're prepared to go to prison is necessary.

But I think the other thing that we can learn from the anti-apartheid movement, which Mandela taught us, is always to be clear that we are fighting a system, and we're not fighting people. Mandela always was clear about saying we're not fighting white people. We are fighting a system that perpetuates white domination, which is very different. That's why we need to convince the people who are benefiting from the current system that in fact, it is in their interest to change, because both the rich and poor children's lives are threatened by climate change. And hopefully that is a message we can communicate.

Winona, you might have some perspectives on this as well.

LaDUKE: I would agree. As a young student at Harvard, I was involved in a Harvard divestment campaign. We were trying for a long time. And the other

"People will either be retrained for the renewable energy industry, or if they're close to retirement, they should be able to retire with dignity."

thing you learned from that struggle is it takes a while. It doesn't happen overnight. You have to keep building the pressure, and you have to keep transforming it. But my alma mater, Harvard, did divest in fossil fuels or is beginning that process. No such luck for a long time on South Africa. So you see changes happening. I have taken a lot of good heart from the privilege of my experience with South African ANC and the movement there. So take heart. It takes a while.

NAIDOO: Maybe the one last thing I want to add is the critical importance of ensuring that our resistance to the fossil fuel industry and other industries that are driving us to climate destruction needs to be peaceful. I think that there are people in certain governments and in certain industries that are banking on that the anger and the disappointment that young people and others are feeling will manifest themselves in violent resistance activities. I think that if we play into that, we will be doing a disservice to the struggle. Right now, while I can completely understand especially young people feeling an absolute sense of betrayal, I urge and appeal to young people to ensure that our resistance is bold, it's strong, it's courageous, but we ensure that we remain peaceful. Because if we cross that line, we will give those that want to prevent our voices from being heard an excuse to come down and crush us.

And just to be clear, they are crushing resistance to injustices of all kinds at the moment, and that's what we are up against. But I think adhering to peaceful ways is critically important. Sorry, over to you.

Q: My question is about the changing face of colonialism. We're seeing the fossil fuel industry, the Western states increasingly look towards things like nickel, cobalt, lithium as materials that they can extract whilst pretending to be green. So what can we as the 21st century environmental movement do to effectively fight against that?

LaDUKE: Yeah, thank you for saying that, because I just had a pipeline shoved down my throat by Canada.

It was a very colonial experience. (laughter) Didn't have anything to do with any UN declarations on the rights of Indigenous people. That's the way it is with late-state addiction. They're going to keep trying to push these things and push these things. The latest is the green mining projects for the electric cars.

I see that, one, the first thing you got to do is stop your level of consumption. We got to cut back and cut back how we behave, because we behave like a bunch of T. rexes, quite frankly.

Then the other thing we got to do is go for the easy answer. Don't ask me to fill your energy needs in the United States with renewables when you waste 60% of your power between point of origin and point of consumption.

NAIDOO: Exactly.

LaDUKE: So get efficient and be responsible. That's what we do. And that generates a tremendous amount of jobs—insulating, rebuilding grid systems, building local energy. That is more efficient, and it really fundamentally is also about how we relate to each other and how we relate to Mother Earth or our planet.

So the decolonizing involves letting go of your bad behavior and getting back into being the responsible people and societies that we're supposed to be. It's this moment of transformation. We're in the middle of a pandemic. We're sitting here in the bastion of colonialism itself. And I think what we're saying is time to move on. Time to rebuild relationships that are far more just and fair. I'm optimistic, because I believe and I see the change has been made, and I see our prophecies that say which way to go, and I'm all ready. I'm all ready to move on the green path, and I think a lot of us are.

NAIDOO: I'm optimistic even at a time when a lot of the resistance to injustice is being met with force and repression, because as was said many decades ago, first, they ignore you, then they laugh at you, then they fight you, and then you win. The good news is the resistance to injustice is not being ignored, is not being laughed at. It's being fought very hard by those in power. Let's hope that if this wisdom is right, then people are just one step away from winning economic justice, social justice, climate justice, gender justice, Indigenous justice, and so on.

LaDUKE: Yes. In our hearts, I know that our ancestors are with us and that we are ancestors for those who are not yet here. And I want them to look on me and say you did a good job, sister. So that's this time, which is a good opportunity to do the right thing.

NAIDOO: That's beautiful, and I think it's good to leave it there.

Kumi Naidoo & Winona LaDuke (Part 2), December 26, 2021
https://youtu.be/sRZaEjBCWBo

CHAPTER TWENTY EIGHT

LEARNING LESSONS ON **GLOBAL SOLIDARITY**

By William Minter
Unlike authoritarians, who may follow a standard playbook, progressive movements must be aware of the specificity of particular social and political terrains.
May 2021

Editor's Report
Background on the Essay Series

The idea for the US/Africa Bridge Building Project emerged in mid-2020. The project was partially funded by an initial grant from the Ford Foundation beginning in November 2020.

The concept of the project was based on remote conversations among me, as editor of AfricaFocus Bulletin; Imani Countess, then an Open Society Economic Inequality Fellow; and Vera Mshana, then a Ford Foundation Program Officer. All three of us were supporters of the Stop the Bleeding Africa campaign. All three of us agreed that it was necessary to explore new frameworks that moved beyond the conventional paradigms of bilateral relationships between activists and organizations in the United States and Africa. And we were also convinced that the issue of tax justice and illicit financial flows was an essential component of any progressive analysis of other fundamental issues faced by Africa and the world.

In understanding global inequality, we rejected the framework which relies on ranking countries by levels of development and advising poor countries to advance by adopting the policies and receiving assistance from the rich. Instead, we drew on the concept of a system of "global apartheid." More than a metaphor, the term evokes the system of South African apartheid, which was itself embedded in a global history of white supremacy.

"Global apartheid" is multidimensional and fractal, as inequalities are replicated from local to global levels. Similar patterns can be illustrated everywhere in the world. But the United States and the African continent anchor the poles of today's global inequality. Whether the issue is climate change, a global pandemic, or food security, Africa is the most vulnerable region and the United States is still a central force in blocking the needed fundamental changes.

Despite this reality, even most progressive activists in the United States tend to regard issues outside our national borders as "foreign policy" of interest only to a few rather than as integrally connected to our own futures as well as that of those who live in Africa and other regions of the global South. To the extent that U.S. media pay attention to the world, it is overwhelmingly focused on U.S. involvement and on high-profile crises in Europe, the Middle East, or Asia.

> **Whether the issue is climate change, a global pandemic, or food security, Africa is the most vulnerable region and the United States is still a central force in blocking the needed fundamental changes**

Activists may denounce U.S. military interventions and applaud critiques of the "white savior industrial complex." And there are many creative initiatives and projects that focus on specific countries or specific issues on the African continent. But on global issues affecting both Africa and the United States, U.S. activists still lag far behind their African counterparts in recognizing the urgency of global collaboration. African global leadership on tax justice and illicit financial flows provides an opportunity for making new linkages. The essay series was intended to assist in providing a broader framework for understanding such solidarity.

Earlier that year, in January, *AfricaFocus Bulletin* had begun to run a series of short essays by Imani and me under the rubric "Beyond Eurocentrism and U.S. Exceptionalism: Starting Points for a Paradigm Shift from Foreign Policy to Global Policy." In the third essay in that series, in February 2020, we argued that "National and Global Inequalities Are Intertwined," introducing the theme of illicit financial flows. We noted that "The U.S. debate on national inequality between rich and poor households has not yet broadened into a conversation about global inequality between rich and poor countries. This theme remains muted at best, even among progressive activists."

In that essay, we focused on the "often invisible nexus of how money flows to the ultra-rich both within and across borders, how it is linked to deep structural realities of national and global history, and how finding the resources to address acute public needs requires not only higher tax rates but enforcing transparency about hidden wealth worldwide."

This was exactly the time period when the World Health Organization declared COVID-19 to be a Health Emergency of International Concern on January 30 and designated it a pandemic on March 11.

As a result, Imani was forced to cancel planned trips to Africa and to the four cities which had been highlighted as pilot projects for outreach in her Open Society Fellowship. The grant proposal which resulted in the initial Ford Foundation grant beginning in November 2020 was envisaged as supplementing her 1-year fellowship by providing additional support for consultations between African tax justice activists and activists in the pilot communities, as well as for wider dissemination of the themes raised in the AfricaFocus series which continued in 2020.

Beginning In late June 2021, Imani was able to complete exploratory visits and meetings with local activists in Atlanta, Minneapolis, Oakland, and Los Angeles. She also attended the 9th Pan-African Conference on Illicit Financial Flows and Taxation in Nairobi in late October. However, it was not possible to complete the full consultations planned because of the continued impact of the COVID-19 pandemic as well as the need for local activists to focus on pressing domestic issues.

Although the project's series of internet posts, initially called a "Transnational Solidarity Playbook," did not require travel but was managed remotely, the pace of work on it was also seriously affected by the context of the COVID-19 pandemic. We underestimated the difficulty of securing commitments and getting timely submissions from authors. Nevertheless, we published five original essays and one extensive interview we had commissioned as well as ten other resource guides and other educational materials addressing critical issues of global solidarity, beginning in April 2021 and concluding in March 2022.

We are deeply grateful to all who helped make this happen. Donna Katzin, Rosebell Kagumire, Sahra Ryklief, Meredith Terretta, and Joseph Tolton contributed original insights on five critical topics. In addition to resource guides to material available online, the series was enriched by recent reflections from Angela Davis, Varshini Prakash, and Adom Getachew, reproduced with their permission, and open-access reproduction of key documents and videos from the African Feminist Forum, the Solidarity Center, the Indigenous Environmental Network, the Red Nation, Kumi Naidoo, and Winona LaDuke. We are also thankful for the encouragement we received from others we invited to write essays, but who were unable to do so because of their many other commitments, complicated by the additional demands and stresses imposed by the pandemic. These included Roxanne Dunbar-Ortiz, Robin Kelley, Charlotte Bunch, Ken Zinn, Brian Kagoro, and Bobby Peek.

In addition to project founder Imani Countess, other members of the project team who contributed to the series in many different ways included web designers Gail Oring and Miriam Paska; development consultant Mary Semela; editors and writers Jacqueline Asheeke, Zeb Larson, Kassaundra Lockhart, and Margaret Summers; and interns Kadidiatou Diallo and Seamus Love. In addition to the original Ford Foundation Grant, donations also came from the US-Africa Network, USA for Africa, and more than 50 individual donors.

As this report is written in May 2022, the COVID-19

> Billionaires and multinational corporations are getting richer, while governments are denied necessary resources to provide basic human rights and invest in a sustainable future for the planet.

pandemic is still with us, while the unequal distribution of vaccines, treatments, and other health services deepens global apartheid. With economic recovery in Africa still weighed down by the impact of the virus, Africa is being devastated by food shortages and other direct effects of the war over Ukraine. Climate disasters in both rich and poor countries vividly signal a future of apocalyptic catastrophe. The fossil fuel industry and governments have turned from outright denial to deception and delay in the urgent transition to renewable energy. State and non-state violence persists despite much wider awareness and calls for reform.

These cumulative crises are still revealing and deepening structural inequalities around the world. Within and across countries, the people who have suffered most are those already disadvantaged by race, class, gender, or place of birth, reflecting the harsh inequality that has characterized our world for centuries.

At the same time, billionaires and multinational corporations are getting richer, while governments are denied necessary resources to provide basic human rights and invest in a sustainable future for the planet. Fiscal conservatives declare we can't afford it. But money laundering siphons off wealth into the "offshore" realm of secret tax havens, which are everywhere and nowhere, to escape obligations to repair damage to the planet and promote a just society.

In 2022, media attention to fundamental global issues was virtually eclipsed by the latest war in Europe centered on the Ukraine, featuring both an open invasion by Russia and escalation driven by massive U.S. military intervention over many years before as well as after that invasion.

Learning Lessons

What lessons, if any, can we draw from these essays published in the turbulent years of 2021 and 2022?

In my opinion, it is clear that the terminology we used in the series title fell short of the complexity of today's realities. "Transnational" solidarity *between those working for justice in specific countries* is not sufficient to address global problems. The solidarity we strive to build must be *global in scope* and be nurtured *among many diverse partners* to build powerful coalitions capable of confronting vested interests. And, unlike authoritarians, who may follow a more or less standard playbook often cited in the media, progressive movements must constantly be aware of the specificity of particular social and political terrains of struggle. We must also adjust to rapidly changing realities for which respectful and open debate among allies is needed to reach mutual understanding on how our efforts can complement each other rather than weaken our collective impact.

Instead of a checklist in a playbook, therefore, we might consider guiding principles that might serve as watchwords for the years ahead. The five listed below as examples are not intended as definitive in either wording or number, but simply as elements I think it important to stress.

Solidarity Must Encompass Many Levels from Local to Global

In today's world, with the proliferation of virtual, in-person, and hybrid communications, the scope of communities, organizations, movements, and decision-making "places" is less and less defined only by national or other geographic boundaries. Although the technology has changed, the principle of global solidarity has strong roots in the Pan-African movement.

A Fuller Freedom: The Lost Promise of Pan-Africanism

Lawyers Crossing Borders

Pan-Africanist, Christian, and Queer

We Must Respect Each Other and Respect the Planet

Respect for each other's humanity (Ubuntu) must be paired, as indigenous peoples have long been aware, with respect for all creatures on the planet as well as the natural features of the earth itself

Indigenous Action to Save the Planet

Moving Beyond the Green New Deal

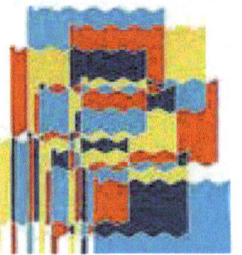

Kumi Naidoo and Winona LaDuke

We Must Recognize Intersecting Inequalities and Fight Against Them

In addition to the classic distinctions of class, race, and gender, human beings have constructed unjust inequalities defined by appearance, physical abilities, or social, political, cultural, or organizational positions.

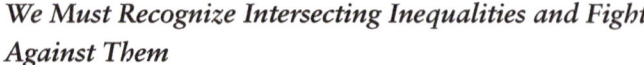

Resisting Beyond Borders

Towards A Partnership of Equals

Today's Global Apartheid is Still Shaped by More Than 500 Years of European Expansion

Struggles against violence and injustice go back for millennia in every region of the world, including centuries of resistance and of influence by those conquered and colonized by European powers. But the period of the the European-driven slave trade in West Africa and across the Atlantic, beginning in the late 15th century, still defines the general contours of global inequality today.

Confronting Global Apartheid Demands Global Solidarity

Diverse New Realities Require Multiple Strategies and Tactics, Both Old and New

Progressive social movements build on each other in creating repertoires for action, such as sit-ins, disinvestment campaigns and many more. But combining specific actions effectively depends on paying attention to specific situations, and openness to constant learning and adaptation.

From Disinvestment to Reinvestment/

Angela Davis at Biko Memorial

Redefining What's Possible

INDEX

A

6th Pan-African Congress, 100
Abrahams, Peter, 101-102
Accra, Ghana, 82
Adeleye-Fayemi, Bisi, 81,126
Adi, Hakim, 101-104
Adu-Amankwah, Kwasi, 93
Africa World Press, iii
AfricaFocus Bulletin, x,22,32,61,80,140
African Feminism, 80
African Feminist Charter, 81
African Feminist Forum, 81,82,140
African Regional Organisation of International Trade Union Confederation (ITUC-Africa), 92-93
African Trade Unions, 92-96
African Union, 21,44,99
African Women's Development Fund, 81
Africans Rising, 104,127
Ajayi, Jacob, iii
Akwei, Adotei, 122
Al Jazeera, 127,133
Algeria, 102
Amnesty International, 29,36,122,127
Anglo-American world, vii
anti-apartheid movement, i,iii,i ,v,4,21,62-64,74,97,127,136-137,146
Asheeke, Jacqueline, 140

B

Bahe, Brian, iv
Barbados, 57-58
Bayton, Naima Natalie, iv
Beinart, Peter, 10
Ben Bella, Ahmed, 102
Bennett, John, iii
Bennis, Phyllis, 10
Berlin Conference, viii
Biden, Joe, 3,6-7,22,50-57,71,105,111,132,134
Biko, Steve, i,63-68
Bing, Geoffrey, 98
Black Lives Matter, i,vi,33,35-39,42,63,67,74,76,80
Blyden, Edward, 103
Bolivia, 113-114
Bop, Codou, 81

Boycott, Divestment, Sanctions (BDS), 76
Brandon, Ruth, iii
British Haldane Society, 98
Burgis, Tom, 22
Burnham, Linda, iv
Butcher, Goler, 100
Butler, Josephine, iii
Buttigieg, Pete, 7,10

C

Cameroon, 97-100
Canada, 3,19,105-108,113-114,131,137
Capital in the Twenty-First Century, 22
Carbon Tracker, 72
Caribbean, 26,100-104,120,126
Celaya, Mrs., iii
Central Africa, 91,94
Checole, Kassahun, iii
Chigudu, Hope, 81
China, ix,13-15,18,23-25,28,31,33,36,41,51-52,54-55,94,114,131
Chinakwe, Albert, iv
Chinakwe, Tapiwa, iv
Chinakwe, Tendai, iv
coal, 13-16,72,106,113-114,133
cobalt, 15,114
Cold War, ix,3,29,43-44,48,52,54,102
colonialism, v,viiiix,4,16,48,83,97,102-104,14,166,122,131,135
Combahee River Collective, 80
Congo, 54,102,114,120
Countess, Colleen, iv
Countess, Gregory, iv
Countess, Jemal, iv
Countess, Kathy, iv
Countess, Lisa, iv
Cullors, Patrisse, 47

D

Dakar, 99
Dakota Access Pipeline, 107-110,113,135
Davis, Angela, i,vi,63,65,67-68,104,140,143,146
Davis, Jennifer, iii
de Carvalho, Jackson, 98
deCOALonize, 13,72

Delgado, Mario, iv
Democratic Liberties Defense Committee of Black Africa, 98
Democratic Party of Côte d'Ivoire, 98
Democratic Republic of Congo, 94,114
Diallo, Kadidiatou, iv,140
Dibango, Manu, 97,101
Dieng, Rama Salla, 80
Diop, Fadilou, 99
Disinvestment, 75
dos Santos, Isabel, 21
Douzon, Henry, 98
Doyle, Nora, iv
Drayton, Jennifer, iii
Du Bois, W.E.B., 65,101-103
Dunbar-Ortiz, Roxanne, viii,10,41,48,116,140

E

Early, James, iv
East Africa, 77,93.98,103
East Timor, v
Egypt, 53,57
Ekine, Sokari, 126
Elder, Joseph, iii
Elkins, Caroline, 100
Equiano, Olaudah, 103
Ethiopia, 26-28,53,101,103
Eurocentrism, 4,140
extractivist, vii,25

F

FeesMustFall, 67,79
Feffer, John, 8
Feminist Africa, 80
Ferguson, C. Clyde, 100
Ferrão, Valeriano , iii
Financial Accountability and Corporate Transparency (FACT) Coalition, 22
Firestone Agricultural Workers Union of Liberia (FAWUL), 94
First Pan-African Conference on Reparations for Slavery, Colonization and Neocolonization, 97,101
Fletcher, William (Bill), Jr., iv,92
Flory, Margaret, iii

Ford Foundation, 139-140
fossil fuels, 5,12-15,34,46,72-76,105,111-112,131,137
Frelimo, iii-vi,ix
Fund for Constitutional Government, iv

G

Garvey, Amy Ashwood, 102
Garvey, Marcus, 103
Garvey, Mary Marcus, 102
Gary, Ian, v
Garza, Alicia, 67
Getachew, Adom, 97,101,104,140
Ghana, 33,80,82,93,98-104,122
global apartheid, 59,61,130-142
Global Inequality, 5,7,15-22,32,88,139-140
Global North, viii,75,114,131
global solidarity, 93,101,139-140
Global South, 57-58,75,114,139
Globalizing Culture Wars: U.S. Conservatives, African Churches, And Homophobia, 122
Gold Coast, 98-99
Grand Bassam, 98
Green New Deal, 11-16,39,46,51,63,72,111-115
Gribben, Peter, iv
Guadeloupe, 98
Guinea, 100,102,104

H

Hill, Sandra, iv
Hill, Sylvia, iv
Hobbs, Loretta, iv
Horn, Jessica, 81
Horton, James Africanus, 103
Houser, Myra Ann, 100
Hovey, Gail, iii
Howard University, 98-100
Hubbell, Stephen, iv

I

I am a homosexual, mum, 123
illicit financial flows, iv,21,55,140
Imam, Ayesha, 81
imperialism, v,83103,112,114
India, 13,69
Institute for Policy Studies, i,10,17

Interfaith Center for Investor Responsibility (ICCR), 75-76
International Consortium of Investigative Journalists, 19.21
International Defense and Aid Fund, 99
International Labour Organization (ILO), 28,92
Iron Eyes, Tokata, vii,12,14

J

James, C.L.R., 100
Japhet, Kirilo, 98
Jenkins, Myesha, iii
Jennings, Keith, iii
Jones, Alethia, iv
Jordan, Joseph, iv

K

Kachingwe, Nancy, 82
Kagoro, Brian, 104,140
Kagumire, Rosebell, iii,77,80,97,140
Kaldor, Pierre, 98
Kaoma, Kapya, 122
Karekezi, Alice, 81
Kato, David, 119
Katzin, Donna, iii,73,105,111,140
Kaunda, Kenneth, ix
Kennedy, John F., vii
Kenya, 13-14,36,72,99-100
Kenyatta, Jomo, 102
Kikuyu, 98-99
Kinloch, Alice Victoria, 103
Kipling, Rudyard, viii
Kitunga, Demere, 81

L

LaDuke, Winona, 110,127-140
Lall, Diwan Chaman, 99
Lamu, 14-15
Landes, David, iv
Landis, Elizabeth, 99-100
Larson, Zeb, x,117,140
Lawyers' Committee for Civil Rights under Law, 99-100
Lehman, Paul, iii
Lenoir, Gerald, iv

LGBTQ, 38,63,117-123
Liberia, 27-28,94,103
lithium, 113-114,137
Lockhart, Kassaundra, 140
Lomé, Togo, 93
Looting Machine, 22
Love, Seamus, iv,140
LuandaLeaks, 21,22
Lucy, William (Bill), iii
Lumumba, Patrice, 102
Lusane, Clarence, iv

M

Machel, Graça, i,vi, 57-58, 146
Machel, Samora, iii,v,vii,ix
Madunagu, Bene, 81
Mali, 44
Mama, Amina, 80,84
Mandela, Nelson, vi,ix,57-66,134,137
Manley, Michael, 102
Manley, Norman, 102
Marley, Bob, 97,101
Martin, Conrad, iv
Mau Mau, 98,100
Mboya, Tom, 99
McDougall, Gay, 100
Meru Land Case, 100
Migration, 4-5,8,42,53,89,103
Milanovic, Branko, 22
Miller, Joseph, iii
Millner, Ralph, 98
Ministry for the Future, 116
Minter, Cynthia, iii
Minter, David, iii
Minter, Diane, iii
Minter, Elizabeth, iii
Minter, John, iii
Minter, Sam, iii
Minter, Sue, iii
Minter, Susan, iii
Mondlane, Eduardo, iii
Moshi, 98
Mottley, Mia, 57-59
Mouton, Adwoa Dunn, iv
Mozambique, i,iv,vi-ix,5,11-12,54,93

Mozambique Liberation Front (FRELIMO), iii,v-vi,ix
Mugisha, Frank, 119
Mukasa, Sarah, 81
Murray, Pauli, 100
Musah, Arthur, 122

N

Naidoo, Kumi, 127-142
Namibia, v,73,78,100
nation of immigrants, viii
national Inequality, 140
NATO, 6,28
natural gas, 14,113
Navajo, 113
Nesbitt, Prexy, iii-vi,32
New Mexico, 41,113
Ngcukaitobi, Tembeka, 97
Ngong, David Tonghou, 122
Nigeria, 36,44,48,54,78-81,93,99,103-104,126
Nile River, 53
Nkrumah, Kwame, 98,102,104
North Africa, 19,95
North Atlantic Treaty Organization, See NATO
Nyerere, Julius, 104

O

O'Dell, Jack, iii
Obasanjo, Olusegun, 104
OccupyWallStreet, 11,17
Oduyoye, Mercy Amba, 126
Open Society Foundation, iv,x,139-140
Organizing Upgrade, 23,49,51,80
Oring, Gail, iii-iv,140
Ortiz, Paul, 10
Ouandié, Ernest, 99
Oxfam, 19,67

P

Padmore, George, 102
Palestine, i,52
Pan African, 21,89,104
Pan-African Conference of 1900, 97,101
Panama Papers, 19
PanamaPapers, 19,21
Paska, Miriam, 140

Patel, Milap, iv
Pauulu's Diaspora, 116
Perez, Carlotta, 15
Perinbaum, Marie, iii
Piketty, Thomas, 22
Pine Ridge Reservation, 12,14
Plummer, Anita, iv
Political Research Associates, 122
Portugal, vii
Portuguese colonialism, v, ix
Power Africa Initiative, 14
Prakash, Varshini, i,63-72
Pritt, Denis Nowell, 99
public country-by-country reporting, 21
Public Services International (PSI), 124

Q

Queer Pan-Africanism, 123
Ransby, Barbara, i,38,80,146

R

Reggy, Anyango, iv
Reinvestment, i,72-76,111
Responsible Statecraft, 50,53-54
Rhodes, Cecil, vii,79,89
Robinson, Kim Stanley, 116
Robinson, Lisa Crooms, 109
Rodney, Walter, 104
Rubin, Leslie, 100
Rusimbi, Mary, 81
Rwanda, 81,120
Ryklief, Sahra, iii,87-83,140

S

Saez, Emmanuel, 17,21-22
Sanders, Bernie, 3,7-8,10-11,15,22,29,39
Saudi Arabia, 8,13,15,25,46,134
Schmidt, Elizabeth (Betsy), iii,43,48,100
scramble for Africa, viii
Seaton, Alberta & Earle, 98
Seaton, Earle, 98
Seidman, Ann, iii
Seidman, Gay, 76
Seltzer, Zachary, iv
Semela, Mary, iv,140

Senegal, 31,34,80-81,99
Senyonjo, Christopher, 118-119
SharedInterest, 76
Sharpton, Reverend Al, 119
Sherrod, Charles, iii
Sierra Leone, 103
Silberman, Bernard, iii
Sindab, Jean, iii
Smith, Damu, iii
SNCC, iii,80
Solidarity Center Africa, 93,140
Southern Africa, 18,50,61,64,74,76,83,93,99-100
Southern Africa Support Project, iv
Sowah, E.N.P., 99
Standing Rock Sioux, ii,105-109
Summers, Margaret, 140
Sunrise Movement, 11,15,39,63,69-72
Sunshine, Catherine (Cathy), iii,x
Sunshine, Jim, iii
Sunshine, Jim, iii
Swan, Quito J., 116
Swaziland, 93
Syrakos, Holly, iv

T

Tamale, Sylvia, 81,126
Tanganyika, See Tanzania
Tanzania, vi,64,81,98,100,104
Tate, Lessie B., 98
Taylor, Keeanga-Yahmatta, 38,80
Terretta, Meredith, iii,97-101,140
the West, vii,118,120
Thunberg, Greta, vi,12,14,124
Tiyende Pamodzi, ix
Tolton, Bishop Joseph W., iii,117,121,140
Tometi, Opal, 67
trade unions, i,28,30,87-96
Transnational Solidarity, i,62,87-91,140
Treason Trial, 99
Trinidad, 97,100
Trusteeship Council of United Nations, 98
Turtle Island, 106,109,113

U

Uganda,

United Nations, 4,6,8,18-19,25-28,32,44,61-62,91, 99-101,106,108
Universal human rights, 19
US-Africa Network, 140

V

Vaccine Apartheid, 75
van Klinken, Adriaan, 122
Verghese, Paul, iii

W

Wainaina, Binyavanga, 123-124,126
Wallerstein, Immanuel, iv
Wanyeki, Muthoni, 81
Warren, Elizabeth, 3,7,10,15,22,39
West Africa, 44,52,93,103
white supremacy, viii,18,28,35,37,43,61,101,106,139
WIEGO, 92
Williams, Eric, 100
Williams, Henry Sylvester, 97
Williams, Paul, iii
Willoughby-Herard, Tiffany, i
Wilson, Shamillah, 81
Win, Everjoice, 81,85
World War II, viii,3-7,18,27-29,41-48,98,102

Z

Zambia, v,ix,93
Zimbabwe, v,81,93
Zucman, Gabriel, 17,21-22